TAN AI G

WHAT MATTERS IN LEARNING?

TEACHING AND LEARNING SERIES

© 2005 Marshall Cavendish International (Singapore) Private Limited

Published 2005 by Marshall Cavendish Academic
An imprint of Marshall Cavendish International (Singapore) Private Limited
A member of Times Publishing Limited

Times Centre, 1 New Industrial Road,
Singapore 536196
Tel: (65) 6213 9300
Fax: (65) 6284 9772
E-mail: mca@sg.marshallcavendish.com
Website: http://www.marshallcavendish.com/academic

ISBN-13: 978-981-210-455-7
ISBN-10: 981-210-455-0
Printed by Times Graphics Pte Ltd, Singapore
on non-acidic paper

London • New York • Beijing • Bangkok • Kuala Lumpur • Singapore

National Library Board Singapore Cataloguing-in-Publication Data

Tan, Ai-Girl.
    What matters in learning?/Tan Ai Girl.–Singapore: Marshall Cavendish Academic, 2005.
    p. cm.–(Teaching and learning series)
        Includes bibliographical references and index.
        ISBN: 978-981-210-455-7
        ISBN: 981-210-455-0

1.   Learning. 2. Teaching. I. Title. II. Series: Teaching and learning series

LB1060
370.1523—dc21
                                            SLS2005037450

I dedicate this book to my parents, Cheng Mun-Mun and Tan Khai-Hum, for their lifelong passion in teaching, belief in education, and love for children.

Contents

Acknowledgements

Words of thanks are due to the following:

- The series editor, Jason Tan, for his invitation, insightful preface, and faith in educational research and publication.
- The editorial team at Marshall Cavendish Academic, for their foresight and expertise in publishing academic books, and their interest in contemporary educational issues.
- My siblings, brothers-in-law, niece, and nephews, for their unconditional support.
- My father, for being a role-model in engaged and dedicated social, educational, and community services.
- My mother, for her unconditional love and positive regards.
- The authors and co-authors, for their insights into the various themes explored in this book.
- The Director, deans, and heads of the various academic groups at the Nationnal Institute of Education, for their support and encouragement.

All faults found in this book are due to my shortcomings to present a comprehensive view of what matters in learning. I take sole responsibility.

Tan Ai Girl, Ph.D.
Singapore
March 2005

Preface

The appearance of this volume is timely. In the midst of a flurry of educational reform initiatives, it is all too easy for educational practitioners to feel increasingly harried and to be groping for answers to practical questions such as "What works? Why does it work? When does it work? How does it work? With whom does it work?" Ai Girl has attempted the brave task of marshalling and summarising a fairly comprehensive amount of research literature both within and outside of Singapore. The topics she has covered are of interest to educational practitioners across different levels of schooling, and include self-initiated learning, group work, class size, problem-based learning, and learning with information and communication technologies. With judicious use of the research findings presented in this volume, educational practitioners will be better placed to bridge the oft-lamented gap between theory and practice, and to make wiser decisions regarding teaching and learning processes and practices.

Jason Tan

Preface

Introduction

TAN AI GIRL

> "Learning is an instinctual, adaptive function of *conscious* agents. The propensity for acquiring knowledge, insights and skills in a *flexible* and an *active* manner is the unique feature of human learning… (P)eople learn in any context in which they are embedded, … at any age … The ubiquity and permanence of learning gives rise to a host of intricate queries, among others: How a context can be manipulated so as to maximize learning effect." (Law 2002, 181; italic in origin)

In this introduction chapter, we pose a question: What matters in learning? As a human activity and social process, learning occurs, when a person socialises, encultures, and accultures with primary and other caregivers, peers and others of similar and different backgrounds. The person learns formally and informally human languages, numeracies, literacies, and artistic expressions to represent her(his) feelings, thinking, will, and needs. Using these different forms of representation, the person gives meanings to her(his) experiences and interpersonal relationships, and makes sense of the world events. Culture contextualises learning.

Central to the question of "what matters in learning?" is our philosophy of learning which addresses the indispensable role of learning for developing personhood (*zuoren*). Learning in developing personhood aims to drive the learner's will, motivation and determination to better her(him)self and her(his) life. In other words, *the person's full development* and *growth* is the outcome of learning (Dewey 1938/1997; Freire 2002); and *the person* is the core of learning, not the learning resources, activities, frameworks, or others.

The learner is a person who is born into "an organized social life … from which s/he draws her (his) mental and spiritual substance, and in which s/he must perform her(his) proper function or become a mental and moral wreck" (added gender pronounces, Dewey 1884, 57). The learner is dependent, relate, and attached to her(his) caregivers and loved ones (Bowbly 1969; Bowbly 1973; Bowbly 1980). S/he is self-determined, self-regulatory, and self-directed in all her(his) experiences which are intrinsically social and cultural. The learner is self-initiated such that s/he regulates her(his) learning her(him)self, being efficacious of her(his) undertakings, and being intrinsically motivated to attain her(his) aspirations.

1

Learning in a *person-centred* environment facilitates individualised, co-operative (every learner is inter-dependent on the others to complete a task) and collaborative learning (all learners work on the same task). The learner engages in a continuum of individualised cognition and social cognition. As an open system, the learner is organised and dynamic (Much 1995). S/he interacts and establishes interdependent relations with other open systems: Her(his) culture and social institutions (Csikszentmihalyi 1988). S/he optimises her(his) human potentials to be with something or someone else, being with the world, and being in the face of meaning to fulfil and of value to realise. The learner is open to the world and to all her(his) experiences, and hence her(his) creativity is ethical, constructive and caring (see Rogers 1961). S/he exercises her(his) capacity to take a stand to be free to shape her(his) character, to be responsible for what may come out of her(him)self (Frankl 1988). In the process of learning "being more fully human" (Freire 2002, 44) the learner restores true generosity, conquests freedom, and uses her(his) power to create and recreate in her(his) power to transform her(his) perceived world. Creativeness in the present experience can become a moving force for growth (Dewey 1938/1997). To allow continuity in growth, the learner values her(his) present experiences that live fruitfully and creatively in subsequent experiences.

"A learned person is one who *seeks* to understand what this world has been and is and how that explains, if only in part, what that person is and wants to become." (Sarason 1993, 28; italic in the original sentence, replaced educated with learned) In order to be or become, learning is constantly made into praxis (Freire 2002). Hence, learning should be viewed as a way of exploring and expanding our understanding of our future optimistically in relation to humanity's history, accomplishments, and purposes (see Sarason 1993). It is an open practice, an activity of understanding meaning and interpretations in the human world. It is an engagement in learning how to live and to be human (Hinchliffe 2001). Learning initiates the person into an understanding identity (Fuller 1989). To orchestrate *person-centred* learning, the teacher has to facilitate personalised learning using self-regulated and -directed learning strategies, differentiated learning, co-operative learning, collaborative learning, tutoring, and the like. Higher mental functions depend on mastery of cultural tools. Considering this, learning can be facilitated through scaffolding, modelling and guided discovery using language as a tool to monitor mental functioning (Wertsch & Tulviste 1992).

The joy of learning and the drive of continuous learning are embedded into the philosophy of holistic education for full human development. Human development is ecological (Bronfenbrenner 1979), evolutionary and ontogenetic (Baltes 1997), neither determined by genes nor by experience (von Bertalanffy 1933/1962). It engages processes that broaden the range of choices to enable human beings to achieve capacities and to fulfil needs to survive, secure, love, belong, esteem, and actualise (Maslow 1943). Full development is facilitated in enriched cultural environments (Bruner 1998). Programs that embed creative and caring learning strategies are designed for the young with learning difficulties (e.g., the learning support program) and for learning with authentic problems (e.g., problem-based learning and project work). These innovative learning programs are meant to optimise the learner's full functioning. Learning is thus purposeful, meaningful, intentional, and directional.

"Learning also involves certain virtues: care and accuracy and conscientiousness, a desire for truth, the willingness to admit mistakes, and so forth." (Wilson 2003, 107) The philosophy of learning for full development highlights basic human values such as dignity and respect, and encourages cultivation of good values such as care, love, and compassion. Care as value-guided practice emerges as a response to a need. It includes everything that we do to maintain, continue, and repair our world (i.e., our bodies, our selves and our environment) so that we can live in the world as well as possible (Tronto 1993). In a care-giving context, a person's dignity and quality of life is of paramount importance (see Saunders 1990). The care of the self concerns a life of receptivity (*Gelassenheit*), or "letting things be" (Edwards 2000). The caregiver and the care receiver are obliged to self-care, knowing where to get, and how to access to resources of all kinds that benefit one's growth.

In a holistic educational context, the learner builds caring human relationships with her(his) contemporaries (i.e., fellow learners) and predecessors (i.e., parents, teachers, and senior students) and successors (i.e., junior students). Holistic care (Engel 1977), dependency (Bowbly 1969; Bowbly 1973; Bowbly 1980; *amae* in Japanese, Doi 1973) and attachment (Ainworth 1982) are some inevitable means that facilitate intimate relatedness among the person and her(his) loved ones. Relatedness of the person to her(his) caregivers, peers, and other adults are significant as it determines the quality of the learner's social and cultural life which in turn determines the degree of intensity and the sense of directedness of her(his) purposeful acts and intentional learning.

LEARNING IN THE SINGAPORE'S EDUCATIONAL CONTEXT

In brief, Singapore's educational development can be divided into several phases: foundation (1965–1979), efficiency-driven (1980–1997), and ability-driven (1998–). In each phrase, foci of education remain, that is, creative education, instructional or pedagogical innovation, and national education or character development. Generally, educational policies move hand in hand with socio-economic and cultural policies.

Singapore gained its independence in 1965. During the first two decades Singapore's leaders put in extensive efforts to ensure as much as possible, that every child receives at least foundation education. In 1979, under the bilingual education policy, all schools adopted the English language as the main medium of instruction, and mother tongues (e.g., Mandarin Chinese, Malay and Tamil) as the languages for cultural transmission and moral development. In the eighties, the country's economy and socio-politics were relatively stable. During this period, developing an efficient work force and cultivating high quality manpower were key on the educational and national agenda. In the nineties, the country attained an affluent life style, and satisfactory educational outcomes. In 1997, a new framework of learning, the Thinking Schools Learning Nation (TSLN) document was released around the same period as the announcement of high achievement in mathematics and science at the Third International Mathematics and Science Study (TIMSS). The TSLN set a new momentum towards independent learning, discovery learning and student-centred learning. Supporting the TSLN framework were the implementation of the information technology (IT) master plan and the program on national education (NE). The learning outcomes and attributes desired for student characters were documented as the desired outcomes of education (DOE). Building on its good profile of high academic achievement, schools went through a series of exercises to improve their physical infrastructures to accommodate the country's aspirations to move towards excellence in education. In addition, relevant infrastructures and programs were initiated to include teacher network, learning circle, professional development, attachment to the

4

teacher educational institution, and the MOE headquarters with the aim of encouraging teachers to interact, exchange ideas, and share good practices.

In Singapore, education has a special role and unique position. This is evident when we examine the country's Prime Minister's (PM) annual address during the national day rally (in August). Among other themes, education is a core. Delivered are major initiatives and directions of education for the next several years. Subsequently, during a one-day annual work plan seminar (around September or October) the education minister addresses school and higher educational institutional leaders and shares his vision of education based on key points disseminated by the PM.

This book attempts to provide a perspective on what matters in learning in the Singaporean context. The question to what really matters in learning is timely, as Singapore has just entered into a new chapter of leadership. The newly appointed leaders in the Ministry of Education (MOE) include the Minister himself (appointment: August 2003), the director-general of education (February 2004), and the director of schools (January 2005). The Minister was formerly the senior minister of state for trade, industry and education; the director-general was a teacher, a principal and a former director of schools (since 2002); and the director of schools was a headmaster of a secondary school. For the past one year or more, innovative and enterprising ways has been introduced in the system to advance the effectiveness of Singapore's school programs.

Innovation and Enterprise

In his keynote at the work plan seminar 2003 the then acting Education Minister encouraged teachers, school leaders, teacher educators, and education leaders to embark on the journey of innovation and enterprise (I & E), a continual effort of the TSLN (Tharman 2003). The spirit of facing new challenges successfully is conceptualised with the intent to encourage Singaporeans to move "out of the box" (i.e., more self-initiative, less close guidance) and "beyond the existing comfort zone" (i.e., having confidence to try something new). Along with the I & E framework the education ministry aims to diversify Singapore's educational structure and create more space for students to pursue their passions and to develop their talents. A broad-based, holistic education means allowing students to draw from a wide range of learning experiences through co-curricular activities (CCAs) such as uniformed groups, volunteered work, self-initiated activities, and community involvement. Teachers are encouraged to extend their experience to the business and community sectors through the professional development leave (PDL) scheme. Multidisciplinary learning is welcome and humanity is included into the curricula. Two teacher conferences were organised in 2003 and 2004, highlighting the roles of teachers as enterprising educators who possess innovative, risk taking, and intrinsic motivated dispositions. Resources and funding are allocated to support such engagement, whenever possible.

New Announcements

Specifically, in January 2004, in a press release the MOE announced two new measures. The first was about giving schools the flexibility to develop their own annual grade four (age: 10–11 years old) streaming examination papers for one subject—the mother tongue. The second was related to the possibility for schools having the flexibility to merge the EM1 and EM2 streams and to prepare the best foundation programme for the EM3. As a matter of fact, until 2004, all children in Singapore sit for the first national examination at the age of ten or eleven years, after four years of elementary schooling. All children learn the English language as a medium of instruction, and their mother tongues (the Mandarin Chinese, Malay language or Tamil language, depending on their home language use and ethnicity). The two languages, i.e., the English language and the mother tongue, are examinable subjects for the first (in grade 4) and second (in grade 6) streaming exercises. In other words, instead of sitting together for a national examination, children of different schools will sit for school-based examinations. The respective schools are allowed to decide on the schedule of the examination and to develop their own assessment and/or to take questions from the national item bank. Students are streamed to three different groups based on the grade 4 national examination results. The first group comprises pupils who are conversant and competent in both the English language and the mother tongue at the first language level (EM1). The second group consists of the pupils whose competencies in the English language and the mother tongue are at the first language level and the second language level (EM2) respectively. The third group is made up of the pupils whose competencies in both the English language and mother tongue are at the communication level (EM3).

In March 2004, the MOE press released two significant announcements worthwhile mentioning here. One of them was about a revised way of ranking for the secondary schools. Instead of using the students' ordinary level results as the indicator for school ranking, twelve bands are employed to rank secondary schools. The other was the launch of a monograph on strategies for active and independent learning with the main contents of learning experiences from 36 piloted schools at the grade three and secondary one levels. In September, to support broad-based education, a press release announced the direct school admission program for seven schools that offer integrated programme (IP) at the secondary one level. These schools can admit students based on their own admission criteria (e.g., school A uses the following criteria: Examination results of grades 4, 5 and 6, results of school based general ability test that evaluates problem-solving strategies, reasoning ability, and IQ for P6 non-gifted education programme students, portfolio, personal statement, and interview, when necessary).

Another innovative move in the educational system was witnessed in April 2004 with the establishment of the Singapore Examinations and Assessment Board (SEAB), a statutory board under the supervision of the Ministry of Education (MOE). The SEAB takes over the role of the former Examination Division of the MOE. In the same month the MOE approved the establishment of two private funded schools (managed by the Anglo-Chinese School Board of Governors, and the Singapore Chinese High School Board of Directors).

In line with the spirit of Innovation and Enterprise in June 2004, co-curricular activities (CCAs) were given a distinct status as an integral part of the holistic, well-rounded education to cultivate qualities such as resilience, tenacity, confidence and perserverance. The range of activities grouped under CCAs was expanded to include student participation in sports and rugged activities (e.g., National Civil Defense Corps), student-initiated activities (SiAs, e.g., Volunteer Adult Leader) and community-based activities (e.g., community club's youth executive committee, and residents' committee youth club).

To realise the aspiration of every child matters, in September the press released the announcement on the availability of developing funding (i.e., 12 millions) to improve nine special education schools. The time frame to carry out this initiative was shortened to until the year 2008 (the original proposal was until 2012). Furthermore, the MOE will work with the Autism Association Singapore to build an additional special education school for autistic children. The developing funding is meant for improving resources, quality teachers, curricular design and leadership courses. In parallel, funding will be released to mainstream schools to improve education for the students with dyslexia and autistic spectrum disorder (ASD). With this funding, mainstream schools are encouraged to enhance in-class support and to introduce specialist interventions to assist students with mild and moderate disabilities to cope with regular school curricula. About 20 primary schools and 30 secondary schools will benefit from this initiative.

Moving Forward

In the year 2004 work plan seminar (Tharman 2004), announcements were made on increasing manpower grants to schools to ease the teachers' workload, broaden their educational experiences and to employ expertise. Specialist services and expertise such as CCA specialists, educational psychologists and teacher educator professionals will be provided to schools and school clusters to support teachers' professional development and to enhance the quality of work. Teacher counsellors are to be trained in the year 2005 to meet the needs of children who need professional help. By the year 2006, it is targeted to have one school counsellor (with at least diploma qualification) in every secondary school and by the year 2008 one school counsellor in all other schools. To include children with mild disabilities and learning difficulties, special need officers (at least with certificate qualification) are trained to aid mainstream teachers. There will be an increase in teacher recruitment, so that by 2010, primary (age: 6–12 years old) and secondary (age: 13–16 years old) schools will have about ten more teachers and junior college (age: 16–18 years old) will have on average eight more teachers. With the increase in the number of teachers and specialists, the pupil and teacher ratio (PTR) in the near future may become smaller than that of today. Given extra resources, teachers are encouraged to adopt a variety of pedagogical approaches such as team teaching and co-teaching. School leaders are empowered with the responsibility and flexibility to optimise the given extra resources.

Teach Less and Learn More (TLLM)

Taking teaching and learning as the processes to develop a person fully and to enable the person to make meaning in life, the child's or the learner's experience has to be called to the forefront (see Dewey 1938/1997). Hence teaching and learning have to be experiential, meaningful, purposeful, self-

8

regulatory, and collaborative. The child/learner constructs personalised meanings when s/he engages in activities and in human relationships.

As a newly developed country, Singapore has in the past nearly four decades put in place sound educational and socio-economic systems, cultivated sufficient number of dedicated and quality teacher educators and teachers, and established research and information and community technology (ICT) infrastructures. The next immediate question is that what do all these new development and initiatives mean to the learners?

In his first rally speech to the Singapore nation in August 2004, the PM announced a new direction in education: "teach less and learn more" which has stimulated continuous reflections and discussions. In his words (Lee 2004), the PM iterated the essence of education that is beyond just getting grades but that is about learning how to live life fully: "We've got to teach less to our students so that they will learn more. Grades are important ...but grades are not the only thing in life and there are other things in life which we want to learn in school".

Learning is individualised, social and ecological. Our book examines contemporary issues of concern in education which include space for learning (e.g., class size), structures of learning (e.g., grouping), relationships in learning (e.g., tutoring), and processes in learning (e.g., the use of information and communication technologies, self-regulation, co-operation and collaboration). We hope our writing to a certain extent provides a perspective on the inquiry into what matters in learning, a quest that is of the interest of the Singaporean leaders, educators and parents.

CHALLENGES

On the continuum of life long learning, *spaces* are constructed and co-constructed through and for reflective, socially engaged, and culturally contextual activities. That means learning is experiential, central around the learners' needs, growth, and optimal development. Learner-centredness values *pedagogies* that cultivate trustful teacher and student relationships, and supports teaching methods and approaches that are inclusive, reflective, engaging, scientific, experiential and iterative. The ultimate aim of education is growth, development of full personhood, and having dignified life. To realise this aim we conceptualise the learners as the problem solvers, researchers, critical thinkers, and knowledge innovators. The learners are self-directed, co-operative and/or collaborative. They regulate their cognition, motivation, perception, and belief in collaborative learning. What challenges do we face given the complexity and interwoven of personal and social relationships in learning? To contextualise our reflections, we discuss three challenges Singapore's education faces.

A Common Platform and Space for Dialogue

The *first* challenge is related to *building a common platform and space of dialogue* among educational researchers, policymakers and practitioners. The annual work plan seminar organised by the Ministry of Education around September or October aims to construct a shared communicative space for these three groups of educational professionals. During the one-day program held in one of the educational institutes, the Education Minister in his opening address outlines the educational landscape for the next one year or more. He outlines educational plans for the next three to five years. Awards of various achievements are given away, followed by group discussions on some key issues outlined in the Minister's speech. The groups brainstorm responses related to key issues and submit them to the planning committee. The permanent secretary to the Education Minister delivers the closing address. The essence of the published speeches serves as a common document to construct a sharing space for communication and interaction. The working team comprises policy markers, researchers, and practitioners working in vertical integration for effective and practical research and development.

Evidence-based Educational Policy

The *second* challenge is about *adopting an evidence-based educational policy*, which demands productive changes. Burkhardt and Schoenfeld (2003) advocate the need to change to an evidence-based endeavour for educational policy making. That means the field of education should operate in the mode of applying scientific method so as to use systematic collection and objective information in policy making. At the National Institute of Education Singapore, the establishment of the Singapore's Centre for Teaching Thinking (SCTT), Centre for Research in Pedagogy and Practice (CRPP) and Learning Sciences Laboratory (LSL), for instance, are meant to facilitate some effective mechanisms to take ideas tested successfully in small scale to everyday classroom practice. Productive changes are essential to ensure large scale research for practice. These include having more research in practice to understand which contextual factors are critical and which are not. Design experiments (Kelly 2003) are primary examples of research that resides in Stokes' (1997) "Pasteur's quadrant", the space of studies that offer potentially significant contributions to both theory and practice. Using an engineering research approach, researchers in education can contribute a great deal to the imaginative design and systematic research-based development of educational materials and their implementation. An excellent catalyst for the growth of the engineering enterprise is to have the medium-term funding of some such large scale projects or a number of collaborative institutes to carry out such projects.

A challenge for the educational research centres mentioned above is to identify and to develop existing small scale studies and to build on work effective for learning and accepted by the research community and the public. To establish general principles with a known range of validity, the work of small group of academics on specific and prevailing educational issues over a year or two is valuable. Academics, educational researchers, curricular developers, and practitioners (i.e., teachers) should make conscious efforts to work directly on the treatment they design for in-depth analysis of potentially important and well-developed treatments. This serves as a much more direct route from research to improved practice.

Also, it is essential to have a reasonably theoretical base and a clear view of the reliable range of each aspect of the theory. Such a theory base allows for a clear focus on important issues and provides sound guidance for the design of improved solutions to important problems. It is important to establish a gradually growing core of research results that are generally accepted within the research community, and publicised as such.

To ensure productive changes, some potentially effective levers would be essential which include training for researchers with a broad range of skills, identifying and rewarding outstanding designers of educational materials and processes, re-balancing the academic value system in recognition of the importance of educational research and development and personal and team accountability, funding to support such work, and the creation of appropriate organisational structures to foster it.

Research Methods

The *third* challenge is to have a good grasp of *research methodology* (Pressley, Duke & Boling 2004). In a true experimental design, the participants are randomly assigned to a treatment group (e.g., an instructional intervention of interest to the researcher) and the control group (e.g., receiving a control intervention or the conventional instruction of the day). If achievement is higher among the participants in the experimental group the most likely explanation is that the treatment causes the achievement difference. In a quasi experimental design, usually in natural settings, groups are matched and/or controlled for characteristics the researcher believes could have an impact on the way the participants respond to the intervention.

Meta-analysis is a statistical procedure to synthesise and review the outcomes when a number of experimental and/or quasi-experimental studies of an intervention, and thus to draw conclusions across these studies from the size of the intervention effect of each experiment. The arithmetically averaged usually give greater weights to studies with large sample sizes. The method illuminates the average effect sizes resulted from intervention, and thus can be used to inform if an intervention produces effects or not. The challenge to conduct meta-analysis lies in the search for studies of which an intervention has been evaluated in several experiments. Meta-analysis requires sophisticated statistical skills, and good understanding of the issues being qualifications should supporting personnel and staff acquire? Some of these questions are highlighted in the previous chapters. Specifically, chapter 6 reviews studies conducted to find out that if class size reduction affects a child's achievement, if this measure is cost-effective, and if there are alternative measures to rectify the same problem. Class size refers to the actual number of the learners at any one time when a teacher teaches. Different from pupil and teacher ratio, class size does not include supporting and non-teaching staff. As a matter of fact the pupil and the teacher ratio is counted from the total number of teaching staff, engaged directly or indirectly (by assisting the teacher) to the total number of students in a school. The ratio does not reflect the actual number of teacher in the classroom teaching the students.

Controversial findings appeared from studies on effects of class size reduction on academic achievement. This is true when the "size" or figure of "small" or "large" is contextual and socio-cultural. Class size in many classrooms in Asia is larger, i.e., more than 30. The number 30 may be perceived as "small" for schools that have been keeping the number 40 or 45 in a class. Evidently large class size has been a fact of life in countries that report high achievements in the international studies on Mathematics and Science, such as Singapore, Hong Kong, Japan, Korea, and China. Does "size" of the class really matter in learning? Or, are there equally or more significant factors that influence achievement?

In chapter 7 we review a pre-referral intervention programme introduced to Singapore to facilitate, nurture, witness, and guide optimising human functioning and full human development. In optimising human functioning, teachers model, scaffold, facilitate, innovate, create, and discover best and sustainable learning, cognitive, emotional and pedagogical strategies and skills. Together with students, teachers co-construct motivating, self-directed, collaborative, and life long learning environments. Teachers negotiate, dialogue, share, and journey with students to paths that are suitable for the latter. In the pre-referral intervention programme, school leaders, teachers and professionals need to work together in a systemic manner to construct learning environments that are caring, warm, enriching, individuating and collaborative.

In Singapore, teachers are socialisation agents for full human development and *keys* to nation building. They are predecessors or *sensei* (in Japanese), respectable masters or *laoshi* (in Mandarin), and the known or *guru* (in Malay). "Those who once show me the way are my teachers." Hence, the term *teacher* may broadly refer to those who are in the teaching work force undertaking the role of a classroom teacher, a specialist who assists children with learning difficulty, or peers who tutor. A Chinese proverb is appropriate to highlight indeed "teacher" emerges when two or more persons doing a same task. The phrase "*sanren xing biyou wo shi yan*" is literally translated as "in a three person (working) group a master emerges." That means, in everyday life and in any social practice, when a few persons (in this case three in a group) attend to a task or a problem together, at least one of them will lead the group. Learning with and teaching others is natural, and is part and parcel of human social life. In team, leadership emerges. Teaching and learning is thus social; it happens in every moment of life between two or more persons in engaged interactions and in inclusive *spaces* of learning and living. As a concluding remark, in the Epilogue, we outline other possible learning modes beneficial to the learners including collaboration among teachers and with parents.

REFERENCES

Ainworth, M. D. S. 1982. Attachment: Retrospect and prospect. In *The place of attachment in human behavior* (3–30). Edited by C. M. Parkes & J. Stevenson-Hilde. New York: Basic Books.

Baltes, P. B. 1997. On the incomplete architecture of human ontogeny: Selection, optimization and compensation as foundation of developmental theory. *American Psychologist, 52(4)*, 366–380.

Bowbly, J. M. 1969. *Attachment and loss, vol. 1: Attachment.* London: Hogarth Press.

Bowbly, J. M. 1973. *Attachment and loss, vol. 2: Separation, anxiety and anger.* London: Hogarth Press.

Bowbly, J. M. 1980. *Attachment and loss, vol. 3: Loss, sadness and depression.* London: Hogarth Press.

Bronfenbrenner, U. 1979. *The ecology of human development.* Cambridge, MA: Harvard University Press.

Bruner, J. T. 1998. Science, brain fiction. *Educational leadership, November,* 14–18.

Burkhardt, H., & A. H. Schoenfeld. 2003. Improving educational research: toward a more useful, more influential, and better-funded enterprise. *Educational Researcher, 32(9),* 3–14.

Csikszentmihalyi, M. 1988. Society, culture and person: A systems view of creativity. In *The nature of creativity* (325–339). Edited by R. J. Sternberg. New York: Cambridge University Press.

Dewey, J. 1884. The new psychology. In *The early works of John Dewey, 1882–1897* (vol. 1, 48–60). Edited by J. A. Boydston. Carbondale, Illinois: Southern Illinois University Press.

Dewey, J. 1938/1997. *Experience and education.* New York: Touchstone.

Doi, T. 1973. *The anatomy of dependence.* New York: Kodansha.

Edwards, J. C. 2000. Passion, activity, and "the care of the self". *Hastings Center Report, March–April,* 31–34.

Engel, G. 1977. The care of patients: Art or science? *The Johns Hopkins Medical Journal, 140(5),* 222–232.

Frankl, V. 1988. *The will to meaning: Foundation and application of logotherapy.* US: Meridian.

Freire, P. 2002. *Pedagogy of the oppressed.* New York: Continuum.

Fuller, T., ed. 1989. *The voice of liberal learning: Michael Oackeshott on education.* Princeton, N.J.: Yale University Press.

Harden, R. M., J. Grant, G. Buckley, & I. R. Hart. 1999. BEME guide no.1: Best evidence medical education. *Medical Teacher, 21(6),* 553–562.

Hart, I. R., & R. M. Harden. 2000. Best evidence medical education (BEME): a plan for action. *Medical Teacher, 22(2),* 131–135.

Hinchliffe, G. 2001. Education or pedagogy? *Journal of Philosophy of Education, 35(1),* 31–45.

Kelly, A. F. 2003. Theme issue on the role of design in educational research (editor of special issue). *Educational Research, 32(1).*

Law, L. C. 2002. Learning theories: Past, current and future perspectives. In *Psychology in contexts: A perspective from the South East Asian societies* (181–208). Edited by A. G. Tan & L. C. Law. Singapore: Lingzi.

Lee, H. L. 2004. *National day rally speech* (August 29). Singapore.

Maslow, A. H. 1943. A theory of human motivation. *Psychological Review, 50,* 370–396.

MOE. 2004. *Nurturing every child: Flexibility and diversity in Singapore schools.* Singapore: MOE.

Much, N. 1995. Cultural psychology. In *Rethinking psychology* (97–121). Edited by J. A. Smith, R. Harre & L. V. Langenhove. London: Sage.

Pressley, M., N. K. Duke, & C. E. Boling. 2004. The educational science and scientifically based instruction we need: lessons from reading research and policymaking. *Harvard Educational Review, 74(1)*, 30–61.

Rogers, C. 1961. *On becoming a person: A therapist's view of psychotherapy.* London: Constable.

Sarason, S. B. 1993. *You are thinking of teaching? Opportunities, problems, realities.* San Francisco, California: Jossey-Bass Publishers.

Saunders, C. 1990. *Hospice and palliative care: An interdisciplinary approach.* London: Edward Arnold.

Slavin, R. E. 2002. Evidence-based education policies: Transforming educational practice and research. *Educational Researcher, 31(7)*, 15–21.

Stokes, D. E. 1997. *Pasteur's quadrant: Basic science and technical innovation.* Washington DC: Brookings.

Tharman, S. 2003. *Work plan seminar key note address* (October 2). Singapore: MOE.

Tharman, S. 2004. *Work plan seminar key note address* (September 29). Singapore: MOE.

Tronto, J. C. 1993. *Moral boundaries: A political argument for an ethic of care.* New York: Routledge.

von Bertalanffy, L. 1933/1962. *Modern theories of development: An introduction to theoretical biology.* New York: Harper & Brothers.

Wertsch, J. V., & P. Tulviste. 1992. L. S. Vygotsky and contemporary developmental psychology. *Developmental psychology, 28(4)*, 548–557.

Wilson, J. 2003. The concept of education revisited. *Journal of Philosophy of Education, 37(1)*, 101–108.

CHAPTER 1

Self-Initiated Learning

TAN AI GIRL AND TAMMY KWONG

INTRODUCTION

A new initiative introduced to the Singapore's schools termed the strategies for active and independent learning (SAIL). The SAIL is an instructional approach that has the potential to engage students in active and reflective learning and to nurture independent learning habits. This approach emphasises learning as a formative and developmental process, in which instruction and assessment point the way for students to continuous learn and improve. Under the aspiration of SAIL a teacher is encouraged to help a student take responsibility of her(his) own learning, and be aware of where s/he is in her(his) own learning, what s/he should know and be able to do, and what s/he needs to do to improve and progress. This awareness likely arises from students' habits of self-directed learning and independent learning. How do teachers monitor students' learning? The SAIL suggests using clear communication of learning expectations and assessment criteria to monitor students' learning. Teachers are encouraged to keep the statements of learning expectations broad, so as to allow them to select open-ended tasks that encourage divergent thinking and alternative responses. Using the assessment criteria, teachers should provide the students qualitative feedback on their strengths and areas for improvement. Teachers should give students the opportunities to use the identified assessment criteria to evaluate their own work and that of their peer. Self- and peer-assessments are perceived as the learning tools for students to reflect on their performance and to articulate their learning. This new approach stimulates learning through active questioning and discussion. It is also hoped that the new approach will be able to assist a two-way interaction between teacher and student and encourage students to adapt to new and unexpected situations. For the past several years, some elementary and secondary schools volunteered to undertake the SAIL project in different subjects. Self-reported feedback from teachers and students was relatively positive, such as active student participation and increasing self-awareness of learning expectations.

In this chapter, we focus our presentation on three constructs, self-directed learning, self-efficacy, and self-regulation that appear frequently in the literature that would substantial part of, if not the whole theoretical framework of the SAIL. We hold on to the claim that individualised cognition happens within the continuum of social cognition, and vice versa. Hence we also explore in this chapter the concept of collaborative learning. Findings on self-regulation from the Singaporean teacher educator researchers will be highlighted.

SELF-DIRECTED LEARNING

Self-directed learning is defined as an approach where learners are motivated to assume personal responsibility and collaborative control of the cognitive (self-monitoring), contextual (self-management) processes in constructing and confirming meaningful and worthwhile learning outcomes (Garrison 1997). It is synonymous with terms such as individualised instruction, student-centred learning, prescriptive learning and even computer-based training (Piskurich 1994).

Essentially, self-directed learning is a form of internal regulation, where learners themselves perform learning and thinking activities, instead of the teacher taking over these activities and explaining the relationships between concepts or theories (Birenbaum 2002). In this way, this approach offers a deep level of learning as learners educate themselves at their own pace, and determine their own level of expertise (Hatcher 1997).

Self-directed learning is a core concept in the study and practice of adult education (Garrison 1997) and is especially significant in the knowledge age like now, when most adults desire to continue to learn. At the same time, learners are increasingly expected to be responsible and motivated towards their own learning. As a result of this shift, the role of the teacher and the nature of the curriculum are also being redefined, as self-directed learning departs from a teacher-centred form of teaching, to a learner-centred approach.

Although the learner is responsible for her(his) own learning, this does not mean that the learner constructs meaning in an isolated world (Garrison 1997). Furthermore, absolute learner control may adversely affect or diminish the efficiency of achieving quality learning outcomes. As such, for self-directed learning, collaborative control is the way to go.

Self-directed learning is viewed from a *collaborative constructivist perspective*, where the learner is responsible for constructing meaning, *while including the participation of others*. This increased learner control alters the transactional balance between the teacher and the learner. This means that instead of the teacher being in control traditionally, management of the learning process now becomes a collaborative effort between the teacher and the learner (Garrison 1997). The teacher becomes more of a facilitator, and less of a teacher who dictates the learning process (Hatcher 1997).

Garrison (1997) proposed a model that nicely integrates three overlapping dimensions of the learning process: self-management, self-monitoring and motivation. A brief outline of the model follows.

Self-management: This refers to an aspect of *external* task control on the part of the learner, in the management of learning activities. This dimension focuses on external activities associated with the learning process such as enactment of learning goals and management of learning resources and support that might be available. Increased learner control through self-management develops greater responsibilities, especially towards the learning process itself and the construction of meaning. There is an increased awareness on the part of the learner, of a need to make learning a meaningful process, which in turn necessitates greater responsibility, in monitoring the process. Henceforth, in order to facilitate the self-directed process, facilitators should provide learners with choices on how they wish to carry out the learning process. In addition, learning resources should be made available to them, with flexible pacing to accommodate learners' different needs, as well as offer feedback when needed.

Self-monitoring: In this second dimension, the learner is expected to take responsibility for the construction of personal meaning (Garrison 1997). Self-directed learning builds upon learners' existing knowledge, so it is essentially up to them to integrate these new ideas and concepts with what they already know in a meaningful manner, to ensure that learning goals are met (Hatcher 1997). Students are largely responsible for their own learning and thus self-direction requires that learners have a willingness and ability to self-monitor their learning process, as well as be able to think critically and reflect on what they have already learnt before. As aforementioned, the learner cannot work alone. Internal feedback alone may lack accuracy and explicitness, and so the teacher is required to provide feedback to the learner, for the purposes of self-monitoring.

This is interesting to note, especially since traditionally, many educational institutions tend to place control of the learning process squarely in the hands of teachers alone. With this shift towards self-directed learning and an ever increasing demand for lifelong learning, facilitators should ensure that balanced control exists between the facilitator and the learner. This balance provides opportunities for instructional support, while allowing and encouraging students to demonstrate responsibility over what and how they learn.

Motivation: Motivation has enormous influence on how students assume responsibility for and control of their learning process. It reflects the perceived value and anticipated success of learning goals at the time learning is initiated and mediates between control and responsibility during the learning process. Garrison (1997) distinguishes between two types of motivation in self-directed learning, namely, *entering motivation* and *task motivation*.

Entering motivation is what the learner experiences in the process of deciding to participate. It results from rational intentions with regard to selecting learning goals. Learners have a higher entering motivational state when they perceive that their learning goals will meet their needs and are achievable. Two factors affect a learner's level of entering motivation: *competency* and *contingency*. *Competency* refers to the perceived skills, ability, and knowledge of the individual while assessing one's learning goals. The learner's perception of his or her personal characteristics affects the decision to participate and the choice of goals implemented. *Contingency* refers to the perceived institutional resources or barriers, and ideological and socio-economic constraints. Mostly, this refers to the contextual characteristics that the learner is in. Both of them combined represent anticipated control, that is, the perceived ability and opportunity to exercise control over the learning process.

Task motivation is the effort that the learner requires to stay on task and persist, as well as maintain the intention of achieving the learning goal. It also refers to the learner's volition, that is, the ability to sustain intentional effort or diligence. This is necessary for the learner to assume responsibility for the achievement of the desired learning goal and outcome.

This form of motivation is influenced by both external conditions and internal states. The challenge then, is to guide learners to internalise their external goals and rewards which are often more dominant in the entering stages of learning. It is also imperative for facilitators to create conditions where students will be increasingly motivated by authentic interest and their own desire to construct personal meaning of the knowledge.

Evidently, self-directed learning has the potential to improve the quality of learning outcomes in the short and long term. Self-direction is necessary for achieving worthwhile and meaningful education outcomes. It is associated with initiating learning goals, maintaining intention and striving for quality outcomes (Hatcher 1997).

The *collaborative constructivist view of learning* encourages learners to approach learning in a deep and meaningful manner. Meaningful learning outcomes are achieved when students are self-directed in their learning as they take responsibility to create personal meaning of new and integrated knowledge, while collaborating with their facilitators. Through this approach, students monitor and manage their thoughts and behaviour while facilitators on their part, create educational contexts that facilitate self-direction, not leaving the learners to learn in isolation. This shared control leads to intrinsic motivation, as well as responsibility.

To put self-directed learning into classrooms and teaching contexts would undoubtedly require time and effort. Both learners and facilitators alike need time to adjust to the new culture, context, and structure of learning (Hatcher 1997). Yet, beyond these short term issues, self-directed teaching is a vital tool in learning if learners are to achieve Dewey's ultimate educational goal of becoming continuous learners who possess the capability for greater educational growth.

SELF EFFICACY AND LEARNING OUTCOMES

Social cognitive theory (Bandura 1986, 2001) provides a framework to understanding the mechanisms that underlie human behaviours. Bandura posits the concept of human agency (humans as agents of action) whereby cognitive processes are instrumental in understanding human functioning. Self-efficacy (Bandura 1982, 1997), a principal component of social cognitive theory, is the process by which an individual evaluates the probability of succeeding in an activity based on s/he abilities and resources relative to the difficulty of the task at hand. The two theories combined provide a model of conceptualising the motivation to achieve in school, in children of different ages.

There are three forms of human agency—personal, proxy and collective agency. Personal agency is of a direct nature whereby goal attainment is largely dependent on a person's sole effort. For example if a student desires to attain a high grade in mathematics, he/she would first engage in self-appraisal of one's abilities, followed by setting a series of realistic goals such as always completing one's homework on time. The student would then engage in the actions or behaviours necessary to attain the goal. No individual has the time nor ability to master all domains of life, neither does one exist in isolation of others. Proxy agency is relying on others for successful functioning (such as a child relying on parents), as well as a collaboration of effort between two people to attain a common goal (e.g., a husband and spouse partnership in raising their child). Collective agency encompasses a bigger social network such as that of a school community in educating a child. Likewise schools belong to a greater system of cultural influences and government policies.

The core precept of human agency is that individuals act purposefully to attain desired goals. Several principles underlie the execution of agency and they are as described by Bandura (2001):

Intentionality: It is assumed that all individuals subscribe to the belief of cause and effect, where one can either choose to act or defer action, with full knowledge that their current decision will lead to an outcome. For example a student can choose to go out and play and neglect his/her studies at the risk of angering their parents or teachers.

The second element of agency is *forethought* and it is related to goal setting. "People set goals for themselves, anticipate the likely consequences of prospective actions and select and create courses of action likely to produce desired outcomes and avoid detrimental ones" (Bandura 2001, 7).

Self-reactiveness is the process of motivating one's self to action, as well as the continued self-regulation of affect and behaviours necessary to attaining the desired goal.

The final component is *self-reflectiveness*, the ability to critique one's functioning. "Among the mechanisms of personal agency, none is more central or pervasive than people's beliefs in their capability to exercise some measure of control over their functioning and over environmental events (Bandura 1997)"—Bandura (2001, 10). The more self-efficacious an individual is, the more likely they will undertake a particular course of action.

The level of self-efficacy can be modulated by four processes, the first being *mastery*, which is the grasp of knowledge an individual has over a particular domain. An individual who is confident of his/her abilities in a specific domain will be more likely to engage in a related activity. For example a student who is comfortable with public speaking will speak up more often in class and engage in extracurricular activities where public speaking is valued, such as debating or the students' council. The second component is the *cognitive reinterpretation of the environment*. How an individual perceives the environment determines the type of response s/he will adopt. For example if a teacher announces a surprise quiz, a student who falls into despair will likely perform worse than a student who views it as a challenge, ceteris paribus. *Social persuasion* is the process whereby the action of others influences the behaviour of an individual. If a parent places a high emphasis on education, it is likely that this value will motivate a child to succeed in school. *Social modelling* is similar to social persuasion, however in this instance it is the individual who chooses to adopt the values espoused by others. This is best exemplified by role modelling.

The self or individual interacts with the educational environment to form learning-related behaviours. The environment can be separated into the social and physical constituents. Depending on the developmental age of the child, the influence of the family, teachers, and peers can differ. The physical environment can be partitioned into the facilities and atmosphere of the school and more specifically the classroom. Government policies and cultural standards tie the social and physical aspects to form the education mesosystem (Bandura 1986).

The self component largely consists of the ideals or goals an individual hopes to achieve as well as the self-knowledge of one's abilities. It is related to cognitive processes, such as the feelings of mastery or competency and relates to the types of goals set and the self-regulatory efforts (e.g., motivation) that are employed in working towards the goal. Parenting styles and parent involvement in their child's studies are forms of social persuasion in which the family can influence a child's academic achievement. Likewise teachers are both instructors and role models for children. Play is especially important to social development, in younger children, whilst later in adolescence, peers may take on the role of confidants. Peers can motivate one another to study or they can intervene directly in peer tutoring arrangements. Physical facilities and a conducive environment for study are the more salient aspects of the physical environment of the school and classroom. The teaching techniques adopted in the class such as problem based learning or a multiliteracies approach can cater to the varying strengths of students thus influencing achievement. Government policies and the emphasis on education determine the funding schools receive. Socio-cultural norms such as the Confucian belief in the importance of education are factors in determining the relative importance of educating the young.

The various factors briefly elaborated contribute to the how self-efficacious a child feels with respect to education. Caution must however be adopted in interpreting self-efficacy in education as a global construct (Pajares 1996). Bandura's original conceptualisation of self-efficacy as the interaction of the self-appraisal of one's abilities with respect to a specific domain of functioning, hence self-efficacy was not meant to be a global trait. Therefore an individual can display high self-efficacy for mathematics but feel hopeless in reading literature. Pajares (1996) makes a case against equating self-efficacy with the constructs of self-concept or self-esteem which are more general domains of functioning. A more appropriate manner to operationalise how self-efficacy is related to education is to consider self-efficacy for performance and self-efficacy for learning as two different perspectives. Self-efficacy of performance is engaged when the parameters of a task are clearly defined, such as in the case of being confident in mathematics. If the task is unfamiliar such as learning a new subject, a student cannot gauge his competency based on past experience and hence must fall upon her(his) perceived ability to learn, which is self-efficacy for learning.

Self-efficacy for learning has high practical value as it describes the mechanisms that underlie how competent an individual feels about the general domain of academic studies. Self-efficacy for performance in specific subjects is less useful in predicting student outcomes, as a student's worth is judged by her(his) ability in an array of different academic subjects, not just one specific field. By intervening in raising a student's self-efficacy for learning, we are engaging in the proverbial process of teaching a man to fish, so that he may feed himself for life.

SELF-REGULATED LEARNING

Self-regulated learning has been the focus of several researchers in the last decade (e.g., Butler & Winne 1995; Olaussen & Bråten 1999; Zimmerman 1990). Although there have been many different operational definitions of self-regulated learning, it is essentially the concept of self-regulated learners being active participants in their own learning (Zimmerman 1990). Self-regulated learning is a style of engaging in activities where learners employ positive skills such as setting goals, deliberating about which strategies to select, monitoring, and evaluating each step of the learning process (Butler & Winne 1995).

All learners generally make use of some form of regulatory process in their learning approach. However, self-regulated learners are differentiated by the fact that they are acutely aware of qualities of their existing knowledge, beliefs, motivation, and cognitive processes, and this allows them to judge how their unfolding cognitive engagement is in line with the standards and learning goals which they set for successful learning (Butler & Winne 1995).

Learners expending effort, persisting and being self-motivated in their learning is a crucial aspect of the learning process in contemporary education and especially so in Singapore, where the curriculum at higher educational levels are steering towards a more cognitively demanding context (Chong 2003). Chang's (1999; cited in Chong 2003) investigation of transitional changes experienced by secondary one students in Singapore indicated that these students report a shift towards a more dependent learning style when entering secondary school, when what is required of them is a greater independence in their learning approach. This reflects a strong dependency on teachers, as well as an unwillingness to be independent and responsible for one's own learning. In order that the future generation of learners will benefit from the schooling system, educators must to this end, provide a learning context where learners are motivated to actively engage and participate.

Educators need to focus on motivating students so that they will become independent, self-directed learners responsible for their own learning process. Students need to know *how* to think, *how* to learn and how to take active control for their own learning. It is imperative that learners assume personal responsibility and control over their learning processes.

Self-regulated learning has been found to have significant impact on the academic achievement of American students (e.g., Zimmerman & Martinez-Pons 1990), with evidence coming from correlational studies that show that higher achieving students are more self-regulated, as well as from experimental studies showing that curricula designed to increase self-regulation have led to better achievement (see Olaussen & Bråten 1999). Drawing from these findings, there exists a need to implement appropriate support that will encourage self-regulation for students who are at risk of failure, academically weaker or in some way disadvantaged. This is especially since the motivation for them to sustain interest in schoolwork is often lacking. We shall look at this in greater detail later in this chapter.

Self-regulated Learning Processes

Researchers have for the past decade been studying the key processes through which students self-regulate their academic learning. Zimmerman and his colleagues (Zimmerman 1990; Zimmerman & Martinez-Pons 1990), in particular, have expressed immense interest in students becoming self-regulated learners in relation to their academic achievement.

Self-regulated learners view the acquisition of knowledge as a systematic and controllable process, one where they accept greater responsibility for their own learning outcomes and achievement (Zimmerman 1990).Essentially, self-regulated learners plan their learning process by setting goals, organising their learning, self-monitoring and self-evaluating their learning process as they acquire new knowledge. These steps make them self-aware, independent, and responsible learners.

Zimmerman (1990) notes that one distinction of the self-regulated learning approach is that it is not characterised merely by the processes of self-regulation and argues that it is the *strategies* that self-regulated learners use which optimise the processes. Strategies specifically refer to the actions and processes aimed at acquiring knowledge or skills. These actions and processes involve agency, purpose and instrumentality perceptions by learners. Essentially, self-regulated learners are distinguished by their awareness of strategic relations between regulatory processes and learning outcomes, and their use of these strategies in order to attain their academic goals. Zimmerman also described the self-regulated learner as one who makes use of metacognitive, motivational, and/or behavioural strategies.

In terms of *metacognitive* processes, self-regulated learners have a conscious awareness of their learning, and conduct frequent self-checking to determine if his or her learning goal has been achieved. This self-monitoring plays a pivotal role in the self-regulatory approach as it underlies the importance of self-awareness in one's ability to regulate performance (Butler & Winne 1995). If necessary, the learner may choose a different and more appropriate strategy in order to reach that goal (Malpass, O'Neil & Hocevar 1999).

Self-regulated learning also entails a "self-oriented feedback" loop (Zimmerman 1990). Feedback, in the learning approach, is an inherent catalyst for self-regulation. The internal self-monitoring within a learner generates feedback that in turn contributes to his or her regulation of subsequent cognitive engagement.

25

Occasionally, self-regulated learners seek feedback from external sources such as the teachers' remark, or peers contributions in collaborative group work (Butler & Winne 1995). Drawing from the feedback they receive, learners may choose to adjust or even abandon their initial learning goals, in order to adapt and invent new methods and strategies for progress to take place.

Along with feedback, learners may find that they need to seek help in order to overcome certain obstacles and difficulties along the way. By seeking help, self-regulated learners are able to move past the obstacles to achieve mastery and autonomy in learning (Dembo & Eaton 2000).

For the *motivational* aspect, self-regulated strategies include the learners' perception of self-control, consisting of a sense of competence, high efficacy and autonomy (Chong 2003). Self-regulated learners are motivated to learn. They do not merely react to outcomes. They proactively seek out opportunities to learn (Zimmerman 1990).

One of the major differences between successful and less successful learners is that successful learners know how to motivate themselves even when they do not feel like performing a task. Less successful individuals tend to have difficulty controlling their motivation (Dembo & Eaton 2000). In order to control motivation, learners need to set goals, develop positive beliefs and self-efficacy, and maintain those beliefs even when faced with obstacles, distractions, occasional failures and possibly interpersonal conflicts in their lives.

Learning and motivation are intrinsically tied together and the end result is learners continually setting and pursuing higher learning goals.

In terms of *behavioural processes*, successful self-regulated learners are able to select and/or construct environments that would facilitate and optimise their learning processes and outcomes (Chong 2003). Self-regulation of the social environment that they work in relates to the learner's ability to determine when they need to work alone, or in a group, or when they need to seek help from other sources such as tutors, peers and even textbooks.

It is evident then that self-regulation is specific to context and learners' choices of strategies are dependent not only on the academic context, but also on personal efforts to self-regulate, as well as the outcomes of the process along the way (Chong 2003). In order to be effective self-regulated learners, learners must be constantly aware of the functional relationships between their thoughts and behaviours, and the contextual variables that they are working in.

Academic Achievement

There exists a considerable body of research that has been conducted on the relationship between self-regulated learning and academic achievement (e.g., Howse, Lange, Farran & Boyles 2003; Malpass, O'Neil & Hocevar 1999). In general, the consistent finding has been that self-regulated learners are likely to have more adaptive cognitive, motivational and achievement outcomes than their peers who do not self-regulate. There is also evidence that the use of cognitive and self-regulatory strategies is an important component of student performance and achievement (Chong 2003).

A study examining sixth grade high-achievers' goals and usage of strategies (Ee, Moore, Atputhasamy 2003) found that the high achieving students reported greater knowledge than usage of strategies. Conducted in Singapore, the study consisted of 566 high-achieving Primary 6 students and 32 teachers in high-achieving classes across 34 schools. Three measures were obtained from students, namely, their academic achievement, goal orientations, and knowledge and usage of self-regulated learning strategies:

- The measure of *academic achievement* was obtained from the Primary Six Leaving Examination (PSLE) results provided by the schools involved.
- *Goal orientations* were obtained using the Personal Goals Scale. This scale assessed students' task, ego and work avoidance orientations in school contexts.
- The Self-Regulated Learning Strategies Scale was used to assess students' reported *knowledge and usage of self-regulated strategies.*

Results revealed that all high-achieving students scored higher on task and ego orientations than on work avoidance orientation. These high-achieving students also demonstrated a tendency for higher task than ego goals. This may be attributed to the high competitive academic context that Singapore has, which "focuses on high achievement through competing and comparing" (Ee, Moore & Atputhasamy 2003, 32). Compared to lower-achieving students in a study by Ee, Moore and Atputhasamy, the high-ability students in this study were found to be more likely to have both higher task and goal orientation scores and tend to demonstrate work avoidance less commonly.

27

Further, the high-achieving students commonly reported "frequently" to "almost always" having knowledge of their self-regulated learning strategies, though they report to use these strategies only "sometimes" to "frequently" (Ee, Moore, & Atputhasamy 2003). This finding of greater knowledge than usage of strategies is not uncommon.

On the teacher level, the Teacher Survey Questionnaire developed was used to assess teachers' classroom orientations and strategy-based instruction. The scale examines teachers' classroom practices in terms of their enhancement of task and ego orientations and promotion of cognitive self-management in the classrooms.

Ee, Moore and Atputhasamy (2003) found that teachers reported a greater frequency of encouraging both task and ego orientations. In addition, the teachers' *task* classroom goal orientation is more frequently encouraged than *ego* classroom goal orientation, which is similar to the findings on students. This suggests that teachers expect their students to achieve high grades and they perceive competing and comparing as a form of motivation that would enhance students' learning. It is also not surprising in a competitive society as Singapore's, where achievement is highly valued, for teachers to use competitive strategies to motivate their students.

Self-regulated learning and low-achievers: Using structured interviews, Zimmerman and Martinez-Pons (1986; cited in Zimmerman 1990) assessed the use of self-regulation levels between students in higher-achieving classes and those in lower-achieving classes. 40 of the students (14–16 years old) were drawn from the advanced academic track, and another 40 were drawn from the lower academic track in a high school.

Students in the higher achieving classes reported greater use of 13 or 14 self-regulatory strategies, twice as often as low achieving students. Discriminant function analyses revealed that students' achievement track could be predicted with 93 per cent accuracy by using their weighted strategy totals across the learning contexts, suggesting that students' use of self-regulated strategies had a strong association with their superior academic performance (Zimmerman 1990).

It was also found that lower achievers tended to demonstrate several common non-self-regulated responses more often than students from the advanced track. These responses express simple resolve (no use of strategies) or a lack of personal initiative ("I just do what the teacher tells me"). This lack of self-regulatory initiative in lower achievers is certainly a cause for concern for educators and parents alike.

Using Likert scales on teachers' ratings of students' strategy use, a subsequent study of another group of 80 15-year old high school students found that self-regulatory strategies could be factorially separated from verbal ability and academic achievement. The items on the scale were focused on learning strategies that were directly observable in school, including several items designed to assess students' intrinsic motivation displayed during class and in their homework assignments. These findings suggest that it is possible to measure qualitative differences in using self-regulatory strategies for studying, and that they are distinct from psychological cognitive constructs like verbal ability or intelligence.

Ablard and Lipschultz (1998) obtained similar findings in their study. 222 high achieving seventh graders were asked to use Zimmerman and Martinez-Pons (1986) Self-Regulated Learning Interview Schedule (SRLIS) to describe their use of self-regulated learning strategies and rate their achievement goals. Students reported frequent use of self-regulatory strategies such as organising and transforming, reviewing their notes, as well as seeking help from adults. All the students scored in the top three per cent of a standardised achievement test and were motivated to participate in special summer programs despite their wide range in use of self-regulated learning strategies. Some students did not report the use of a single strategy while others reported use of almost all the different strategies. Ablard and Lipschultz (1998) suggest that this might be because high achievers are not aware that they use such strategies since these might have become automated processes for them. Drawing from these findings, future research may look into how high achievers attain such high levels of academic performance without necessarily using any self-regulated learning strategies.

Interestingly, in their study, Ablard and Lipschultz (1998) also noted that girls reported using strategies that optimise the immediate environment or personal regulation, in particular learning contexts, in tasks that were exceptionally difficult or that involved reading and writing, more often than boys. This finding, Chong (2003) notes, supports existing research on gender differences and leads to more questions as to whether boys and girls attain high achievement through different methods of learning.

In Singapore a survey was conducted with 831 secondary school students and 129 junior college students from various academic streams, educational levels and with a wide variety of subject combinations. Using a questionnaire containing 42 items, adapted from the Motivated Strategies for Learning Questionnaire (MSLQ), they found above average scores for self-regulation, which suggests that Singaporean students were equally capable of purposeful, responsible and strategic learning and monitoring of their own learning process in different subjects. The study also shows that high achieving students (in the Express and SAP streams) do indeed have better self-regulated learning abilities than the low achievers (in the Normal streams) (see Chong 2003).

In another study, Chong (2003) adapted a training framework and implemented an intervention programme with 89 Normal Academic students to investigate the usefulness of self-regulatory and motivational concepts in aiding them in developing more positive self-perceptions and their role in personal agency. Using self-report questionnaires to assess their perceptions towards the use of self-regulatory strategies (both academic and social), and about their efficacy beliefs, self-concept and affiliation-based motivation in relation to academic and social engagement.

Quantitative analyses indicated a positive impact of the intervention on the Academic Efficacy and Academic Self-Regulation of low ability students in the Experimental group. These analyses supported the effectiveness and appropriateness of the concepts that were introduced to enhance students' academic and social learning (Chong 2003).

These findings (Chong 2003) show that it is feasible to implement a training model that links cognition, perceptions, emotions, and behaviour which influence students' self-regulatory capability and personal agency beliefs. In particular, the results from this study indicate that a social cognitive model that incorporates self-regulation and personal agency beliefs of self-efficacy is beneficial to Singapore secondary school students in allowing them to become more effective learners. However, what this study did not cover were the specific conditions under which the efficacy beliefs of the students enhanced or facilitated their academic self-regulation. As such, further research in this aspect would be worthwhile.

Self-regulated learning and economically disadvantaged children: Research and policy literatures document that young children from economically disadvantaged homes often enter school at a significant disadvantage in scholastic skills as compared to their more affluent peers. Howse, Lange, Farran and Boyles (2003) in their writing mention that children's early self-regulation difficulties stem from the negative environmental conditions of poverty. They stand a greater risk of school failure. These at-risk children from low-income families face the possibility of poor achievement because of motivational factors. Further, to the extent that these children have lesser family and community support, as well as more scholastic failures than their more advantaged peers, it may be assumed that they have lower levels of self-efficacy and poorer attitudes towards school-related activities. All these factors cumulate to result in poorer achievement motivation during their early schooling years. However, there is a lack of research that backs this explanation.

Howse, Lange, Farran and Boyles (2003) conducted a study based on five of the motivational measures on 43 kindergarteners and 42 second graders. Two measures were affective measures regarding the children's worries about, and positive feeling towards the school environment. The other three measures tapped into motivation-related cognitions associated with self-perceived competence and preference for challenge. The researchers sought to investigate the potential effects of the different and potentially unrelated aspects of motivation on early-achievement outcomes. In particular, they wanted to look into the roles of motivation and self-regulated task activity for early-achievement differences between the economically-at-risk and not-at-risk children.

The analysis of the study included a comprehensive measure of children's motivational dispositions, as well as children's reported attitudes and concerns about doing well in school, and teachers' ratings of students' self-motivated behaviour in the classroom. The researchers found no evidence that at-risk children suffered from less motivation to engage in achievement-related activities as compared to their more advantaged peers. Attitudes towards school and levels of self-efficacy were remarkably positive in both groups of children. Teachers' ratings also seemed to support this finding.

Stipek and Ryan (1997; cited in Howse, Lange, Farran & Boyles 2003) reason however, that the high confidence levels reflected in their findings could be a reflection of defensiveness on the part of the children who are least confident about their competence. Nonetheless, there is little evidence that exists to suggest that children from economically impoverished households are at a motivational disadvantage during their early school years.

There were very diverse results from comparisons of children's self-regulation of task attention. The researchers found that although the younger at-risk kindergarteners exhibited high levels of motivation, they demonstrated poorer self-regulation abilities especially in regulating their attention in goal-directed task activities, as compared to their more advantaged peers who showed no apparent attentional decline. This implies that for at-risk young children, their performance in academic tasks may not be as good as their more advantaged peers if tasks require attentional regulation. For second-graders, the research findings showed that both risk-status groups showed moderate but comparable distraction levels in forced-distractor condition. From these findings, there are implications that educators should encourage young students to adopt self-regulatory strategies. They should also show them methods to engage in task activities in deliberate, planned and strategic ways.

COLLABORATION

Smith and MacGregor (1992) term collaborative learning as an "umbrella term" describes the many educational approaches involving join intellectual effort by students, or students and teachers together. According to Cabrera, Crissman, Bernal, Nora, Terenzini and Pascarella (2002), collaborative learning is a way of restructuring the classroom to small groups work, requiring intensive interaction between students and the faculty member while working through a complex projects. Through completion of projects, learning is suppose to have taken place as well as enhanced. During the process of completing projects, students enhance personal experiences while working with other students. In collaborative learning, the faculty undertakes the role of a facilitator rather than of knowledge source. Three major characteristics of collaborative learning:

- Collaborative learning represents a significant shift away from the typical teacher-centred approach.
- Collaborative learning emphasises social and intellectual engagement and mutual responsibility.
- In collaborative learning situations, students work in groups of two or more, mutually searching for understanding, solutions or creating a product.

Collaborative learning covers approaches ranging from classroom discussion to study on research teams. The collaborative learning approach includes co-operative learning, problem-centred learning, writing groups, discussion groups and seminars, peer teaching and learning communities. There is some difference between "co-operative learning" and "collaborative learning." The term "co-operative learning" refers to a learning environment where students work together to achieve a common goal. In achieving the goal, tasks and responsibility are divided among the members. In collaborative learning, members of the team work together on all parts of the given projects (Underwood 2003). Collaborative learning involves share authority for the idea generation, mutual accountability for success and sharing of resources and rewards (Salisbury, Evans & Palombaro 1997). It involves joint-structuring of activity with share participation of two or more persons in which outcome for each individual are typically documented. Collaborative activities are divided between four to six member groups and gains are often gauged by group-level performance (Wentzel & Watkins 2002). Collaborative learning involves an interdependent relationship among two or more people to achieve a common goal. This relationship calls for commitment to mutual goals, a structure for shared responsibility (Salisbury, Evans & Palombaro 1997).

Some Reviews

Cabrera, Crissman, Bernal, Nora, Terenzini and Pascarella (2002) studied the impact of collaborative learning on college students' development and diversity. Using a sample of 2050 students in 23 institutions, researchers attempted to examine how gender and ethnic differences affected preference to collaborative learning, effects of collaborative learning on students learning outcome and factors that determine openness to diversity among students. Student development in this study was measured by understanding of science and technology, personal development, appreciation for fine arts and analytical skills. Openness to diversity was measured by students' attitudes and predisposition towards interacting with people from different background.

Using regression analysis, collaborative learning was found to be the single best predictor for the four cognitive and affective outcome of students' development. This study found that women and minorities were more predisposed towards collaborative learning. There was no significant difference between white female and male in their preference to collaborative learning. However, minorities were found to be more predisposed to collaborative learning compare to the whites.

Moalem (2003) evaluated the effectiveness of using an interactive design model as an approach of collaborative learning in developing an online course. He looked into how an interactive design model was use to enhance collaborative learning and co-operative learning; and how activities were structured to promote the level and quality of communication among peers and instructor

The participants of this study were 24 graduate students seeking a master degree in instructional technologies course. This course expect students to develop knowledge of theoretical foundations of instruction design and to apply these theories in the design and developmental of instructional materials.

Major findings of this study were as follows:

- It was found that course management and delivery system seemed to influence student interaction. Support systems like chat rooms, e-mail and electronic file sharing seemed to limit students interaction in some ways. The students and instructors of the study had to spend hours to mange a discussion that could have been competed within 30 minutes in a face to face situation. However, this problem was resolved after the researchers adopted the Web collaborative learning. The students in the study were then able to participate in several chat rooms at the same time. They felt supported and had better interactions.

- The problem solving tasks appeared to influence student discussion and conversation. Generative problem solving tasks created a better environment for discussion and construction of knowledge than did the intellective problem solving tasks.

- Individualised assignments improved the quality of interaction and encourage student participation. In conclusion, the researchers indicated that communication tools do not enhance learning by themselves. They provide the avenue for learning, when placed in the capable hands of skilful teachers and designers of instruction.

Salisbury, Evans and Palombaro (1997) looked into the use of Collaborative Problem-Solving (CPS) among the children of disabilities. The children of an elementary school participated. They were students with mild to profound disabilities physically placed together. Both teachers and students participated in this study. They underwent process training session and then used CPS to identify and solve issues related to physical, social and instructional exclusion of students in the classrooms. Data were collected over a period of 24 months, from 12 different classes. Major findings were as follows:

- The use of CPS became familiar in most classes. Teachers found that CPS was easily incorporated into existing practices. Over the period of two years, teachers reported that they internalised the process, making it difficult to recognise when exactly they got used to CPS.

- Although both students and teachers were trained to use CPS, results found that most of the CPS sessions were initiated by teachers.

- Teaching staff judged CPS as an important strategy in promoting the physical, social and instructional inclusion of students with disabilities in the classrooms.

IMPLICATIONS FOR EDUCATORS AND PARENTS

Educators

A study conducted by Ee, Lee and Potter (2004) examined teachers' understanding and use of strategy-based instruction in developing students' self-regulatory behaviour in learning. Using a 50-item questionnaire on classroom practices across Primary 6 teachers of English language across five countries (Australia, Cambodia, Hong Kong, Singapore and Vietnam), the researchers found that teachers' understandings of self-regulated behaviour were vague.

Although educators in Australia, Hong Kong and Singapore indicated awareness of the importance of self-regulatory behaviours, ironically, they also reported that they were least likely to ask students to stop and self-evaluate their use of strategies during a task, or whether they were meeting particular learning criteria. While the educators said that they value students' ability to self-regulate and they report using strategy-based instruction to enhance these skills, educators' understanding of the learning and teaching processes involved still come across as lacking. As a result, there was an inconsistent approach to teaching, and instead of leading into a student-centred learning approach, teachers were still very much in control of students' learning.

Hence, there is a need for teachers and educators to be well-tuned into the strategies that govern self-regulation. On the same note, teachers have to be exposed as much as possible to the different and appropriate types of strategies that would assist them in teaching students to self-regulate. Project-based activities would also serve to harness students' learning and thinking. Ee, Lee and Potter (2004) also suggest that the Ministry of Education (MOE) could implement a more metacognitively-based curriculum in Singapore schools, in order to focus on encouraging critical, independent thinking in students.

Further, in light of the achievement-oriented educational environment that Singapore schools function in, it is imperative that teachers do not perceive learning as merely a process of *obtaining* information. Instead, they should focus on learning as a process of active knowledge construction, where the student is motivated to learn, think critically and ask questions. Educators should form self-regulatory strategies for students to adopt and customise for independent learning. By employing instructional practices that enhance students' cognitive assessment of their ability in task engagement and self-regulatory strategies, teachers would encourage active and responsible learning in students.

In addition, with increasing emphasis in Singapore schools on project-based learning, Chong (2003) notes how self-regulatory learning can be useful in such collaborative attempts. This would take the focus off the end-product and instead have students become more aware of their effort, strategies and self-regulation as they formulate solutions, plans and evaluate their task approach, while revising their final product. While working on such collaborative projects, students learn to monitor their thoughts and understanding, as well as compare these with the thoughts of others. Such self-directed initiatives undoubtedly "require considerable cognitive and metacognitive sophistication and motivation to work effectively with others" (Chong 2003, 379–80).

In order that project-based instruction to be successful, students need to become aware of and examine their own conceptions, develop and use various problem-solving strategies and through their self-regulatory efforts, generate an approach to learning. Teachers need to plan their teaching such that they are creating opportunities for students to generate positive feelings about one's efficacy in order to maximise their potential learning outcomes, which would have implications on further development of project-based learning programmes.

Parental Involvement

Howse, Lange, Farran and Boyles (2003) suggested that children's ability to internalise control and become independent learners was dependent largely on the presence and availability of responsive, consistent parenting.

Furthermore, children's ability to self-regulate stems from whether they are given the opportunities to practise such behaviours. These opportunities might be absent in many economically impoverished households. It is important that schools implement programs and adopt a more proactive stand in making sure that parents are involved in their children's learning. Activities such as reading programmes, or parents running school clubs or extracurricular activities all help in getting parents involved with the school, and indirectly, their children's learning.

Importantly, the parents' participation should allow them to interact with the students, giving the children opportunities to have hands-on experience in dealing with challenges by actively participating in the activity. Mentorship or career guidance programmes put various professional parents in good positions to help out in schools and guide the students in choosing their career paths. Other programmes such as counselling also help foster good adult-child relationships, as well as aid children in monitoring and dealing with their personal or school problems. By learning to monitor and regulate their emotions, children are likely to be in better steed in the acquisition of knowledge. As such, attempts to help students' efforts to internalise and regulate their social behaviours would likely be assisting in their academic self-regulation.

Other Remarks

Education reforms in schools have tended to focus on structural changes in school organisations. These changes have undoubtedly brought about enhanced learning contexts with better academic achievement, but maybe what remains to be done is attention needs to be focused on the way students are taught to learn. Educators should not neglect the student's own role in her(his) own learning, as suggested by Dembo and Eaton (2000). Educators need to be acutely aware of each and every learner's needs, and students on their part need to learn to take charge of their own learning process as they are the ones who have most control over their success.

Researchers (e.g., Graham & Harris 1993) may develop self-regulated strategies with the goals of this technique to help students to master the higher-level cognitive processes involved in writing, develop autonomous, reflective, self-regulated use of effective writing strategies, and form positive attitudes about writing and about themselves as writers. The method advocates using a variety of mechanisms for promoting active involvement, thus its effectiveness in targeting the learning disabled.

Lemaire, Lecacheur and Farioli (2000) in their study on the strategies children used to solve basic arithmetic problems (mental estimation of the sum of two 3-digit numbers) found that children are generally adaptive in their strategy choice, using different tools depending on the characteristics of the problem.

The self-regulated learning approach has massive appeal and even greater repercussions for learners and their achievement. It has major implications for educators and the way in which they should interact with their students, as well as how schools should be organised. Research has revealed that similar self-regulatory processes are used in disciplines such as music, writing, sports, arts and computing (Chong 2003). This means that teaching self-regulatory strategies for studying may prove to be well suited for learners to attain the goal of self-education and self-direction throughout their lives. It is imperative that educators teach students the strategies involved and allow them to be independent self-regulators in their learning process, able to overcome obstacles and failures to achieve their personal and learning goals.

Wentzel and Watkins, (2002) argue that peers have the potential to provide context for learning. They highlighted Vygotsky's framework on peer interaction in collaborative learning. According to the Vygotskian framework development is likely to occur when a co-operative exchange of ideas takes place within a zone of proximal development. Zone of proximal development refers to the range spanning from where a child can function independently in a cognitive sense, to a more advance level where s/he has the potential to develop when collaboration with a more capable peer. Vygotsky stated that the role of the child's social partner must be different in level of expertise and the partner should have an understanding of the abilities of the less advanced child. According to Wentzel and Watkins, research on collaborative peer learning has a positive impact of child learning, but children do not always naturally develop constructive interaction patterns without specific training. Thus when paring the more competent child, the child tends to offer help in the form of lectures and demonstration, and rarely elaborates her(his) explanations or ignores the less competent one.

Among the learners, collaborative learning is useful in improving reading competence (McMaster, Prentice, Kazdan & Saenz 2001), as in the case of the known Peer-Assisted Learning Strategies (PALS). In PALS, a stronger and a weaker student pair up and engage in activities such as partner reading, paragraph shrinking and "prediction relay" (drawing inferences/predictions from the material). The activity is made fun through by introducing a competitive aspect (e.g., correct responses earn points for a pupil's team). The effectiveness of PALS has been documented among students in grades 2–6 for improving reading fluency and comprehension for students with learning disabilities. In the study by McMaster and colleagues (2001) the system was extended downwards (to kindergarten and grade 1 and upwards (to high school). Results were encouraging, although the authors indicated the need for further research to be done.

Scaffolding is a process by which adults (and more knowledgeable peers) guides children's (or less knowledgeable persons) learning and development. It is assumed to result in better understanding on the part of the child, thus the technique may be petered out over time as the child shows improvement in her(his) work. Stone (1998) found that parents were sensitive to their children's needs, adjusting their level of support as a function of task demand and communication status. The mothers of learning disabled children tended to use scaffolding more, taking more direct responsibility for task assembly that the mothers of normally developing children, and engaging in lengthier chains of titrated assistance. By doing all this, educators will develop a future generation of self-regulated learners who will approach their educational tasks with confidence and diligence. They will be resourceful learners, aware of their abilities, as well as the abilities which they do not have. Self-regulated learners will eventually be able to work around difficulties and poor learning conditions that they may encounter. They will demonstrate responsibility for their own learning and be motivated to set higher goals and achievement outcomes.

REFERENCES

Ablard, K. E., & R. E. Lipschultz. 1998. Self-regulated learning in high-achieving students: Relations to advanced reasoning, achievement goals, and gender. *Journal of Educational Psychology, 90(1), 94–101.*

Bandura, A. 1982. Self-efficacy mechanism in human agency. *American Psychologist, 37, 122–147.*

Bandura, A. 1986. *Social foundations of thought and action. A social cognitive theory.* Englewood Cliffs, NJ: Prentice Hall.

Bandura, A. 1997. *Self-efficacy: The exercise of control.* New York: Freeman.

Bandura, A. 2001. Social cognitive theory: An agentic perspective. *Annual Review of Psychology, 52, 1–26.*

Birenbaum, M. 2002. Assessing self-directed active learning in primary schools. *Assessment in Education, 9(1), 119–138.*

Butler, D. L., & P. H. Winne. 1995. Feedback and self-regulated learning: A theoretical synthesis. *Review of Educational Research, 65(3)*, 245–281.

Cabrera A. F., J. L. Crissman, E. M. Bernal, A. Nora, P. T. Terenzini, & E. T. Pascarella. 2002. Collaborative learning: Its impact on college students' development and diversity. *Journal of College Student Development, 43(1)* 20–34.

Chong, W. H. 2003. *The role of self-regulatory and motivational processes on the academic and social functioning of secondary one students.* Unpublished doctoral dissertation, National Institute of Education, Nanyang Technological University, Singapore.

Dembo, M. H., & M. J. Eaton. 2000. Self-regulation of academic learning in middle-level schools. *The Elementary School Journal, 100(5)*, 473–549.

Ee, J., Lee, O. K., & G. Potter. 2004. Teachers' understanding and practices of strategy-based instruction and goal orientation for students' self-regulation: Findings across cultures. In *Thinking about thinking: What educators need to know* (108–141). Edited by J. Ee, A. Chang & O. S. Tan. Singapore: McGraw Hill.

Ee. J., P. J. Moore, & L. Atputhasamy. 2003. High-achieving students: their motivational goals, self-regulation and achievement and relationships to their teachers' goals and strategy-based instruction. *High Ability Studies, 14(1)*, 23–29.

Garrison, D.R. (1997). Self-directed learning: Toward a comprehensive model. *Adult Education Quarterly, 48(1)*, 18–33.

Graham, S., & K. R. Harris. 1993. Self-regulated strategy development: helping students with learning problems develop as writers. *The Elementary School Journal, 94(2), 169–181*

Hatcher, T. G. 1997. The ins and outs of self-directed learning. *Training & Development, 51(2), 34–39.*

Howse, R. B., G. Lange, D. C. Farran, & C. D. Boyles. 2003. Motivation and self-regulation as predictors of achievement in economically disadvantaged young children. *The Journal of Experimental Education, 71(2)*, 151–174.

Lemaire, P., M. Lecacheur, & F. Farioli. 2000. Children's strategy use in computational estimation. *Canadian Journal of Experimental Psychology, 54(2)*, 141–148.

Malpass, J. R., H. F. O'Neil Jr, & D. Hocevar. 1999. Self-regulation, goal orientation, self-efficacy, worry, and high-stakes math achievement for mathematically gifted high school students. *Roeper Review, 21(4)*, 281–288.

McMaster, K. N., K. Prentice, S. Kazdan, & L. Saenz. 2001. Peer-assisted learning strategies in reading: extensions for kindergarten, first grade and high school. *Remedial and Special Education, 22(1)*, 15–21

Moalem, M. 2003. An interactive on-line course: A collaborative design model. *Educational Technology, Research and Development, 51(4)*, 85–103.

Olaussen, B. S., & I. Bråten. 1999. Students' use of strategies for self-regulated learning: Cross-cultural perspectives. *Scandinavian Journal of Educational Research, 43(4)*, 409–432.

Pajares, F. 1996. Self-efficacy beliefs in academic settings. *Review of Educational Research, 66(4)*, 543–578.

Piskurich, G. M. 1994. Developing Self-directed Learning. *Training & Development, 48(3)*, 30–36.

Salisbury, C. L., I. M. Evans, & M. Palombaro. 1997. Collaborative problem solving to promote the inclusion of young children with significant disabilities in primary grades. *Exceptional Children, 63(2)*, 195–209.

Smith, B. L., & J. T. MacGregor. 1992. What is collaborative learning? In *Collaborative learning: A sourcebook for higher learning*. Edited by A. Goodsell, M. Maher & V. Tinto. National Center on Post Secondary Teaching, Learning & Assessment (NCTLA).

Stone, C. A. 1998. The metaphor of scaffolding: Its utility for the field of learning disabilities. *Journal of Learning Disabilities, 31(4)*, 344–364.

Underwood, J. D .M. 2003. Student attitudes towards socially acceptable and unacceptable group working practices, *British Journal of Psychology, 93*, 319–337.

Wentzel, K. R., & D. E. Watkins. 2002. Peer relationships and collaborative learning as contexts for academic enablers. *School Psychology Review, 31(3)*, 366–377.

Zimmerman, B. J. 1990. Self-regulated learning and academic achievement: An overview. *Educational Psychologist, 25(1)*, 3–17.

Zimmerman, B. J., & M. Martinez-Pons, M. 1990. Student differences in self-regulated learning: relating grade, sex, and giftedness to self-efficacy and strategy use. *Journal of Educational Psychology, 82*, 51–59.

---

[*] Wong Soo Fei and Bryan Tang assisted in literature search.

2

Grouping and Psychoeducational Group*

INTRODUCTION

"I have always found myself rather unable to think productively as a single person. I hope that this handicap may, ..., turn out to be of some advantage. ... collectives have had and will, I think, always have their place in scientific work." (Lewin 1936, ix)

Early in the twentieth century (1900–1920), Kurt Koffka (1886–1941) conceptualised group from the gestalt psychological perspectives. Koffka regarded groups as *realities* (just like human beings are realities), and a group as a gestalt (i.e., a product of organisation). According to him, a sociological (geographical) group presupposes a psychological (behavioural) group. Sociological group properties are mediated by psychological groups; "... we experience a 'we', a belonging to a psychological group ..." (Koffka 1962, 652). The nature of psychological groups includes unification (" ... 'we' meaning 'I within the group' ..." [Koffka 1962, 665]) and segregation ("...'I and they', 'I *opposed* to the group' ..." [Koffka 1962, 665]), stability (connected with the closedness of the group), and articulation (closure; animal groups).

For about two decades (1920s and 1930s) Lewin advanced the study of group or collectives by bridging the gap between theory and research. One of Lewin's students, Morton Deutsch (1920–) conducted the study of group with a theory of cooperation and competition (Deutsch 1949). In his theory, Deutsch (1949) clarified some essential concepts: the "strength" of a gestalt as the degree of interdependence; "we", the reality of the psychological group implies the feeling of unity in joint action; the psychological group as an individual life space, and the sociological group as a group space. Deutsch (1949, 150) innovated Koffka's concepts of psychological and sociological groups, and proposed the following definitions:

- A sociological group exists (has unity) to the extent that the individuals or sub-units composing it are pursuing promotively interdependent goals.
- A psychological group exists (has unity) to the extent that the individuals composing it perceive themselves as pursuing promotively interdependent goals.
- A psychological group has cohesiveness as a direct function of the strength of goals perceived to be promotively interdependent and of the degree of perceived interdependence.

For Deutsch, "The way in which participants' goals are structured determine how they interact, and the interaction patterns determine the outcomes of the situation" (Johnson 2003, 936). Hence, the effect of group goals can be both cooperative and competitive; and so as social interdependence, positive and negative. The social interdependence theory by Johnson and Johnson in the 1970s is a well-researched framework that relates to practices in the classrooms and other settings. "A group is the interdependence among members ... (g)roup members are made interdependent through common goals." (Johnson 2003, 935) To begin, we share with the readers basic concepts of groups and grouping.

This chapter builds on the earlier chapters on self-initiated and differential learning. Our view on individualised and social cognition is in line with Koffka's and Lewis' that is we experience individualised learning when we engage in social learning. To behave in a group (psychological) we need a group (sociological). In this chapter, we discuss the sociological group, i.e., grouping and its effectiveness and the psycho-educational group for effective group guidance.

GROUPING

Common Grouping Practices

Grouping can simply refer to physical placement of students into small groups for the purpose of learning. Such placement is related to the organisational structure of the classroom (Gamoran 1987). Grouping alone does not always guarantee learning. For learning to occur, the learner has to engage in cognitive restructuring or elaboration through taking part in activities such as giving feedback and engaging in debate, interacting with peer, working in collaboration or cooperation, and generating idea (Kramarski & Mevarech 2003). Grouping in general may facilitate cooperative learning, building on communication skills; it can discourage competitive learning (Lou, Abrami, Spence, Poulsen, Chambers & d'Apollonia 1996).

According to Tieso (2003) there are three common grouping practices, namely *whole class*, *between class* and *within class*.

Whole class grouping is where students are taught as a single, large group. The emphasis for whole class grouping is on uniformity of instruction (Lou, Abrami, Spence, Poulsen, Chambers & d'Apollonia 1996). Whole class instruction is characterised by the utilisation of a traditional, textbook dominated curricular movement through the curriculum at the same pace, using the same methods and materials. This form of instruction allows a large number of attendance within a classroom of a same grade. The teacher prepares lessons based on a single ability or readiness level (Tieso 2003). Students move through curriculum with less regard to their prior knowledge, interests or levels of readiness. Whole class instruction may either be teacher-centred or student-centred.

The teacher-centred whole class instructional classroom has the teacher as the principal "actor". The teacher asks a question to which there is only one answer. Students' learning relies on teacher-initiated drill and recitation.

The student-centred whole class instructional classroom occurs when the class is divided up mainly into small groups or individually. Students' needs are infused into the organisation of contents to be learned. The teacher determines rules of behaviour and enforcement and uses of varied instructional materials for individual or within small group learning. Classroom is organised in such a way that it allows students to move independently within their work space.

Between class grouping refers to a school's practice of separating students based on their achievement into different classes, courses or curricular tracks. One of the well known between classes grouping is the *Joplin Plan*. Students are grouped by ability in a particular subject in the *Joplin Plan*, regardless of their age or grade. Students from the same grades or across grade levels may be grouped by ability for reading or mathematics instruction. Schools may have remedial classes for low achievers and enrichment courses for the gifted students. The advantages of the *Joplin Plan* lies in its temporary nature of grouping arrangement, allowing students to move into and out of groups based on their current demonstrated achievement (Kulik & Kulik 1982; Slavin 1990).

Within class grouping is also known as *flexible* grouping (Tieso 2003). This grouping places students within the same class into smaller groups for specific activities and purposes (Kulik & Kulik 1992). Typically, the teacher presents a lesson to the whole class and then places students into small groups, based on demonstrated performance, interest, and level of prior knowledge. *Flexible grouping* groups students on a subject by subject basis, according to their current levels of performance, to provide instruction that meets students' current needs. A student may be in the most advanced group for one subject but in a less advanced group in another subject. This method of grouping is better than tracking as it groups students according to their current needs in various subjects. Tracking places students in a given track and are taught on the same level in all subjects.

Skill grouping is a term used (Mosteller, Light & Sachs 1996) to refer to placing students according to ability or performance. Skill grouping emphasises the learners' current skill level, whereas tracking or ability grouping entails a sense of permanence in quality. Similar to flexible grouping, in skill grouping, students who share a similar current skill level are grouped for the purpose of instructions.

In both *between* and *within* class grouping students can be placed according to their perceived ability which is also known as *ability grouping*. Tracking or streaming refers to placing students solely based on their learning ability (Slavin 1993). Often, *ability grouping* and *tracking* are used interchangeably. As a matter of fact, tracking was coined to address the problem of teachers having difficulty in handling students of different capacities in the whole class grouping. Ability group can be further divided into *homogeneous* (i.e., groups made up of student of the same ability) and *heterogeneous* group (i.e., groups made up of students with mixed ability).

Other forms of grouping include *cluster* grouping and *combination class* grouping.

Cluster grouping places small groups of students with similar instructional needs clustered within a primarily heterogeneous classroom (Fiedler, Lange & Winebrenner 1993). The form of grouping enables gifted students, for instance to be with their intellectually compatible peers so that they are appropriately challenged and so that they are able to view their abilities in a more realistic manner.

Combination class grouping can be used for uneven enrolments and fiscal constraints that prevent schools from hiring more teachers and using smaller classes. Students are purposefully assigned to classes, unlike the heterogeneous random assignment of students. Students with higher ability or more independent, or both, are usually assigned to combination classes. Consistent results show that combination classes have higher class mean scores, less variation in ability and independence, fewer low-ability and low-independence students and more high-ability and high independence students. Hence, students are able to make more productive use of seatwork time and complete meaningful work without direct teacher supervision. This, in turn, allows for better classroom management and reduces management problems associated with two-group instruction (Burns & Mason 2002).

Types of Grouping

Homogenous versus heterogeneous grouping: Grouping may be based on common (homogeneous) or diverse (heterogeneous) interests, goals or skills (Lou, Abrami, Spence, Poulsen, Chambers & d'Apollonia 1996). Lou, Abrami, Spence, Poulsen, Chambers and d'Apollonia (1996) found that the optimal grouping size was 3–4 members, resulting in a significant difference in achievement. There was no significant difference in achievement shown in 6–10 member groups. The average student had an improved positive attitude towards subject matter through grouping, but their attitude towards institutional approach was not significantly different. Students also showed improved general self-concept, but no significant difference in domain specific academic self-concept.

According to Cheung and Rudoxicz's study (2003), students in homogeneous groups had significantly higher academic achievement and self-esteem. Homogeneous grouping improved the learning pace and level for high ability students and commensurate pace with other members in the group. For low-ability students, it improved attention and increased review of material. Homogeneous grouping based on friendship created cohesiveness and improved performance. The Lou, Abrami, Spence, Poulsen, Chambers and d'Apollonia (1996) review confirms that homogeneous groupings were found to be effective for reading.

Heterogeneous groupings are good for discussions that need multiple perspectives and creative controversy. It allows elaborate explanations by high ability students to weaker students. Effects were found to be greatest for mathematics and science in heterogeneous grouping, but this grouping was not effective for reading, language, arts and other courses. It has been found that low ability students perform better in heterogeneous groups. Medium ability students perform better in homogeneous groups. High ability students perform just as well in heterogeneous and homogeneous groups. Achievement effects increase when group formation is based on mixed sources, not on ability alone (e.g., physical placement, modified teaching methods and instructional materials maximises effects) (Lou, Abrami, Spence, Poulsen, Chambers & d'Apollonia 1996). Varying instructional materials produces a higher treatment effect than using the same materials. This is known as curricular adjustment, made uniquely to the needs of the group, rather than a "one size fits all" approach. Curriculum "remodelling" strategises critical thinking (affective strategies/cognitive strategies) (Tieso 2003).

Ability grouping: Ability grouping is the grouping of students into classes based on their abilities (Cheung & Rudoxicz 2003). It allows teachers to tailor their teaching instruction for a homogeneous group of students, who benefit from cooperation, mutual facilitation and studying at the same pace in class. However, ability grouping is seen as undesirable as it may lead to deficits in academic self-concept and academic achievement.

The rationalist argument to this claim is that in fact there are no rational criteria for grouping students. Any chosen criterion would largely reflect on the student's socio-cultural characteristic. Hence, grouping as such fails to uphold the rationality of meritocracy.

The egalitarian argument states that ability grouping is unfair, especially to low-ability students as it does not provide students with equal chances of achievement. All students receive different instructions and treatments from teachers and schools. Hence, students are vulnerable to contextual influence of the grouping, resulting in polarising of ability between high and low ability students. This aggravates social inequality, reproducing class differences and suppressing mobility and opportunity in class structure. Moreover, past research on ability grouping has found equivocal findings. Some studies found strong effects and others, minimal, null or negative effects for high ability students and low ability students. Findings show that high-ability students have better conduct, learning strategy, educational expectation, chance for university enrolment and more attention, support and encouragement, have better life chances but lower self-concept, higher test anxiety, resulting in poorer mental health. It is recommended that culture specific studies be done as most research is done in the West. The Asian collectivistic culture might influence the effect of ability grouping (Cheung & Rudoxicz 2003).

Class composition would have effects on the achievements of students. Students in high ability classes receive more or higher quality instruction, having more motivated or better qualified teachers, and high-ability classmates contributing to the academic climate. They are exposed to more positive normative climate, resulting in a more positive reference group for self-evaluation and better self-concept. However, in low-ability classes, teachers hold inappropriately low expectations (stigma) for the students, causing students to behave in harmful ways towards their academic interests (Burns & Mason 2002).

Tracking: Tracking is an attempt to group students of like ability to make instruction more effective. It can be done based on school type, course of study, stream, ability grouping, and geographic location (LeTendre, Hofer & Shimizu 2003). Tracking alone may not be able to provide information of a student's current instructional needs in specific subject areas. It is true that grouping without curriculum differentiation specifically to the students' needs serves only to stratify, not to educate students.

Tracking is considered an extreme form of ability grouping, where students are sorted according to a general measure of ability or achievement, such as IQ, achievement tests or GPA. Tracking judges and evaluates students before placing them into classes, groups, schools, receiving differentiated curriculum as they progress through the education system (LeTendre, Hofer & Shimizu 2003). This form of grouping has a negative effect on a student's ultimate educational trajectory. Students remain in these homogeneous tracks for all their instruction, without consideration for how much they vary in their performance in different subject areas. Schools rarely offer opportunities for students to move from one track to another (Fiedler, Lange & Winebrenner 1993). Hence, educational tracking is the major mechanism where inequality of educational opportunity is transmitted or maintained, with issues concerning social equity, rewarding individual merit and maximising student academic potential (LeTendre, Hofer & Shimizu, 2003). It causes students to be sorted by race and socioeconomic status. Upper tracks disproportionately consist of middle and upper-middle class, White and Asian students. Lower tracks consist of lower and lower-middle class children of colour. As such, tracking is seen as racially and economically discriminatory.

One may argue that it can be the perceived ideal goal of schooling and the nature of education, rather than the eventual outcomes of education that contributes to the social perception of tracking as a problem in society. LeTendre, Hofer and Shimizu (2003) reported that Germans are comfortable with tracking as long as the tracks were fairly determined. What is considered "fair" remains a subject of discussion or for debate. The Japanese believe that all children should be given similar education. In the United States, references of the Third International Mathematics and Science Study (TIMSS) case study project claimed tracking as problematic. Detracking is thus the current trend to keep students from being labelled and limited in developing to the best of their potential, emphasising on autonomy, choice and range of curricular options.

Cooperative learning: Cooperative learning can be either homogeneous or heterogeneous in grouping (Fiedler, Lange & Winebrenner 1993). Peterson and Miller (2004) compared the quality of students' experiences during cooperative learning and large-group instruction. Their study showed that the overall quality of experience was greater during cooperative learning than in large group activities, especially for thinking on task, student engagement, perceptions of task importance, and optimal levels of challenge and skill. Cooperative learning engaged students more actively. Students were more likely to be thinking about something on task or related to the task during cooperative learning. They were more likely to be thinking of something off task during large group instruction.

High achieving students had higher attending behaviours in smaller groups than in larger groups but low achieving students did not show any significant difference. Low achievers were less active during small-group instruction than high achievers, though attending behaviours were the same with high achievers. This is due to the dominance of the high achievers in small group discussions. Nonetheless, low achievers enjoyed the social nature of cooperative learning and looked forward to it.

It was noted that students felt more self-conscious and had more difficulty concentrating but could concentrate more intensely during cooperative learning. This is due to the social nature of small group discussions that students feel a greater sense of self-consciousness, making concentration more difficult. However, with the greater degree of engagement in small group discussions, it counteracts with self-consciousness, allowing students to concentrate on higher levels. The levels of challenge, concentration, and enjoyment were higher for small groups (cooperative learning), but perceptions of importance for future goals were higher for big groups. There was greater cognitive efficiency during large group instruction. Students' thinking was clearer and was less self-conscious.

The implications of cooperative learning are teachers have to design and monitor cooperative tasks that will help students achieve future goals. Tasks should be challenging to the students and should require the use of skills that they feel capable of using to maximise their involvement in tasks. Teachers should closely monitor the involvement of lower achieving students in all learning activities regardless of instructional context. Teachers have to learn how to structure and monitor meaningful learning experience for students. Cooperative learning with metacognitive training was found to be an effective method in comprehending mathematical reasoning (Kramarski & Mevarech 2003). Elaboration is important to enhance understanding. Hence, cooperative settings are appropriate to encourage students to elaborate information.

Cooperative learning may be executed by using small heterogeneous groups, with changes made to the organisation of the classroom and ways in learning, the teacher's roles, metacognitive guidance, selection, and use of mathematical tasks. These small group activities have to be structured to encourage students to engage in questioning, elaboration, explanation, verbal communication to express ideas, give and receive feedback. However, students with poor communication skills are less likely to benefit from cooperative learning as they are unable to communicate their mathematical reasoning to others, do not know how to ask questions, reflect on the solution process to explain to peers and offer constructive criticism. Hence, placing students in cooperative groups is not sufficient for enhancing mathematical reasoning. Implementing metacognitive training, together with cooperative learning, is an effective means of facilitating mathematical reasoning, even in individualised settings.

EFFECTIVENESS OF GROUPING

The effectiveness of grouping has been the focus of educational researchers for some time. The research on ability grouping on achievement has been quite extensive. Several meta-analyses and research syntheses have been published (Kulik & Kulik 1982 & 1992; Lou, Abrami, Spence, Poulsen, Chambers & d'Apollonia 1996; Slavin 1990).

Effects of Grouping Programs

In a meta-analytic paper, Kulik and Kulik (1992) stated that research on grouping has a long history but unable to have a conclusive finding whether one actually benefits from grouping or how one benefits from this practice. Further, grouping practice has also come under strong attack recently, citing the discrimination and inequality as the reason. Therefore, this article wish to re-examine the findings of grouping practice by focusing on five different groups, i.e., multilevel classes, cross grade programs, within-class grouping, enrichment classes for the gifted, and accelerated classes.

The findings showed that the effects are a function of program type. Multi level classes usually have little or no effect on student achievement. Within class programs that entail more adjustment of curriculum to ability shows positive effect, and enrichment and accelerated classes programs, which involve the greatest adjustment to curriculum indicated the largest positive effects on student learning. As conclusion, these results do not support the claim that no one can benefit from grouping practices or lower ability students are harmed by this practice.

Within-class Grouping (Lou, Abrami, Spence, Poulsen, Chambers & d'Apollonia, 1996)

The effect of within-class grouping has been the interest of educational research for some time since 1950s. The aim of this meta-analysis is to integrate quantitatively the research findings on the effect of within class grouping on achievement, attitude and self-concept. This study also aims to explore which features explain variability in previous research findings and which time of grouping are most optimum to facilitate learning.

Meta-analysis combines results of independent experiments with a purpose to integrate their findings. The analysis is conducted on a group of studies with a common conceptual hypothesis or common operational definitions of independent or dependent variables. Meta-analysis is applicable to the research on goal structures and achievements, as there is considerable research that used identical or at least conceptually similar variables.

In total there were 66 studies included in this meta-analysis. Two groups of studies were identified and analysed independently. The first analysis compared within-class grouping with no grouping on students' achievement, self-concept and attitude. The second analysis compared homogeneous groups with heterogeneous groups.

51

The findings for the first analysis, grouping versus no grouping, showed that overall students in small group performed slightly above average compared to students in classrooms without groups. Students placed in small groups showed more positive achievement had more positive attitudes and higher self-concept than students in non-group class.

The findings for the second analysis, homogenous grouping versus heterogeneous grouping, seemed to favour homogeneous grouping over heterogeneous group on student achievement. Nevertheless, low ability students learned significantly more in heterogeneous ability groups than in homogenous ability groups (d+ = - 0.06). Medium ability students, however benefited significantly more in homogenous ability group than in heterogeneous ability group (d+ = 0.51), whereas for high ability students, group ability made no significant difference (d+ = +0.99). However, factors such as outcome measures, source and type, instruction treatment, teacher's training, class size, and subject area had significantly moderated students' achievement within class grouping. The effect of group ability showed no significant difference with the homogenous groups performed as well as the heterogeneous groups. However, homogeneous ability groups learned significantly more than heterogeneous groups in reading (d+ = +0.36). In conclusion, the practice of small class grouping in facilitating learning is supported.

Ability Grouping

Kulik and Kulik (1982) synthesised research of ability grouping. The researchers gave some overview of the development of age graded school in the United States and how it developed into ability grouping practice. The data of their review came from 52 comparative studies of grouping on examination scores of students. The findings showed that students who were grouped in classes according to ability performed only slightly better compared to the non-grouped ones. However, students in gifted programs performed better than they would in heterogeneous classes. There was no difference for lower ability students in both groups; they neither performed better or worse than they would in a mixed-ability group. The effect of self-concept of grouping was positive but minor. Students who were grouped for a particular subject (English or Mathematics) had better attitudes towards the subject.

In conclusion, this meta-analysis showed that only one of the high ability students placed in a special honour class yielded significant positive results. High ability students apparently benefited from special curriculum. Other types of groupings reported trivial effects, where students learned as much in the heterogeneous classes as in the homogeneous classes. These results did not support the view that grouping has unfavourable effects on the achievement of low ability students.

Ability grouping and secondary school students' achievement: Slavin (1990) presents a review of research that evaluated the effects of ability grouping on students' achievement in secondary schools. This paper incorporates features of meta-analysis and traditional review. The studies included had to involve comprehensive ability grouping plans that incorporated most of the students in the school and studies had to be in English. Studies of within class ability grouping are included but studies related to special education program for the gifted or remedial program are excluded. In total, six randomised experiments, nine matched experiments and 14 correlational studies compared ability group to heterogeneous plans over a periods of from one semester to five years.

Across 29 studies used, achievement effects were found to be essentially zero at all grade levels. These findings were similar for all subjects except for social studies, which there was a trend of favouring heterogeneous group. This finding contrasts with those studies comparing the achievement of students in different tract where results generally find positive effects of ability grouping for high achiever and negative effect for low achiever. Slavin (1990) also discussed some of the limitations in this review. One of them is that there were no systematic observations made of teaching and learning in all the studies reviewed in this paper. Therefore questions like how do teachers of low-tract classes adapt instruction to the need of their student, or what level and pace of instruction is provided in heterogeneous group or the variation from teacher to teacher in instruction behaviour in high, low and heterogeneous classes relate to the outcome of ability grouping are not answered.

In conclusion, Slavin (1990) reported that comprehensive between-class ability grouping plans have little effect on achievement of secondary school students. Different forms of ability grouping are equally ineffective. Ability grouping is equally ineffective for all subjects. Assigning students to different levels of the same course has no consistent positive or negative effects on students of high, low or average abilities.

Cooperation: Meta-analyses

In proposing the theory of cooperation and competition, Deutsch (1949) reviewed his predecessors' works such as May and Doob, Mead, Lewis, Maller and Barnard. He postulated that cooperation seems to bring out more positive outcomes than competition. In this and the following sections, we examine the essence of cooperation and meta-analytic reviews on cooperation.

Deutsch (1949) states that on a social level, we cooperate with one another under four different conditions: When we are striving to achieve the same or complimentary goal that can be shared; when we are required by the rules of the situation to achieve this goal in nearly equal amounts; when we perform better when the goal can be achieved in equal amount; and when we have relatively many psychological affiliative contacts with one another. In cooperation, the goal-regions for each of the individuals in the group are defined so that a goal-region can be entered by any individual only if all the individuals, to some degree, can enter their respective goals. Given the same conditions, in competition the individuals will not able to reach their respective goals. Hence, in cooperation, the individuals have "promotively interdependence goals" as opposed to in competition they have "contriently interdependence goals". We are aware that in real-life situations, most of us will involve in a complex set of goals and sub-goals instead one competitive or one co-operative goal. We, in a group, may work together to achieve the same goal yet at the same time compete with each other towards another goal. Or we could be working together towards the same sub-goal yet competing with each other towards the main goal. "Interdependence" (Deutsch 1968) in essence is that of promotive or cooperative.

To summarise our learning on cooperation, we examine meta-analyses put forward by the following questions.

1.   What are the effects of cooperative, competitive and individualistic goal structures on achievement?

Deutsch (in Johnson, Maruyama, Johnson & Nelson, 1981) conceptualised in his theory of how people may interrelate from the perspectives of three types of goal structures: *cooperative, competitive,* and *individualistic*. In a *cooperative* social situation, the different individuals' goals are linked together in such a way that there is a positive correlation among their goal attainments. To attain her(his) goal, an individual is dependent on the other individuals. Only if the other individuals in the group can attain their goals, will the goal of the individual be attained. Thus, the individual seeks an outcome beneficial to all those whom s/he is cooperatively linked. In contrast, in a *competitive* social situation, the goals of the different individuals are so linked that there is a negative correlation among the goal attainments. Under the situation that the other individuals in the group cannot attain their goal an individual's goal will then be attained. Hence, the individual seeks an outcome that is personally beneficial. There is no correlation among the goal attainment of the different individuals in an *individualistic* situation. Hence, the individual seeks an outcome that is also personally beneficial.

Johnson, Maruyama, Johnson and Nelson (1981) conducted a meta-analytic study. They used three methods of meta-analysis, i.e., the voting method, the effect-size method and the z-score method. A total of 122 studies with 286 findings were reviewed. Johnson, Maruyama, Johnson and Nelson (1981) compared four conditions, namely cooperation, cooperation with intergroup competition, interpersonal competition, and individualistic effort. The results of the study showed that cooperation is superior to individualistic efforts and competition in promoting achievement and productivity; cooperation without intergroup competition promotes higher achievement and productivity than cooperation with intergroup competition; and there is no significant difference between interpersonal competition and individualistic efforts on achievement and productivity. From these results, we learn that an increase in the use of cooperative learning procedures can promote higher student achievement. Group reward systems may enhance productivity.

2. What is the impact of positive interdependence and academic group contingencies on achievement?

We learn that cooperation promotes higher achievement among students. Does positive goal interdependence or positive reward interdependence mediates the relationship between cooperation and achievement? Two conditions need to be fulfilled. First, positive goal interdependence will exist when students perceive that they can achieve their goals when their fellow colleagues with whom they are cooperatively linked achieve their goals. Second, positive reward interdependence will exist when the reward for every member of a cooperative learning group is the same when a joint task is successfully completed.

How can we translate this to mainstream education? The assumption of mainstreaming is that achievement of the academic challenged students will increase when they are placed in cooperative groups. Will the high-achievers suffer from high achievement when they are placed with academic challenged students? How to ensure that neither groups suffer, and every group benefits? One strategy to this situation is to ensure that group-to-individual transfer can take place. When individuals performing within a cooperative group demonstrate mastery of the material being studied on a subsequent test taken individually, group-to-individual transfer will occur.

Mesch, Johnson and Johnson (1988) conducted a long-term study of cooperative learning, for about six months. The participants comprised two advanced tenth grade social studies classes from a suburban middleclass school district in the Boston area. A total of twenty-six students were in the control class; and a total of twenty-eight students were in the experimental class, of which four were academically challenged and isolated students. The teacher was trained in the strategies of conducting individualistic learning experiences. Students were randomly assigned to learning groups of four members, stratified on the basis of sex and academic ability. The experimental class was taught by one social studies teacher and one special education teacher. Both of them were trained for one year in the principles of behaviour analysis and cooperative learning.

The results of the study showed that positive goal interdependence in and of itself increased achievement over individualistic efforts. The combination of positive goal and reward interdependence had an even greater effect, especially for the academically challenged and isolated students. Group-to-individual transfer took place for all students in the cooperative condition, who achieved more than did the subjects in the individualistic condition. The results indicated that the achievement of other students was not hindered by working with low-performing peers. The academically challenged and isolated students also seemed to benefit academically from working with medium- and high-achieving students.

3. What is the relation between interdependence and interpersonal attraction among heterogeneous and homogenous individuals?

Johnson, Johnson and Maruyama (1983) performed a meta-analysis to find out if interdependence has an effect on heterogeneous or homogeneous individuals. They reviewed in total 98 studies with 251 findings using three methods of meta-analysis, namely the voting method, the effect-size method, and the z-score method. Four conditions were compared: cooperation, cooperation with inter-group competition, interpersonal competition, and individualistic effort. The results showed that cooperative learning experiences promote *greater interpersonal attraction among heterogeneous peers* than do competitive or individualistic learning experiences. *Cooperative learning experiences have been found to promote greater cognitive and emotional perspective-taking abilities* than competitive or individualistic learning experiences.

4.   Does competition enhance or inhibit motor performance?

Stanne, Johnson and Johnson (1999) examined the relative impact of cooperation and zero-sum, unclear, and appropriate competition on self-esteem. They investigated a total of 64 studies relevant to the analysis. Social interdependence was the independent variable for cooperation versus zero-sum competition (e.g., sport championships and business competing for contracts), cooperation versus unclear competition, cooperation versus appropriate competition, and cooperation versus individualistic efforts. Dependent variables were achievement or performance on motor tasks, interpersonal attraction, social support, and self-esteem. Moderating variables were factors that might potentially influence the relationship between dependent and independent variables. The results of the study indicated that cooperation under all the conditions stated above was found to result in higher performance on motor performance tasks than competitive or individualistic efforts. More research is needed to find out under which conditions competition may be used to create positive relationships, social support and self-esteem

Other Evidence

What is the relation between grouping and class size? Mosteller, Light and Sachs. (1996) tried to explore empirical evidence for grouping and class size to clarify two questions:

- Should students be placed in heterogeneous classes or tracked classes?
- What is the impact of class size on student learning?

Mosteller, Light and Sachs (1996) used the term "skill grouping" opposed to ability grouping or tracking, because they felt that skill grouping emphasised current ability which can be modified by training and education, rather than tracking which classified student permanently.

Four types of grouping were identified:

- Whole class or mixed grouping versus heterogeneous grouping within grades.
- Between class grouping or XYZ skills grouping versus homogeneous grouping within grades.
- Cross-grade grouping or the Joplin Plan versus homogeneous grouping across grades.
- Within class grouping versus homogeneous grouping within classes.

Using 15 experiments involving skill grouping, Mosteller, Light and Sachs (1996) found little evidence that skill grouping has any major impact, either positive or negative on students' cognitive learning. With regard to class size, the Tennessee study demonstrated that student achievement was better in smaller classes for grades K-3 (less than 15) and that this enhanced achievement continued even when students moved to regular size class in the 4th grade and beyond. Mosteller, Light & Sachs (1996) suggested in their conclusion that education would benefit from a commitment to sustained inquiry through well designed, randomised controlled field trails of education innovations.

THE PSYCHOEDUCATIONAL GROUP

Psychoeducational group is one method to implement effective group guidance. *Group guidance* is the study of the nature of social interactions within and between groups, the process of the individuals' social positions in groups, and ways to help the individuals function effectively within and between groups (Shertzer & Stone 1981). It is the process of managing groups to develop effective groups. Gutsch and Alcorn (1970) describe group guidance as having the following characteristics:

- The group leader serves as a facilitator or an advisor.
- The group leader is able to adjust her(his) leadership style depending on the situation. Leadership styles range from being democratic to autocratic.
- Group members have a common purpose.
- Group members usually work towards creating a more cohesive and harmonious group.
- The type of group tasks being completed influence the group structure. Certain tasks would require a clear and well-defined structure while other tasks are easier to complete using a loose structure.
- The group size can be changed to meet the demands of the task being completed.
- Group members interact with each other along a range of high formality to a more personal informal nature.

Lim (2004) reorganised Wheelan's (1994) list of 40 characteristics of effective groups according to Handy's (1993) framework of structure of groups:

- Group members: Goals and roles, norms, relationships, and roles of subgroups.
- Leadership styles.
- Tasks and situations: Task, communication, problem-solving and resources and time.

Psychoeducational groups are designed to help participants develop knowledge and skills for adaptively with potential and/or immediate environment challenges, developmental transitions, and life crisis (Association for Specialists in Group Work, 1992; cited in Jones & Robinson 2000). Many specialists in the area of counselling such as Morrill, Oetting and Hurst and Ivey introduced psychoeducational groups with the objective for the roles of prevention, development, skills training and remediation in therapy and helping role. Psycho-educational groups can be used in a variety of populations, age groups and group themes in a short period of time, in various settings such as hospitals, schools, social service agencies and even universities. Topics covered in psycho-educational groups include emotional, existential and cognitive and behavioural issues (Furr 2000). The hallmark feature of a psycho-educational group is its significant educational component (Brown, 1998 cited in Jones & Robinson 2000). In every psycho-educational group, there is a group leader and structural exercises.

The roles of group leaders include planning the topics for group sessions; determining the curriculum by taking into consideration group members' stage of readiness; and deciding the sequence of the groups exercises (Jones & Robinson, 2000).

Drum and Knott (1977) descried the first framework on designing *structured groups*. According to them, structured groups have predetermined plan and goals. Structured groups serve the purpose of imparting knowledge and skills as well as provide support and sharing. These groups have become one of the most popular modalities especially in the short-term treatment settings (Furr 2000).

Given the role functions of group leaders mentioned above, it is important that the group leaders are educated about the stages of group development, frameworks or models of group approaches and some available group exercises or activities.

Stages of Group Development

According to the *group model theory*, all groups develop and move to different stages as they progress. Groups move from a beginning stage to middle or working stage, and then to an ending or a closing stage (Jones & Robinson 2000).

There are five stages of group development: *Forming, storming, norming, performing and adjourning* (Tuckman 1965; Tuckman & Jensen 1977). Group leaders have to deal with different sets of challenges and opportunities in each of these stages (Lim 2004).

During the *forming* stage, group leaders help group members to understand their individual and group roles and expected behaviours, and to clarify group procedures and rules (Tuckman 1965; Tuckman & Jensen 1977).

The *storming* stage occurs when group members challenge or disagree with the group (Tuckman 1965; Tuckman & Jensen 1977). During this stage, group leaders need to guide the group in identifying and establishing boundaries and autonomy (Johnson 1979, 1980); and in building mutuality and trust (Johnson & Johnson 1989).

These beginning stages are characterised by members' anxieties. Anxieties are mainly due to members being new with unfamiliar group members and group rules. Conflicts and confusion may arise in these stages.

The *norming* stage occurs when a group agrees on group values, norms and beliefs (Johnson & Johnson 2000). Self-enforcement and policing by group members of these procedures is a clear indicator of the success of the norming stage. The role of group leaders is to gradually reduce the amount of monitoring for compliance of group norms and rules (Lim 2004).

During the *performing* stage, which is the fourth stage, the group has established sufficient levels of cohesiveness, trust, commitment to be able to perform their roles effectively (Tuckman 1965; Tuckman & Jensen 1977). In this stage, the group leader should ideally change from being a directive task-oriented leader to a more consultative relation-oriented leader (Johnson & Johnson 2000).

As the group moves forward to the middle stage, group members start to experience universality and group cohesion. Members, at this stage, are more willing to explore underlying issues, feelings and needs with more intensity and depth (Jones & Robinson 2000).

The last stage is the *adjourning* stage, in which, the group members prepare to disband, either because they have completed their mission, or because they could not resolve conflicts (Tuckman 1965; Tuckman & Jensen 1977). Some groups do not experience this stage and can continue performing for many years. In the last stage, where groups are moving forward to termination process, members will deal with feelings associated with this termination process (Jones & Robinson 2000).

Intensity of Group Activities

Jones and Robinson (2000) highlighted about the "intensity" of group members engaging in the group as they move these stages. *Intensity* (Jacobs, Masson & Harvill 1998) is defined as the extent to which the group topic, structured exercises and group techniques involved in:

- evoking anxiety among group members;
- challenging group participants to self-disclosure;
- increasing awareness;
- focusing on feelings;
- concentrating on the here and now; and
- focussing on threatening issues.

Group intensity, according to the psychoeducational model follows the stage of the group development, progressing slowly at the beginning to a height at the middle stage, and then subsiding as the group moves towards termination. The whole process can be illustrated with a normal bell curve. During the *beginning* stage, members tend to feel less comfortable in sharing. As such, group members tend to focus on topics such as developing trust and safety that is less intensive. At the *working* stage, where the participants have built more trust among them, group activities that can be appropriate include encouraging members to express their own opinions, exploring different behaviours and dealing with personal issues. By the *final* stage, members may wish to continue dealing with intense issues, but group leaders should direct the group dynamics towards closure of the groups, by decreasing the intensity and shifting attention to focus on meaningful and integration of learning (Jones & Robinson 2000).

Selection of Appropriate Group Activities

One central feature in the planning of an effective psychoeducational group is choosing the appropriate structured group activities. This effort needs to take into consideration timing and issues, objectives or goals of the groups. Jones and Robinson (2000) provide the following step-by step guidelines in choosing activities in groups:

Step 1: Brainstorming group activities appropriate for the group theme. The group leader and members list as many activities as possible from a variety of theoretical framework such as gestalt, behavioural and cognitive perspectives.

Step 2: Assessing the intensity of each activity. The group evaluates the extent that each of these activities will evoke and challenge the participants' emotion, self-awareness, and readiness.

Step 3: Choosing activities for the early stage of groups. The activities chosen should help the group to facilitate the development of trust among members, teaching of basic group processes, or assisting members in expressing their fears and expectations of the group.

Step 4: Choosing activities for the middle stages of group. Group activities should include those that encourage members to recognise, express and deal with their feelings, conflicts and fear. It is appropriate for groups to use activities that invoke greater intensity, such as self-disclosure, dealing with the current realities and enhancing self-awareness.

Step 5: Choosing activities for the ending stage. Activities at this stage can include activities that make members evaluate the impact of the group and decide what changes they want to make and how to go about doing it.

Model of Structured Group Design

Furr (2000) proposed a two phase development model of structured group:

- *The conceptual phase* includes a) statement of purpose, b) establishing goals, and c) setting objectives.
- *The operational phase* includes a) selection of content, b) designing experiential activities, and c) evaluation.

Counselling theories are used as the foundation of the conceptual phase. These theories guide the belief that changes occur in individuals may occur at the individuals' levels of awareness, knowledge, insights or behaviour (Gladding 1990).

The steps in the conceptual phase are:

Step 1: Statement of purpose. An explicit statement of the reasons for the group's existence must be established. The statement will address the following questions:

- What is the primary content focus of this group?
- Which population will benefit from participation of this group?
- What is the purpose of intervention? Is it remediation, prevention or development?
- What is the expected outcome of participation of this group?

Step 2: Establishing goals. Furr (2000) argued that goals indicate how an individual may change as a result of participation in a group. These changes can occur at the cognitive, behavioural, existential and physical levels. Hence, group leaders should specify the type

63

of changes expected from group participation. Furr (2000) further highlighted a few criteria to be met for a goal to be effective in guiding the group design. The goal must be reasonable, achievable, clear, and written in measurable forms so that participants can conduct self-evaluation on their own level of achievement. Short term goals may also be helpful in providing steps that will lead to the attainment of long term goals. Furr (2000) noted that clearly defined goals will assist members of the groups in recognising that the group has a certain limitation in its scope, rather than the group being able to solve all issues. In addition, well-defined goals allow participants to evaluate if the outcomes facilitated by the group are consistent with her(his) personal value systems.

Step 3: Setting objectives: As goals set the direction for the group, objectives provide the road map on how to get there. Objectives indicate what must be done, or happen if the goals are to be achieved. Objectives establish the connection between theory and application and specify the steps needed for reaching the goals (Furr 2000).

Step 4: Selection of content: Furr (2000) organised the group content into three components: didactic, experiential, and process. The didactic component focuses on direct imparting of information. Experiential learning allows the material to be encountering on a more personal level. Instead of just listening, participants learn by engaging in the 'doing' of the topic taught. Again, Furr (2000) emphasised the importance of experiential activities to be grounded on a theoretical perspective.

The process component aims to help participants connect the experiential and didactic components. By linking the experience with theory, the participants are better equipped to generalise the experience to a broader life situation and to integrate the new awareness to an individual conceptual framework. Processing can involve activities such as discussion about what happens in a certain activity; what are participants' reaction (thoughts, feelings, insights generated) to the activity.

A type of processing component includes sharing leaders' observations on group interaction or sharing concerns arising for participants.

Furr (2000) suggested that cognitive and behavioural dimensions focus more on the didactic aspect whereas affective and existential dimensions demand more experiential and processing activities. For a group to be effective, the group leader must balance the three components appropriately. Furr (2000) suggested the following timeline for each component:

- Cognitive: 60 per cent didactic, 15 per cent experiential and 25 per cent processing
- Behavioural: 40 per cent didactic, 40 per cent experiential, and 20 per cent processing
- Affective: 30 per cent didactic, 40 per cent experiential, 30 per cent processing
- Existential: 20 per cent didactic, 40 per cent experiential and 40 per cent processing
- Physical: 25 per cent didactic, 50 per cent experiential and 25 per cent processing.

Step 5: Designing exercise: Without structural group exercises, psychoeducational groups, according to Furr (2000) would only convey information rather than would change perception and behaviour. In choosing appropriate exercises, Furr (2000) listed the following factors to consider:

- Identifying the theory and goals behind the exercise to ensure that the exercise is congruent with the current group theory and goals.
- Considering the age and experience level of group members.
- Having some exercises such as self-assessment, cognitive-structuring, role-playing, imagery, creative arts, body awareness, and homework.

Step 6: Evaluation: Furr (2000) suggested two types of evaluation to test group activities and to determine which components facilitate change.

- *Process evaluation* refers to testing the effectiveness of the session-to-session activities. This is an on-going activity as it is important to know the participants' perceptions of their

65

connectedness to the group. Evaluation can be conducted informally, asking members about their perception of the group and the activities. It can also be conducted midway to see if the group's needs are being met.

- *Outcome evaluation* refers to the degree of individual change. One of the most rigorous ways in outcome measure is the pre- and post-test method. A number of instruments have been designed to measure specific construct. One should nonetheless select the instruments carefully as the construct addressed by the group may not change much in the short span of structured groups (Baldwin, Collins, Kostenauer & Murphy 1988). Examples of outcome assessment are evaluations of goal attainment, members' satisfaction, leadership styles, as well as contents and activities in the group (Furr 2000).

Cognitive Appraisal Theory

Another useful approach to psychoeducational group is the cognitive oriented model for group work based on appraisal theory (Roseman, Antoniou and Jose 1996). Appraisal theory attempts to specify the precise links between cognitive evaluations of an event and resultant discrete emotions. Appraisal theory presents a model how the individual's thoughts are translated into emotions in various ways due to one's subjective evaluation/interpretation of an event.

Roseman, Antoniou & Jose (1996) postulated that cognitive appraisal of events are based on the following specific dimensions:

- *Situational state* is when a person considers whether an event is consistent or is inconsistent with one' desires.
- *Motivational state* refers to whether the individual is seeking something positive striving to avoid something painful.
- *Probability* refers to the perceived likelihood of an event's occurrence.
- *Control potential* refers to the degree to which individuals believe they can control or influence a given situation.
- *Problem source* refers to whether a negative event is caused by something inherent to the person or object (characterological) or merely with the behaviour or non-central attribute of the person or object (non-characterogical).

- *Agency* consists of three separate sub-dimensions:

    i)   *agency-self*, the degree to which the event is perceived as caused by oneself.
    ii) *agency-others*, the degree to which the event is perceived as caused by another person.
    iii) *agency-circumstances*, the degree to which the event is perceived as caused by external circumstances.

By measuring appraisal along these dimensions, an individual's emotional reaction could be predicted. This theory postulates that there are 11 negative emotions (disgust, distress, sadness, fear, unfriendliness, anger, frustration, shame, regret, guilt, and contempt) and five positive emotions (joy, relief, affection, pride, and hope). For example, in an event that is appraised as motive inconsistent (low on situational state dimension), appraised as caused by another person (high on the agency-other dimension) and appraised as having low control potential is likely to result in dislike. To change one's appraisal of this event, appraisal on all the above dimensions need to be changed.

A four stage psychoeducational model for using appraisal theory with groups: McCarthy, Mejia and Liu (2000) noted that although the four-stage model psychoeducational group can be useful, it is important to be aware that each stage can vary depending on the group goals. The group leader may introduce this model after two to three group meetings. The model is rather complex, and may only be beneficial to adults or late adolescents.

Stage 1: Introduction: Cognitive intervention typically begins with a didactic introduction (D'Zurilla 1986; Meichenbaum 1985). From the outset, group leaders will introduce some negative emotions common in therapy. The group leader may refer to Roseman, Antoniou and Jose's model (1996) and try to create awareness of how an undesirable event occurs. As the model can be complex, the group leader should check the level of understanding of each member.

Stage 2: Discovery: The group leader's role at this stage is to clarify aspects of the model. Members at this stage are asked to identify an emotion they experience and wish to understand better. Using a structured exercise, members should be asked to write about the event in general and about the situation that caused them to feel that way. Next, members will proceed to systematically evaluate how each appraisal dimension led to the experience of the emotion. The group leader should process the experience and should encourage members to evaluate the usefulness of this approach for their own lives.

Stage 3: Deeper insight: According to Mahoney (1988, cited in McCarthy, Mejia & Liu 2000), the primary goal of insight is to generate awareness with the assumption that insight can accelerate adaptive changes. Common understanding among members can be explored. Structure exercise at this stage can involve having group members recount an event in which they feel specific emotions with further details about their subjective evaluation of the event. This is to improve members' understanding of the model and to find alternative ways of appraising an event. The group leader's role at this point is to pay specific attention to the information provided to gather relevant materials about the types of appraisal made by the members. The group leader can also invite other members to evaluate the extent to which the members' appraisal matches those hypothesised by the model.

Another important task at this stage involves the group leader helping group members process experiences by having them talk about their reactions so as to explore their appraisals. Questions should be addressed include the following: Do the members need that further help in understanding the model? Are they comfortable talking about their appraisal and emotion?

Stage 4: Integration and appraisal flexibility: By this stage, members should be able to reflect on past events which resulted in negative emotions and decide on alternative appraisal patterns. The group leader should emphasise that one appraisal is not better than the others, but "what seems optimal is the ability to appraise the situations in the most adaptive, constructive and socially useful terms" (McCarthy, Mejia & Liu 2000, 118).

The Types of Leaders and Nature of Leadership

The group leader comprises an important component of group guidance and psychoeducational groups. To a large extent, the effectiveness and efficiency of the group leader determines the success or failure of group guidance (Lim 2004).

Democratic vs. autocratic, relation-oriented vs. task-oriented leaders: Democratic leaders share and delegate power, responsibilities and decision-making roles with group members, while authoritarian leaders prefer to keep all the decision-making power (Handy 1993). Leaders who use democratic leadership styles are more likely to be successful leaders than those who use the authoritarian approach. Some of the positive impact of democratic leadership styles are higher satisfaction among subordinates, lower turnover, lower grievance rates, less inter-group conflicts, higher group productivity, and higher level of subordinates commitment and loyalty (Handy 1993; Schmuck & Schmuck 2001).

Blake and Mouton (1964) state that leaders who are high in both relation orientation (more concerned with the welfare of group members) and task orientation (more focus on successful completion of group tasks) are more likely to be successful and effective leaders. Relation orientation leadership behaviours include developing relationships with group members and developing a sense of trust, respect, understanding, support, and obedience. Task orientated leaders tend to focus more on the quality and quantity of group production at the expense of the welfare of group members. Effective and successful leaders are able to judge the situation (e.g., subordinates, tasks, situational factors, and available resources) and to use different leadership styles (Fiedler & Chemers 1974; Handy 1993; Hersey 1984; Hersey & Blanchard 1976; Kennedy 1982; Miner 1992; Vroom & Yetton 1973).

Psychoeducational groups are useful approaches, yet a number of possible constraints need to be addressed:

- Group leaders may have too broad a focus for psychoeducational groups (Furr 2000).
- Another challenge is making the time commitment to document the group design. Group leaders need to recognise that a natural evolution of the group exists and that the nature of sessions will change as the group progresses, at the beginning with more support and safety net and shifting to more challenge activities (Furr 2000).
- Group leaders need to be aware of members that might benefit from further referrals for additional individual or group therapy or services

(Furr 2000).

- Group leaders are sometimes not aware of the diverse range of experiences, definitions, feelings, opinions and thoughts that each group member brings to the psychoeducational group (Villalba 2003).
- Group leaders must be aware of their own biases (Villalba 2003).

FINAL WORDS

Finally, we iterate our wish—teachers should adapt flexibly and appropriately their methods of instruction and materials to different groups of students. It is important to understand that to achieve the maximum achievement effects grouping practices have to be complemented with appropriately modified and differentiated curricula (Tieso 2003). In socialisation, peers are "all individuals who work in the same group as the focal group member" (Chattopadhyay, George & Lawrence 2004, 892). This chapter examines forms of *work groups* (Hackman 1983). A work group is defined as "intact, bounded social systems, with interdependent members and differentiated member roles, for pursuing shared, measureable goals" (Chattopadhyay, George & Lawrence 2004, 892). One central idea throughout all forms of effective groups is that individuals need to feel that they are valued and welcome in these groups, a crucial component for the development of positive experiences.

REFERENCES

Baldwin, C. L., J. R. Collins, T. Kostenbauer, & C. B. Murphy. 1988. Research choices for measuring outcome of high school groups. *Journal of Specialists in Group Work, 13,* 2–8.

Blake, R., & J. Mouton. 1964. *The managerial grid.* Houston, TX: Gulf.

Burns, R. B., & D. A. Mason. 2002. Class composition and student achievement in elementary schools. *American Educational Research Journal, 39(1),* 207–233.

Chattopadhyay, P., E. George, & S. A. Lawrence. 2004. Why does dissimilarity matter? Exploring self-categorization, self-enhancement, and uncertainty reduction. *Journal of Applied Psychology, 89(3),* 892–900.

Cheung, C. K., & E. Rudowicz. 2003. Academic outcomes of ability grouping among junior high school students in Hong Kong. *Journal of Educational Research, 96(4),* 241–254.

D'Zurilla, T J. 1986. *Problem-solving therapy: A social competence approach to clinical intervention.* New York: Springer.

Deutsch, M. 1949. A theory of cooperation and competition. *Human Relations,*

2, 129–152.

Deutsch, M. 1968 Field theory in social psychology. In *The handbook of social psychology* (2nd ed., Vol. 1, 412–487). Edited by G. Lindzey & E. Aronson. Reading, MA: Addison Wesley.

Drum, D. J., & J. E. Knott. 1977. *Structured groups for facilitating development: Acquiring life skills, resolving life themes, and making life transitions.* New York: Human Sciences Press.

Fiedler, E. D., R. E. Lange, & S. Winebrenner. 1993. In search of reality: unraveling the myths about tracking, ability grouping and the gifted. *Roeper Review, 16(1),* 4–7.

Fiedler, F. E., & M. M. Chemers. 1974. *Leadership and effective management.* Glenview, IL: Scott, Foresman.

Furr, S. 2000. Structuring the group experience: A format for designing psychoeducational groups. *Journals for Specialists in Group Works, 25,* 29–49.

Gamoran, A. 1987. Organization, instruction, and the effects of ability grouping: Comment on Slavin's "best-evidence synthesis". *Review of Educational Research, 57,* 341–345.

Gladding, S. 1990. Let us not grow weary of theory. *Journal for Specialists in Group Work, 15,* 144.

Gutsch, K. U., & J. D. Alcorn. 1970. *Guidance in action: Ideas and innovations for school counselors.* Parker.

Hackman, J. R. 1983. *A normative model of work team effectiveness* (Technical Report No. 2). New Haven, CT: Yale University, School of Organization and Management.

Handy, C. 1993. *Understanding organizations* (4th Ed.). London: Penguin Books.

Hersey, P., & K. H. Blanchard. 1976. Leader effectiveness and adaptability description (LEAD). In *The 1976 annual handbook for group facilitation* (vol. 5). Edited by J. W. Pfeiffer & J. E. Jones. LaJolla, CA: University Associates.

Hersey, P. 1984. *The situational leader.* Escondido, CA: Center for Leadership Studies.

Jacobs, E. E., R. L. Masson, & R. L. Harvill, R. L. 1998. *Group counseling: Strategies and skills.* Pacific Grove, CA: Brooks/Cole.

Johnson, D. W. 2003. Social interdependence: Interrelationships among theory, research, and practice. *American Psychologist, 58,* 934–945.

Johnson, D. W., & F. P. Johnson. 2000. *Joining together: Group theory and group skills* (7th Ed.). Boston: Allyn and Bacon.

Johnson, D. W., & R. T. Johnson. 1989. *Cooperation and competition: Theory and research.* Edina, M.N.: Interaction Book.

Johnson, D. W., R. T. Johnson, & G. Maruyama. 1983. Interdependence and interpersonal attraction among heterogeneous and homogeneous individuals: A theoretical formulation and a meta-analysis of the research. *Review of Educational Research, 53(1),* 5–54.

Johnson, D. W., G. Maruyama, R. Johnson, & D. Nelson. 1981. Effects of cooperative, competitive, and individualistic goal structures on achievement: A meta-analysis. *Psychological Bulletin, 89(1)*, 47–62.

Jones, D. K., & E. H. M. Robinson III. 2000. Psychoeducational groups: A model for choosing topics and exercises appropriate to group stage. *Journal for Specialists in Group Work, 25*, 356–365.

Kennedy, J. K. 1982. Middle LPC leaders and the contingency model of leadership effectiveness. *Organizational Behaviour and Human Performance, 39*, 1–14.

Koffka, K. 1962. *Principles of gestalt psychology*. London: Routledge & Kegan Paul Ltd.

Kramarski, B., & Z. R. Mevarech. 2003. Enhancing mathematical reasoning in the classroom: the effects of cooperative learning and metacognitive training. *American Educational Research Journal, 40(1)*, 281–310.

Kulik, J., & C-L. C. Kulik. 1982. Research synthesis on ability grouping. *Educational Leadership, 36(8)*, 619–621.

Kulik, J. A., & C-L. C. Kulik. 1992. Meta-analytic findings on grouping programs. *Gifted Child Quarterly, 36(2)*, 73–77.

LeTendre, G. K., B. K. Hofer, & H. Shimizu. 2003. What is tracking? Cultural expectations in the United States, Germany and Japan. *American Educational Research Journal, 40(1)*, 43–89.

Lewin, K. 1936. *Principles of topological psychology*. New York: McGraw-Hill.

Lim, K.M. 2004. Developmental group guidance in the classroom. In *Counselling in schools: Theories, processes and techniques* (1–22). Edited by E. Tan. Singapore: McGraw-Hill.

Lou, Y., P. C. Abrami, J. C. Spence, C. Poulsen, B. Chambers, & S. d'Apollonia. 1996. Within-class grouping: a meta-analysis. *Review of Educational Research, 66(4)*, 423 –458.

McCarthy, C., O. L. Mejia, & H. T. T. Liu. 2000. Cognitive appraisal theory: A psychoeducational approach for understanding connections between cognition and emotion in group work. *Journal for Specialists in Group Work, 25*, 104–121

Meichenbaum, D. 1985. *Stress inoculation training*. Elmsford, NY: Pergamon.

Mesch, D., Johnson, D.W., & Johnson, R. 1988. Impact of positive interdependence and academic group contingencies on achievement. *The Journal of Social Psychology, 128(3)*, 345–352.

Miner, J. B. 1992. *Industrial-organization psychology*. New York: McGraw-Hill.

Mosteller, F., R. J. Light, & J. A. Sachs. 1996. Sustained inquiry in educational: Lesson from skill grouping and class size. *Harvard Educational Review, 66(4)*, 197–212.

Peterson, S. E., & J. A. Miller. 2004. Comparing the quality of students' experiences during cooperative learning and large-group instruction. *Journal of Educational Research, 97(3)*, 123–133.

Roseman, I., A. A. Antoniou, & P. Jose. 1996. Appraisal determinants of emotions: Constructing a more accurate and comprehensive theory. *Cognition and Emotion, 10*, 241–277.

Schmuck, R. A., & P. A. Schmuck. 2001. *Group processes in the classroom* (8th Ed.). Boston: McGraw-Hill.

Shertzer, E. F., & S. C. Stone. 1981. *Fundamentals of guidance* (4th Ed.). Boston,

Mass.: Houghton Mifflin.

Slavin, R. E. 1990. Achievement effects of ability grouping in secondary schools: A best evidence synthesis. *Review of Educational Research, 60(3)*, 471–499.

Slavin, R. E. 1993. Ability grouping in the middle grades: *Achievement effects and alternatives. Elementary School Journal, 93(5)*, 35–52. 1999. Does competition enhance or inhibit motor performance: A meta-analysis. *Psychological Bulletin, 125(1)*, 133–154.

Tieso, C. L. 2003. Ability grouping is not just tracking anymore. *Roeper Review, 26(1)*, 29–36.

Tuckman, B., & M. Jensen. 1977. Stages of small group development revisited. *Group and Organizational Studies, 2*, 419–427.

Tuckman, B. 1965. Developmental sequence in small groups. *Psychological Bulletin, 63*, 384–399.

Villalba, J. A. 2003. A psychoeducational group for limited-English proficient Latino/Latina children. *Journal for Specialists in Group Work, 28*, 261–276.

Vroom, V. H., & P. W. Yetton. 1973. *Leadership and decision making*. Pittsburgh, PA: University of Pittsburgh Press.

Wheelan, S. A. 1994. *Group processes: A developmental perspective*. Needham Heights, MA: Allyn and Bacon.

---

* This chapter summarises the essence of a co-authored book: Tan, A. G., & K. M. Lim. 2004. Working in group. Singapore: The authors.

3

Learning Support Programme and School Counsellors

TAN AI GIRL, WONG SOO FEI, CHUA KIA
CHONG, AND BRYAN TANG

INTRODUCTION

This chapter has a main focus—to present theoretical discourses on "disability" from the Vygotskian perspectives. Specifically, the position of Vygotsky for disability is discussed. The discourse of disability is relevant to Singapore's learning support programme (LSP) which aims to assist mainstream children with learning difficulties in the English language and/or Mathematics. It is timely to reflect upon the discourse of disability as Singapore in the near future embarks on including more special needs children to mainstream schooling by training and employing special education officers and school counsellors.

We have organised this chapter into three parts. In the introduction we visit the discourse of disability advocated by Vygotsky. In the second part, we present a general overview of Singapore's learning support programme, findings of two efficacious studies, and some general recommendations. As a concluding remark, we refer to current literature for some insights into possible benefits of school counsellors.

L. S Vygotsky (1986—1934), the founder of socio-cultural analysis and activity theory, explained how our mind and the world interact and how they are transformed by this interaction. Vygotsky formulated a unique theoretical frame-work for special education. He highlighted the human being as the subject of cultural rather than natural processes. He shifted away from biologically based understanding of human behaviour to social-cultural explanations of human activity. Vygotsky developed and approached the connected social and mental processes and described the essential mechanisms of socialisation and human development. According to Mahn (1999), Vygotsky used dialectics to develop his major theoretical contributions on the following:

- The role played by language and other forms of semiotic symbols.
- The function of social interaction in the development of human mind.
- The role of word meaning in complex and conceptual thinking.
- Relationships between elementary and higher mental functions.
- Zone of Proximal Development (ZPD) to explain learning and teaching.

In *the cultural-history activity theory* (Gindis 1999), Vygotsky considered learning as a *shared* process in a responsive social context. According to him, psychological phenomena are "social." They depend on social experiences and treatments, and they embody cultural artifacts. Social experiences include the manner in which people stimulate and direct one's attention, model behavior, respond to behaviour, control bodily movement, and organise spatial relations among individuals. Vygotsky (Cole, Steiner, Scribner & Souberman 1978) posited that the mind emerges from the interaction with social others and environment, mediated by artifacts, signs and languages.

Cultural artifacts include signs and symbol, languages, and human produced objects. According to this theory, tools shape the way human beings interact with reality. From the principle of *internalisation* and *externalisation*, shaping external activities ultimately results in shaping internal ones. Tools usually reflect the experience of people who have tried to resolve similar problems in the past. Therefore, the use of tools is a means for accumulation and transmission of social knowledge. Tools influence nature, external behaviour, and the mental functioning of individual. Taking children's interaction with the world as an example, children interact without initial understanding what they are doing. However through a process of internalisation-externalisation, they gradually notice patterns in their behaviour and come to understand their external activity (Hung & Nichani 2002).

One of the major contributions of Vygotsky was that he viewed language and symbols as a *psychological tool* for human development and learning. Psychological tools are different from technical tools, as they direct "mind' and "behaviour." Vygotsky argued that the higher voluntary forms of human behaviour have their roots in social interactions, in the individual's participation in social behaviour mediated by speech (Hung & Nichani 2002).

Vygotsky investigated the origin of human development of consciousness by examining the mediating role played by tools and symbol systems in human interactions with nature. The mediating function of language and other symbolic system is known as *semiotic mediation*. For Vygotsky, languages and other tools mediate social and individual functioning, connecting the external and the internal. The internalisation of language's social regulatory function and the consequence transformation of human activity lead to the development of higher psychological processes. For example, when speech is unified with a child's activities, a new organisation of behaviour occurs and the child begins to use speech to regulate her(his) activities (Mahn 1999). Other semiotic means include various ways of counting, mnemonic techniques, algebra symbol systems, writing, schemes, diagrams, maps, and mechanical drawing. These semiotic means are tools that facilitate co-construction of knowledge and these means are internalised to aid future independent problem-solving activities (Palincsar 1998).

In social interaction, a child learns self-regulatory behavioural aspect of speech as speech truncates to the child's internalised speech. Vygotsky claimed that the function of this inner speech will orient intellectual endeavours, developing conscious awareness, problem solving, and stimulating creativity. Vygotsky examined the developmental relationships between thinking and speaking. He felt that due to new functional relationships between memory and speech, the use of words bring about the formation of a new psychological system. Children, via social interactions will develop systems in thought or concept formation as they acquire languages. Concepts formation can be divided to *spontaneous concepts* and *scientific concepts*

Spontaneous concepts are concepts acquired by the child outside the context of explicit instruction. These concepts are mostly taken from adults in everyday situations, but not in a systematic fashion. *Scientific concepts* are concepts that have been explicitly introduced by a teacher at school or within a well established scientific field. Nevertheless, Vygotsky pointed out the importance the interdependent nature of these two concepts. According to him, the two concepts are interrelated and constantly influence each other (Mahn 1999).

In this history-cultural theory, human development is a sociogenic process carried out in social activities. Education leads development and results in social learning through the internalisation of culture and social relationships. Development is not a straight patch of quantitative gain but a series of qualitative, dialectic transformation—a complex process of integration and disintegration (Gindis 1999).

Disability as a Cultural Phenomenon

According to Vygotsky, "(a) child whose development is impeded by disability is not simply a child less developed than her(his) peers; rather s/he has developed differently" (Vygotsky 1983, 96; cited in Gindis 1999, 336; gender pronounces introduced by the author) That means, the development of a child with disabilities is not slowed down or missing, but her(his) development projects a qualitative uniqueness. Specifically, the child with disabilities has major qualitative differences in the "means and ways" to internalise her(his) culture. These differences emerge from the child's needs to form compensatory strategies and from social complications due to her(his) disabilities. The effectiveness of the compensatory strategies may be relatively independent of the severity or type of disability. More important are the timeliness and appropriateness in the methodology used. Hence, to counter any negative social consequences of primary disability special education programmes one should include sociocultural goals of the general education programmes (Rieber & Carton 1993).

A phenomenon termed a "two-sided nature" of handicap refers to the underdevelopment or absence of functions due to an organic defect and the formation of adaptive-compensatory mechanism. The effectiveness of the adaptive-compensatory mechanism depends on the adequacy and timeliness of the corrective methods used in educating the child. A child's physical or mental impairment could be overcome by creating alternative but equivalent roads for her(his) cultural development. Common laws of development include internalising the external cultural activities into internal processes via *psychological tools* and *mediated learning* provided by adults. In the field of special education, the concepts of internalisation of psychological tools as the main mechanism of development are important for rehabilitation (Gindis 1999).

Students with special needs may benefit in the academic and socioeconomic domains from being in an organised peer group (termed as "a collective"). The peer mediated activities serve as a powerful means to form higher psychological function in children with disabilities. It is believed that a child with disability is likely to extent her(his) zone of

77

proximal development (ZPD) when s/he works with a group of peers under the guidance of an educator. Considering that the development of a child with disability as determined by social aspects of her(his) organic impairment would create an alternative perspective for the child's socialisation and overall remediation.

In his early career years, Vygotsky advocated "normalisation" through "mainstreaming" all children with disabilities—the full inclusion model today. Social inclusion of children with disabilities into the sociocultural life of their communities serves as a condition of effective rehabilitation and compensation. A negative model of special education is a combination of lowered expectations, a kind of water-down curriculum. In his later works, Vygotsky expressed firm conviction that only in a truly differentiated learning environment can a child with disability fully develop her(his) higher psychological functioning.

Vygotsky (Rieber & Carton 1993) believed that by incorporating the child with disabilities into a supportive social environment is likely to allow her(him) to develop her(his) higher functions. Creating a learning environment would give students with disabilities alternative means of communication and development, and using psychological tools most appropriate to compensate for a particular disability. To Vygotsky, a child with disability must be educated with special set of psychological tools, and this should take place within her(his) ZPD and in mainstreamed sociocultural milieu where compensation for secondary defects should take place through the experiences and opportunity as close as possible to those of the normal (Gindis 1999)

In essence, the Vygotskian approach taught that an individual has a natural inclination to compensate for deficiency. Both the problem of disabilities and its solution are sociocultural. The main goal of special education, therefore, is not only to compensate for primary defects but, also to prevent, correct, and rehabilitate secondary defects. The challenge is to create "new tools" to connect with the spontaneous survival strategies of the person and to enable the realisation of goals in new situations (Miltenberg & Singer 1999).

In the *theory of disontogenesis* (distorted development as cited in Vygodskaya 1999, 330), Vygotsky claimed that "a disability in and of itself is not a tragedy. It is only on occasion to provoke a tragedy." The uniqueness of Vygotsky approach lies in his understanding of the *disability* not as a biological impairment having physiological consequences, but as *a social cultural* development phenomenon. He perceived disability as a "social dislocation" (Grigorenko 1998). Vygotsky argued that a disability is perceived as an abnormal only when it is brought into the social context. Impairment of any part of our body leads to a restructuring of social relationships and to a displacement of all the systems of behaviour. Moreover, a defect varies psychologically in different cultural and social environment. Vygotsky pointed out that from the social perspective, the primary problem of disability is not the organic impairment itself, but it social implication (Gindis 1999).

Vygotsky (Cole, Steiner, Scribner & Souberman 1978) introduced concepts of primary disability and secondary disability and their interaction: *Primary disability* refers to organic impairment due to biological factors, and *secondary disability* refers to distortion of higher psychological functions due to social factors. *Lower function* refers to elementary perception, memory, attention, and the like, everything that creates a biological predisposition of the child's development. *Higher function* refers to abstract learning, logical memory, attention, and decision making that appears in the course of transformation of the lower functions. This transformation is made through a process called *"mediated activity"* and *"psychological tools."*

An organic impairment prevents a child from mastering social skills, and acquiring knowledge at a proper rate. The child social milieu may modify her(his) course of development and lead to distortion and delay. Vygotsky therefore argued that from the psycho-education perspective, the primary problem of a disability is not the organic impairment itself but its social implications. An organic defect is recognised by society as a social abnormality in behaviour. Expectation and attitudes of social conditions created by the society influence the access of the child with disability to social-cultural knowledge, experience, and opportunity to acquire psychological tools.

Psychology function of the child appears twice, first on the social level, between people (inter-psychological) and later, on the individual level, inside the child (intra-psychological). The formation of individual consciousness takes place through socially meaningful activities that shape her(his) make-up.

Disturbance in higher psychological functions (which often caused by social impoverishment) can be treated by restructuring the child's social environment. Changing negative societal attitudes towards an individual with disability therefore should be one of the goals of special education. Vygotsky advocated for a favourable societal outlook on a child with disability by searching for positive capacities and qualitative characteristics of the disabled child. He called this a *positive differentiation*, where identification of a child with disability from the point of strength and not weaknesses. Vygotsky also pointed out the dynamic nature of disability. He argued that constant change in the structure and content of a disability takes place during development and under the influence of education or remediation. In a nutshell, the essence and uniqueness of human development resides in its *mediation* by *material instruments* and social signs (*language*). Culture is acquired through internalisation of social signs, starting with language (Gindis 1999).

THE LEARNING SUPPORT PROGRAMME

The Learning Support Programme (LSP) was first introduced by the Ministry of Education (MOE) Singapore in 1992 as an early intervention for primary school students (i.e., primary 1) who are at risk in the English language competencies (LSP[EL]). The programme extended in 1999 to those at risk in the mathematical competencies (LSP[Mathematics]). The primary school children are screened at the beginning of the school year using a pencil-and-paper test (i.e., School Readiness Test, SRT) which assesses basic language and literacy skills (EL) as well as numeracy skills (Mathematics). Only children with SRT levels 0–2 (in all five levels, i.e., 0–4) are placed on LSP (EL). In addition to SRT taken at the beginning of P1, throughout the school year, the LSP is open to the following school children: those who fail SA1/SA2, reading age below chronological age, and based on teacher recommendations. The similar procedure is used to identify P2 children for LSP. Children who obtain a pass for SA1/SA2, whose reading age approximates chronological age, and who receive positive feedback from EL teacher will be discharged from LSP.

Students placed on the LSP(EL) are withdrawn daily from their mainstream English language classes to attend LSP lessons (i.e., half an hour each day). For students placed on the LSP(Mathematics) are either withdrawn from mainstream mathematics classes (i.e., two hours per week) or are supported after school hours (for the same duration). Like the LSP(EL), children in LSP(Mathematics) are taught in small groups (i.e., 8–10 or 8–12) to allow a high level of teacher-pupil interaction, and lessons are carried out using multi-sensory and activity-based learning. Every year a total of 12,000 children are admitted to the LSP, approximately 20 per cent of primary 1 and ten per cent of primary 2 students.

Efficacy Studies of LSP

At for to-date, two local Master theses examined the effectiveness of LSP (Ang 2002; Yang 2004). Results of their studies are summarised below.

Ang (2002) examined effectiveness P2 LSP(EL) in a primary school in Singapore. The purpose of this study was to find out how effective the primary 2 LSP(EL) was in a primary school in Singapore. It focused on reading remediation of the programme for the pupils who lived in a multi-racial environment. The participants of the study were 44 primary 2 "at risk" mainstream students, of which 29 (69 per cent male, 31 per cent female) were in the LSP programme and 15 (40 per cent male, 60 per cent female) were in the non-LSP programme. Three instruments were used for the participants:

- Singapore Word Reading Test to assess reading age of the participants for pre-LSP and post-LSP intervention periods.
- Deberry Reading Attitude Survey to measure the participants' "reading for fun percentile" (13 items) and "students" reading when required percentile (11 items).
- EL SA1 (as pre-test) and SA2 (as post-test). Items in the tests carried equal set of difficulties.

Participants in LSP were given reading remediation by the Learning Support Co-ordinator (LSC) for two semesters. They received 20 weeks of programme reading intervention from January to May and another 20 weeks of reading intervention from July to November. The participants in LSP were tutored four times a week and each lesson took 30 minutes. In these interventions pupils were taught reading, listening, and writing skills. Besides this, pupils also received instruction in the mainstream lessons. Those not in LSP did not attend the remedial lessons. They only attended the mainstream lessons. In addition, 58.6 per cent of participants in the LSP attended remedial classes from outside the school and 80 per cent of non-LSP did.

An LSC administered the test. LSCs are mainstream teachers with at least three years of teaching experience who attended a three-week LSP training course. The LSC conducted the pre- and post tests of the Singapore Word Readiness Test. Two teachers conducted the Deberry Reading Attitude Survey.

The LSP pupils showed significant differences (i.e., higher) in Singapore Word Readiness Test post-test scores and in English Language Semester two results, as compared to Singapore Word Readiness Test pre-test scores in Semester 1 results. There was no difference the LSP and non-LSP pupils in their reading attitude.

The sample size of the study was small (n = 44). Pupils in the treatment group were identified as being weaker than pupils from the non-treatment group. Findings might not be applicable to other schools. This study can be extended to LSP (Mathematics).

Yang (2004) examined effectiveness the Learning Support Programme in a primary school. The similar study was carried out for 88 LSP English children primary one. Instruments used were the Singapore Word Reading test, school's continuous assessment (CA1) and Semestral Assessment (SA2), and survey questionnaire on English language proficiency. Results of the study suggested that the LSP students made a significant improvement in reading. Marginally significant correlation (at the level of $p < .10$) was found between the final school examination results and the final scores of the Singapore Word Reading Test (i.e., "reading age") for LSP children.

Roles and responsibilities of an LSC (MOE 2004):

- Conduct the SRT for all P1 pupils at the start of the school year.
- Identify P1 and P2 pupils for LSP.
- Set up and maintain the LSP resource room.
- Develop a wide range of materials and resources for LSP.
- Plan and conduct differentiated, small group teaching drawing from a wide range of teaching approaches and materials.
- Implement Buddy Reading Programme.
- Monitor pupil's performance and progress.
- Liaise regularly with class teachers in teaching, supporting and monitoring pupils in LSP.
- Develop and implement Individual Educational Plans (IEPs)/ Group Educational Plans (GEPs) for pupils with persistent literacy difficulties.
- Provide regular feedback to MOE and school leaders on the programme.
- Evaluate the effectiveness of LSP and follow up with action plans.
- Conduct briefings and workshops for parents to inform them about LSP.

- Establish good home-school collaboration.
- Advise on and assist teachers with referral to MST or external agencies.
- Manage the referral process, including follow-up and monitoring.

Recommendations

The bulk of special education research to date has been on teaching and learning strategies. Reviews of empirical studies have identified an array of classroom practices, teaching techniques and learning strategies that are effective in achieving positive learning outcomes among children with special education needs (Davis & Florian 2004; Martin & Lloyd 1998; NCAC[1] 2003; National Reading Panel 2000; Sturomski 1997; Swanson 1999). Extant evidence base hence indicates that the benefits of research-based instructional tools for these children are significant and reliable. Notably, studies on the efficacy of multiple strategies also tend to report that a combination of strategies produces more powerful effects than a single strategy solution. The question is no longer which approach is best but how teachers can apply a multi-method response to produce positive learning outcomes in students with learning difficulties (Davis & Florian 2004). Teachers should therefore be trained to realise that the first and most important requisite to effective teaching is obtaining the knowledge and skills necessary to select and properly use research-based instructional tools (Lovitt 1996).

Currently, teachers in the LSP, also known as LSCs, are teachers with at least three years experience in mainstream teaching. Conversion to become an LSC involves a three-week training course, followed by monthly workshops during the first year as LSCs. Thereafter, on-going training takes the form of zonal workshops, annual seminars, and on-the-job supervision by educational psychologists (EPs). With this training scheme, the professional and educational qualifications of our LSCs are generally at a diploma/degree level. In contrast, a higher percentage of special education teachers (57 per cent) than general education teachers (47 per cent) in the US have attained masters or doctorate degrees (NICHCY[2] News Digest, 1997). Would channelling funds or having more qualified LSP teachers (through recruitment or training) lead to significantly higher success rates in the LSP?

It is noteworthy to consider M. M. Clay's contention (as cited in Vellutino, Fletcher, Snowling & Scanlon 2004) at this juncture. M. M.

Clay's classic article "Learning to be learning disabled" (1987, published in New Zealand Journal of Educational Studies from www.readingrevocery. org) pointed to the importance of effective instructional strategies. Clay asserted that reading difficulties in beginning readers are, in most cases, caused by experiential and/or instructional deficits. In a review of past four decades of dyslexia research, Vellutino, Fletcher, Snowling and Scanlon (2004) presented evidence to support this contention. Intervention studies showed that most impaired readers can acquire at least grade level reading skills if they were identified early and provided with comprehensive and intensive reading instruction tailored to their individual needs. Classroom observation and intervention studies showed that comprehensive and well-balanced reading instructions can prevent long-term reading difficulties in children who would otherwise qualify for a diagnosis of reading disability.

Equally compelling support also came from a longitudinal study that incorporated an intervention component to distinguish between cognitively versus experientially impaired readers (Vellutino, Fletcher, Snowling & Scanlon 1996). They reported that while impaired readers identified by typical diagnostic criteria represented about nine per cent of the study population, the number who continued to qualify for the diagnosis of "disabled readers" dropped to only 1.5 per cent after one semester of remediation. This stood in stark contrast to the incidence estimates (10–15 per cent) of reading disability in extant literature. Vellutino, Fletcher, Snowling and Scanlon (2004) therefore cited this finding as evidence that inadequate instruction and/or other experiential factors have led to the reading skills deficiencies that mimic the effects of basic cognitive deficits.

The implication of this assertion is that while interventions like the LSP can be effective, a good LSC must possess the knowledge and skills in using a variety of instructional methods (Fuchs & Fuchs 2000; Lovitt 1996), which are most responsive to the unique needs of each child (Heward 2003). For LSP intervention to be effective, it must be "focused, intense, urgent, precise, structured, and continually monitored for procedural fidelity and effects" (Heward 2003). The quality of teacher training is likely to be intimately linked to the all of these aspects. Channelling funds to raise the level of qualifications of LSP teachers (through training or recruitment) is hence an option that can arguably raise the effectiveness of the LSP.

Special education and mainstream education are grounded in the same basic research (Davis & Florian 2004; Heward 2003). Many teaching strategies and tactics have in fact been derived from relatively few basic principles (Heward 2003). Hence, a special education teacher can work with a general education teacher to assist in developing lesson plans and curriculum. This collaborative effort would serve to improve or add to current instructional strategies to best meet the learning needs and styles of all children. Where feasible in their scheme of work, special education teachers can also team-teach with general education teachers, teach specific learning strategies and study skills, provide small-group support or individual tutoring as needed, and adapt materials for individual students (NICHCY News Digest 27, 1997).

Nearly two decades of research has shown academic achievement gains by student with disabilities when their teachers use curriculum-based assessment, or CBA (Heward 2003). The CBA is one form of direct and frequent measurement that enables teachers to make data-based instructional decisions. Interpreting student performance trends is a complex task (Bielinski & Ysseldyke 2000). Research training for LSCs is essential. Armed with this training, LSCs would be well-placed at the frontline to study the process of student learning (LD Online 2004). They can also serve as the scientist-practitioners who can help translate research into practise. In view of the multiple roles that can be filled by LSCs, channelling the new wave of funding to have more qualified LSCs is a viable alternative.

SCHOOL COUNSELLORS

Singapore's schools in the next few years will receive a school counsellor. The following session refers to the international databases for some insights into models of school counsellors and the effectiveness of school counsellors for full development. School counsellors do not replace the roles and responsibilities of the learning support co-ordinator. Hence, what roles and responsibilities do school counsellors have? Do they adopt the roles of teacher-counsellors, specialist counsellors, and/or pastoral care and student welfare officers? What is the school counsellor and student ratio? The American School Counselor Association (ASCA) in a position statement stated that 100:1 is ideal while 300:1 is the upper limit. In the US, various high schools' counselling programmes propose a ratio of 225:1 as the optimum number.

The availability and accessibility of school counsellors is an issue of concern. There should be sufficient counsellors to cater to the whole student population of the school and they should be *accessible* to students. Students should be knowledgeable about the services counsellors provide and know how to approach counsellors for help. Counsellors should provide weekly calendars about their activities and have free slots whereby students can either walk in or make appointments to meet them.

Another issue of concern is the available resources for physical facilities, i.e., rooms for individual and group counselling, and physical materials—assessment tools, telephone (hotline: also for anonymity should student desire), secure storage for student records (confidentiality).

Other issues of concern are such as the issue of stigma for students to seek the services of a counsellor. And what can be done to address this? How do school counsellors work with parents in school activities (e.g., parent volunteers)?

Some International Models

The role of school counsellors can be conceptualised as facilitating three aspects of positive student functioning. They are academic development, vocational development, and personal and social development (ASCA 2003). Rather than reacting to problems as they arise (e.g., counselling delinquents), developmental advocacy (e.g., Galassi & Akos 2004; MacDonald & Sink 1998) seeks to promote healthy development according to various developmental stage models, thereby reducing the likelihood of developing emotional or behavioural problems. The cultivation of personal attributes such as self-efficacy and resilience, along with problem solving and self-regulation skills, fosters independence in students and allows them to better handle life stressors.

School counsellors have a beneficial effect on the developmental and educational outcomes of students (e.g., Borders & Drury 1992; Lapan, Gysbers & Petroski 2003; Whiston & Sexton 1998). School counsellors perform a wide array of activities, but just what aspects of students' functioning are improved and by what interventions? Two models provide a comprehensive framework for understanding school counseling and guidance, and they function to complement each other. The ASCA National Model was recently developed in 2003 and as such remains to be empirically tested. The Missouri Comprehensive Guidance Programme or Missouri Model has been a project in development since the 1970s with the most recent 3rd edition of the model being published in 2000 (see Gysbers & Henderson 2000; Gysbers & Henderson 2001). The Missouri model has since been implemented in part or whole across many states in the USA (Sink & MacDonald 1998) and its efficacy has been the subject of empirical testing. Each of these models will be examined in turn.

The American School Counselor Association (ASCA) National Model (from the ASCA National Model Executive Summary 2003): The ASCA National Model was constructed to aid schools in "designing, developing, implementing and evaluation a comprehensive developmental and systematic school counselling programme." The model consists of four interrelated components: foundation, delivery system, management systems, and accountability.

Foundation: It is necessary to articulate a set of beliefs or philosophy of the desired outcome of the programme. From this mission statement several key principles are formulated and are applied to each stage of the development, implementation, and evaluation of the programme. A common consensus should be reached amongst all personnel involved and their commitment elicited.

Delivery system: The delivery system consists of four sub-components. The guidance curriculum are structured lessons designed to assist students in achieving "desired competencies and to provide all students with the knowledge and skills appropriate for their developmental level. Individual student planning works with students to form personal goals and provide them with a future-orientated outlook. Responsive services fill the traditional role of providing immediate assistance to students in the form of counselling or professional referrals. Systems support emphasises the need for school administrators to provide the necessary assistance to the counsellors for the successful implementation of a comprehensive guidance programme.

Management system: The management system "incorporates organisational processes and tools to ensure the programme is organised, concrete, clearly delineated and reflective of the school's needs." There are six sub-components. Agreements describe the need to work with administrators at the planning stages of the school year to reach a general consensus about the content of the guidance curriculum. An advisory council composed of students, parents, teachers, counsellors and administrators should be formed to collaboratively review programme results and make recommendations for future work. The use of student data provides a firm justification of the activities of school counsellors. Counsellors must show that each initiative implemented was formulated from a "careful analysis of students' needs, achievement and/or related data." The time of school counsellors is limited and hence all effort should be made to exempt them from non-counselling related activities like general school administrative work. Finally school counsellors should make available monthly and weekly calendars of upcoming activities and services to keep their clients and school administrators informed.

Accountability: To evaluate and justify the effectiveness, school counselling programmes should have a system in place to "collect and use data to link the programme to student achievement." Results should be reported and analysed for effectiveness and improvements. Stakeholders should be regularly updated on the programme's progress. School counsellors' performance should be systematically evaluated to establish comparative standards with other school counsellors. This would also serve as a source of self-evaluation. All information pertaining to the programme should be organised and stored for any future audits.

The ASCA National Standards outline competencies that are the foundation for the ASCA National Model. It focuses on three aspects of student development, namely the academic development, career development and personal and social development. For more information on the ASCA National Model please see the publication titled "ASCA National Model: A Framework for School Counseling Programmes."

The Missouri Comprehensive Guidance Program (or The Missouri Model) (Gysbers & Henderson 2001): The conceptual foundation of the Missouri model is based on a "life career development" framework. It is defined as "self-development over a person's life span through the integration of the roles, settings, and events in a person's life." The life career development concept seeks to unify the various roles an individual will assume (e.g., student, worker, citizen, & parent) with the settings they will find themselves in (e.g., home, school, workplace, and community) and the events they will encounter in life (e.g., job entry, marriage and retirement). It is an all encompassing, holistic approach to preparing an individual for all the different developmental stages of life. The Missouri model consists of three elements: Content, an organisational framework, and resources.

Content: The content aspect of the programme identifies the competencies students ought to achieve as result of participation in the programme. Competencies or desired outcomes are formulated with consideration of the associated human developmental stages. For example there will be more focus on cultivating pro-social behaviours in younger children, whereas there will be additional focus on vocational development in high school students. These competencies can be grouped into domains similar to the academic, career, and personal/social development standards discussed earlier in the ASCA National Model.

Organisational framework: There are two aspects to the organisational framework. They are the structural and programme components. The structural component provides the theoretical groundings of the programme. The structural component has three parts. The first element includes the mission statement and defines who delivers the programme, who the clients are, how the programme is organised as well as the desired outcomes. The second element provides the rationale for the programme. It involves a needs assessment of students, schools, and the community, and how a comprehensive guidance programme would be beneficial.

The third element—assumptions, provides a broad objective: that is the desire to improve students' outcomes. It includes statements of basic expectations of the counsellors themselves and what they hope to achieve.

The programme component is the operational core of the model as it provides methodological guidelines for implementing the programme. It consists of four parts, namely guidance curriculum, individual planning, responsive services, and system support.

Guidance curriculum consists of activities that target the improvement of each of the competencies previously elaborated (academic, career, and personal/social). They could be conducted in the classroom where the counsellor either advises the teacher in planning the activity or is directly involved in team-teaching. School counsellors could also be involved in school-wide activities such as organising educational/college/ vocational days.

Individual planning concentrates on "assisting students, in close collaboration with parents, to develop analyse, evaluate, and carry out their educational, occupational, and personal goals and plans." Some strategies include appraisal, where counsellors or other advisors assist students in interpreting their abilities and interests through interviews or personality assessments for example. With this self-appraisal and other relevant information sources, counsellors then advice students in planning and realising their goals. Counsellors could assist in securing job placements and assist in the transition from school to work.

Responsive services provide diagnostic and remediation to various problems students may encounter, such as "personal identity issues, drugs, and peer and family relationships." Counsellors would consult relevant parties (e.g., teachers, families and community agencies) to gain a better understanding of the student's problem. Depending on the severity of the issue and the counsellor's abilities, personal or group counselling could be employed. In cases requiring professional assistance such as that of a mental health professional, the counsellor would make the necessary referrals and subsequently follow-up on the student.

System support is necessary to facilitate the implementation, functioning, and continued improvement of the programme. Apart from providing basic financial resources, opportunities should be made to allow counsellors to conduct research to contribute new ideas to the field. Counsellors should be allowed to update their professional knowledge and skills when necessary. Just as system support is necessary to the functioning of counsellors, counsellors themselves can work towards improving the community's understanding for the need for comprehensive guidance and counselling of the young. They could be involved in public relations matters through the use of the local media such as newspapers. Counsellors could serve on advisory committees and conduct outreach programmes like encouraging their students to volunteer their time in social service agencies.

Resources are the final component of the Missouri model. It takes stock of the human, financial, and political resources available. Human factors include the support of teachers, administrators, parents, and members of the community. Financial resources include the budget available as well as physical facilities (such as counselling rooms) that counsellors have at their disposal. Political resource describes the political will and vested interests of policy makers in the programme's success. For additional information on the Missouri model please read Gysbers and Henderson's (2000) book: "Developing and managing your school guidance programme."

EFFICACY STUDIES

The contributions made by school counsellors to students' outcomes can be evaluated in two forms. The first would be to consider the impact of comprehensive guidance models like the Missouri model on student outcomes. This is usually accomplished by comparing the various degrees to which a comprehensive programme has been implemented across schools and comparing the outcomes of the different student populations (e.g., Lapan, Gysbers & Sun 1997; Lapan, Gysbers & Petroski 2003).

The second approach is to examine specific counsellor actions on specific student outcomes. For example, goal orientations of high school students could be enhanced by brief individual counselling sessions in which solution-focused strategies were taught to the student (Whiston & Sexton 1998). We shall examine how each of these approaches highlight the contribution of counsellors.

Evaluation of the Missouri Model

The impact of comprehensive guidance and counseling was examined in 22,601 seventh graders and their teachers across 184 schools in Missouri (Lapan, Gysbers & Petroski 2003). The researchers found that school counselling programmes that were more fully implemented showed significantly positive findings. The programmes predicted positive students' perception of being safer in schools, better relationships between students and teachers, greater satisfaction of students with the education they were receiving in their schools, and positive perceptions of education that was more relevant and important to one's future. Schools with more fully implemented model guidance programmes had students who were more likely to report positively. They had earned higher grades. Their education was better in preparing them for their future. Their school made more career and college information available to them, and their school had a positive climate (Lapan, Gysbers & Sun 1997).

From the two studies examined, comprehensive guidance and counselling programmes like the Missouri model appear to be beneficial for student outcomes. Despite being helpful to all students, comprehensive programmes did not close the gap between the academic achievements of high and low socioeconomic status (SES) students. Two common limitations were highlighted by the authors of both studies. First, the data used for analysis were based on self-report data of students and teachers. For a more confident evaluation, future studies should focus on objective data such as academic grades. The second concern is that though tests conducted were statistically significant, the effect sizes were small.

To recapitulate, desirable outcomes as described by the Missouri model can be examined from students' accomplishments in the academic, vocational, personal, and social development domains. Less clear however are the pathways leading to a positive student outcome and how the three domains are interrelated. For example, does the development of a positive self concept lead to better academic achievement? Or does drawing logical links between future vocational requirements encourage students to perform better in academia? Additional research could be conducted on the pathways to academic achievement and perhaps establish casual inferences between each of these domains.

Specific Interventions and their Evaluations

Research on counselling and guidance (as opposed to comprehensive guidance models) has a rich history and its scope is wide and varied. Whiston and Sexton (1998) conducted a comprehensive review of the counselling and guidance literature published between 1988 and 1995. The various studies and their findings that will be presented shortly are derived from Whiston and Sexton's (1998) review. Their review and data has been reorganised into a manner pertinent to this report. We shall examine how specific school counsellor actions are related to the outcome of students as defined by the three domains (academic, vocational, and personal/social). Studies are further sub-divided into the target student population they involved (primary, lower-secondary, and upper-secondary/junior college levels). Finally studies were categorised as to whether they were serving the general student population or specific segments of the student population.

Academic achievement: The effects of school counsellors on academic achievement in elementary school students will be examined first. Second grade students who participated in a guidance curriculum programme encompassing varied activities such as "developing understanding of self and others (DUSO), Most Important Person, and 100 ways to improve self-esteem in the classroom" achieved higher reading scores than a control group that did not participate. The mathematic scores of fourth to sixth graders were similarly improved after participating in a "succeeding in school programme" (Whiston & Sexton, 1998).

Dramatic increases were found in the standardised achievement scores of fourth graders who received training to increase "self-efficacy, awareness of metacognitive skills and knowledge of learning styles" (Whiston & Sexton 1998). Their student sample involved was however unrepresentative as most students were from high socioeconomic background. Therefore generalisability of the study is limited.

Less is known about specific interventions to improve academic achievement at the lower and upper secondary levels. As previously discussed, comprehensive guidance and counselling programmes (e.g., Lapan, Gysbers & Sun 1997; Lapan, Gysbers & Petroski 2003) are generally beneficial to students' academic achievement.

In working with specific student populations such as minority students reported were gains in social development of third graders from diverse backgrounds after participating in a "multicultural guidance project" (Whiston & Sexton 1998).

Personal and social development: In a review Whiston and Sexton (1998) stated some benefits of school counselling programmes for personal and social development. Interventions to improve self-concept and self-esteem in elementary school kids has had mixed success. Neither classroom guidance nor individual counselling had a measurable effect in facilitating self concept development in kindergarten children. Likewise no substantive improvement was found in second graders.

Perhaps it was premature to evaluate self-concept or self-esteem in younger children (kindergarten and second grade) as the two previous studies has done. If one were to subscribe to the Eriksonian stage model of development, the formation of a self-concept does not reach critical mass until the "self identity versus role confusion" stage encountered by older children or adolescents. Suggestive of this hypothesis, the self-esteem of fifth graders was increased by participating in "wellness programmes."

Peer mediation strategies can involve students working in small groups with their peers in activities such as role-playing. Fourth graders who participated in a peer mediation programme to improve conflict management skills reported using the skills learnt, in both school and home.

School counsellors could work with selective high school students and train them to be effective peer counsellors. One such peer counselling intervention improved the communications skills of its participants. Enhancing the goal orientation of high school students is another avenue where school counsellors can play a part. School counsellors working with groups of high school students in a cognitive intervention training programme to enhance stress management skills also demonstrated positive results.

Group counselling techniques are effective in engaging children facing family problems such as divorce. Studies involving Kindergarteners and fourth to sixth graders showed positive results. Behavioural problems can be disruptive to teaching and learning in the classroom. Anger control group counselling was employed targeting aggressive and hostile behaviours in fourth to sixth graders; whilst family systems counselling was employing in treating chronic problem behaviours in elementary school students. Both interventions were successful.

School counsellors play a vital role when tragic incidents occur in school, such as fatal shootings or a student committing suicide. When a student takes her(his) own life, it evokes strong responses in fellow schoolmates and can nudge students who were contemplating suicide to go through with the act. This phenomenon is related to suicide ideation or thoughts about committing suicide. An intervention to reduce suicide ideation following the death of one student was however unsuccessful. Limited empirical research can be conducted on this considering the circumstances necessary for the behaviour to be analysed.

Vocational knowledge and maturity: Research on vocational maturity has been generally focused on high school students for the sensible reason that they will soon make the transition from school to work, or school to college. Findings regarding the effects of counselling and guidance on vocational maturity have generally been positive.

Individual planning activities involve counsellors working with individual students to develop future goals and explore vocational options. In a variation of individual planning, a class of tenth graders was trained in a career decision model; and whilst other groups of counsellors worked with individual students and their families. All these interventions were reported to be successful.

Vocational counselling is similarly effective for promoting career maturity in ethnic minority students and learning disabled individuals. In working with gifted students, vocational counselling had limited success in facilitating career decision making, due to the students' multi-potentiality or potential in many areas (Whiston & Sexton 1998).

In summary, knowledge of specific counsellor interventions on student outcomes is fragmented. It is useful to know how the specific actions undertaken by a counsellor is related to a particular student outcome, such as whether it can readily pinpoint shortcomings or gaps in the current knowledge. This approach is more difficult when evaluating a comprehensive guidance and counselling programme as a whole as counsellors perform many duties, and it is problematic to see the specific effects of each of these actions.

CONCLUSION

In conclusion, we highlight Vygotsky's understanding of disability as a socio-cultural, development and qualitative specific phenomenon which has brought about two concepts useful for education: Zone of Proximal Development and Dynamic Assessment.

Zone of Proximal Development (ZPD)

Vygotsky insisted that it is through others, we develop ourselves (Hung & Nichani 2002). The concept of ZPD highlights Vygotsky's concern of how learning takes place or makes progress. Overall Vygotksy was interested in assessing the child's potential level rather than her(his) current level. Vygotsky argued that human development emerges through interactions with others, through the environment mediated by signs and tools, and through the process of internalisation of external activity. A child interacts with others and forms new understanding of her(his) activities. Gradually, the child relies less on the external support of people and external objects to cue her(his) behaviour as the behaviour has become directed by internal mental processes (Hung & Nichani 2002). ZPD can refer to a range of tasks that the child can accomplish with the aid of *scaffolding*, but alone s/he cannot accomplish these tasks. ZPD extends only to tasks that are comprehensible when the child is given supportive networks (e.g., language, mediator, shared activity, and tutor).

Vygotsky introduced ZPD to differentiate between two levels of development, i.e., the actual level of development achieved so far and the potential level of development with assistance or collaboration with an adult or more a capable peer. The actual level is measured by what the child is capable of achieving on her(his) own. The potential level refers to what a child can accomplish with assistance of another expertise. Zone, according Vygotsky, is where children learn, the area just beyond where they can function independently. Adults and peers interact with children in this zone, "*scaffolding*" children's learning and help them to reach a higher level of functioning (Berk & Winsler 1995; cited in Jacobs 2001).

According to Vygotsky, children are capable of competent performance when they have proper assistance—*scaffold learning*. In this theoretical framework, scaffolding is a process of providing the learner with tools to work on higher level tasks, and gradually withdrawing assistance as students are capable to do more on their own.

Vygotsky (Cole et al 1978) made it clear that the role of the child as a social partner is critical to her(his) learning process. Indeed, Vygotsky proposed that not only is there a difference in the level of expertise between partners that is necessary, it is also necessary to understand the abilities of an advanced partner and of a less advanced child, so that information can be presented at a development appropriate pace and level.

Dynamic Assessment (DA)

This concept highlighted a central tenet in social-cultural theory: the inter-dependence of individual and social processes in the co-construct of knowledge. In the height of popularity of IQ testing during the 1930s, Vygotsky pointed out the limitation of this testing, notably that disability is a process and not a static condition, where IQ testing fail to distinguish impairment that was due to organic damage or due to cultural deprivation. Vygotsky insisted that evaluation or assessment should focus on mental processing and certain qualitative meta-cognitive indicators such as:

- cognitive strategies employed by the child.
- the types of mistakes.
- the child's ability to benefit from assistant provided.
- the child's emotional reactions to success and failure.

Vygotsky regarded this type of evaluation as *Dynamic Assessment (DA)*. DA is an interactive procedure that follows a test intervene-retest format, focusing on the cognitive processes and metacognitive of the child. Through pre- and post- test performances following a test-embedded intervention, an evaluator is informed of a child's cognitive modifiability, responsiveness to an adult's mediation and amenability to instructions and guidance. Today, DA is widely used as a supplementary procedure to measures a child's intelligence (Gindis 1999).

REFERENCES

Ang, M. K. 2002. *Effectiveness of primary 2 learning support programme (English) in a neighbourhood primary school in Singapore.* Unpublished Masters Dissertation, National Institute of Education, Nanyang Technological University, Singapore.

ASCA Publications. 2003. The ASCA National Model: A Framework for School Counseling Programs. An Executive Summary. *Professional School Counseling, 6(3),* 165–168.

Bielinski, J., & J. E. Ysseldyke. 2000. *Interpreting trends in the performance of special education students* (Technical Report 27). Minneapolis, MN: University of Minnesota, National Center on Educational Outcomes. Retrieved 20 October 2004, from http://education.umn.edu/NCEO/OnlinePubs/TechReport27.htm

Borders, L. D., & S. M. Drury. 1992. Comprehensive school counseling programs: A review for policymakers and practitioners. *Journal of Counseling and Development, 70(4)*, 487–498.

Cole, M., V. J. Steiner, S. Scribner, & E. Souberman, eds. 1978. *Vygotsky, L.S.: Mind and society: The develoment of higher psychological process.* Harvard: Harvard University Press.

Davis, P., & L. Florian. 2004. *Teaching strategies and approaches for pupils with special education needs: A scoping study.* Retrieved 20 October 2004, from http://www.dfes.gov.uk/research/data/uploadfiles/RR516.pdf

Fuchs, D., & L. S. Fuchs. 2000. Inclusion versus full inclusion. In *Exceptional children: An introduction to special education* (5th Ed., 72–74). Edited by W.L. Heward. Upper Saddle River, NJ: Merrill / Prentice Hall.

Galassi, J. P., & P. Akos. 2004. Developmental advocacy: Twenty-first century school counseling. *Journal of Counseling and Development, 82(2)*, 146–157.

Gindis, B. 1999. Vygotsky's vision: Reshaping the practice of special education for the 21st centuty. *Remedial and Special Education, 20(6)*, 333–340.

Grigorenko, E. 1998. Russian "defectology": Anticipating perestroika in the field. *Journal of Learning Disabilities, 31(2)*, 193–207.

Gysbers, N. C., & P. Henderson. 2000. *Developing and managing your school guidance program.* (3rd Ed). Alexandria, VA: American Counseling Association.

Gysbers, N.C., & P. Henderson. 2001. Comprehensive guidance and counseling programs: A rich history and a bright future. *Professional School Counseling, 4(4)*, 246–256.

Heward, W. L. 2003. Ten faulty notions about teaching and learning that hinder the effectiveness of special education, *The Journal of Special Education, 36(4)*, 186–205.

Hung, D., & M. R. Nichani. 2002. Bringing communities practice into schools: Implication for instructional technologies from Vygotskian perspective. *International Journal of Instructional Media, 20(2)*, 171–183.

Jacobs, G. M. 2001. Providing the scaffold: A model for early childhood/primary teacher preparation. *Early Childhood Education Journal, 29(2)*, 125–130.

Lapan, R. T., N. C. Gysbers, & G. F. Petroski. 2003. Helping seventh graders be safe and successful: A statewide study of the impact of comprehensive guidance and counseling programs. *Professional School Counseling, 6(3)*, 186–197.

Lapan, R. T., N. C. Gysbers, & Y. M. Sun. 1997. The impact of more fully implemented guidance programs on the school experiences of high school students: A statewide evaluation study. *Journal of Counseling and Development, 75(4)*, 292–302.

Learning Disabilities (LD) Online. 2004. *Teachers-researchers.* Retrieved 20 October 2004, from http://www.ldonline.org/ld_indepth/research_digest/teacherresearchers.html

Lovitt, T. C. 1996. What special educators need to know. In W.L. Heward (Ed.). *Exceptional children: An introduction to special education* (5th ed., 84–86) Upper Saddle River, NJ: Merrill/Prentice Hall.

Macdonald, G., & C. A. Sink. 1998. A qualitative developmental analysis of comprehensive guidance programmes in schools in the United States. *British Journal of Guidance and Counselling, 27(3),* 415–430.

Mahn, H. 1999. Vygotsky's methodalogical contribution to sociacultural theory. *Remedial and Special Education, 20(6),* 341–350.

Martin, K., & J. Lloyd. 1998. *Effective teaching techniques.* Retrieved 20 October 2004, from http://curry.edschool.virginia.edu/sped/projects/ose/information/interventions.html

Miltenberg, R., & E. Singer. 1999. Culturally mediated learning and the development of self-regulation by survivors of child abuse: A Vygotskian approach to the support of survivor of child abuse. *Human Development, 42(1),* 1–17.

Ministry of Education (MOE). 2004. *Learning Support Programme Handbook.*

National Center on Assessing the General Curriculum (NCAC). 2003. Department of Education's Office of Special Program.

National Information Center for Children and Youth with Disabilities (NICHCY). 1997. *Teaching students with learning disabilities to use learning strategies.* In NICHCY News Digest, 27. Retrieved 20 October 2004, from http://www.nichcy.org/newsdig.asp#nd27

National Reading Panel. 2000. *Teaching children to read: An evidence-based assessment of the scientific research literature on reading and its implications for reading instruction.* Retrieved 20 October 2004, from http://www.nichd.nih.gov/publications/nrp/smallbook.htm

Palincsar, A. S. 1998. Social constructivist perspective on teaching and learning, *Annual Review of Psychology, 49,* 345–375.

Rieber, R., & A. Carton, eds. 1993. *Vygotsky, L. S.: The collected works of L. S. Vygotsky, Vol 2: The fundamentals of defectology.* New York: Plenum Press.

Sink, C.A., & G. MacDonald. 1998. The status of comprehensive guidance and counseling in the United States. *Professional School Counseling, 2(2),* 88–94.

Sturomski, N. 1997. Teaching students with learning disabilities to use learning strategies. In NICHCY News Digest, 25. Retrieved 20 October 2004, from http://www.nichcy.org/newsdig.asp#nd25

Swanson, H. L. 1999. Reading research for students with LD: A meta-analysis of intervention outcomes. *Journal of Learning Disabilities, 32,* 504–532. Retrieved on Oct 20, 2004 from http://www.ld.org/research/osep_swanson.cfm

Vellutino, F. R., J. M. Fletcher, M. J. Snowling, & D. M. Scanlon. 2004. Specific reading disability (dyslexia): what have we learned in the past four decades? *Journal of Child Psychology and Psychiatry, 45(1),* 2–40.

Vellutino, F. R., D. M. Scanlon, E. R. Sipay, S. G. Small, A. Pratt, R. S. Chen, & M. B. Denckla. 1996. Cognitive profiles of difficult to remediate and readily remediated poor readers: Early intervention as a vehicle for distinguishing between cognitive and experiential deficits as basic causes of specific reading disability. *Journal of Educational Psychology, 88,* 601–638.

Vygodskaya, G. L. 1999. Vygotsky and problem of special education. *Remedial and Special Education, 20(6)*, 330–332.

Whiston, S. C., & T. L. Sexton. 1998. A review of school outcome research: Implications for practice. *Journal of Counseling and Development, 76(4)*, 412–426.

Yang, P. C. T. 2004. *Effectiveness of the learning support programme in a primary school.* Unpublished Masters Dissertation, National Institute of Education, Nanyang Technological University, Singapore.

NOTES

1   National Center on Accessing the General Curriculum (NCAC) is collaboratively established by the Center for Applied Special Technology (CAST) and the U.S. Department of Education's Office of Special Programs (OSEP), to provide a vision of how new curricula, teaching practices, and policies can be woven together to create practical approaches for improved access to the general curriculum by students with disabilities.

2   National Information Center for Children and Youth with Disabilities (NICHCY) is funded by the Office of Special Education Programs (OSEP) at the U.S. Department of Education, to serve as a central source of information on children with disabilities.

CHAPTER 4

Problem-based Learning and Project Work

TAN AI GIRL AND LAURA LYNN LEE

INTRODUCTION

The origins of problem-based learning (PBL) and the theoretical orientations can be traced to early works of Kilpatrick, John Dewey, Jerome Bruner, and Jean Piaget under the rubric of the inquiry approaches to teaching science (Baker 2000). The recent history of PBL is often accredited to Howard Barrows and colleagues at the McMaster University in Canada in the sixties. At the Faculty of Medicine PBL was incorporated into medical education to increase the competence of doctors in managing health problems using their knowledge and ability. By 1991, various aspects of PBL have been implemented in a majority of medical programs in United States, Canada, Australia, the United Kingdom, the Netherlands, the Middle East, South Africa, and Asia (China, Japan, Thailand) (Baker 2000). Today, most medical schools in the United States and many in almost every country of the world are implementing (or are planning to implement) PBL in their curricula to a greater or lesser extent (Camp 1996). Besides this, PBL has been integrated for nearly a decade in some nursing schools in countries such as Canada, Australia, and the United Kingdom (Baker 2000). It has been endorsed as an educational strategy by the World Federation of Medical Education and the World Health Organisation. In addition, at the college level, PBL has recently been adopted by most health sciences (dentistry, occupational therapy, pharmacy, physical therapy, public health, veterinary medicine) and other disciplines (architecture, business, education, engineering, forestry, police science, and social work). The movement has also extended to the K-12 (Camp 1996).

In line with the world trends, in 1996, ten per cent of the dentistry curricula adopted the PBL approach at the National University of Singapore (NUS). The Faculty of Medicine of NUS in 1999 used PBL in 20 per cent of its medical curricula. Subsequently, in 2001, a whole curricular approach of PBL was implemented by the Temasek Polytechnic for a marketing program at the Diploma level. This new curricular approach was granted by the Enterprise Challenge of the Prime Minister Office (awarded in November 2000). In January 2002, H. Barrows was appointed as the international advisor to the Temasek Centre for problem-based learning. Around the same period, at the National Institute of Education (NIE), PBL was introduced to part of a core-module of educational psychology. In 2003, Singapore hosted the Asian Pacific Medical Education Conference. Many papers on PBL were read in this conference.

This chapter outlines core features of PBL, discusses effectiveness of PBL, and presents how PBL can be integrated into project work. Project-based learning is viewed as a learning approach used by students of almost all levels, ages, and abilities; it complements mainstream learning methods (Burns 2000). Our discussion of PBL encompasses that of project-based learning. It is especially relevant for the Singaporean school contexts where project work has been integrated into the curricula. Project-based learning may enhance teachers' professionalism and collaboration and increase students' self-reliance, attendance, and improved attitudes towards learning.

PBL AND ITS EFFECTIVENESS

In general, PBL aims to facilitate acquisition of a retrievable and usable knowledge base, professional reasoning, and self-directed learning. The educational objective for PBL was then to educate medical students to acquire basic scientific knowledge that is better retained, retrieved, and later applied in the clinical context (Barrows 1985). Core features of PBL (Barrows 1985) include student-centred learning, small student groups, tutor acting as facilitator, authentic problems introduced before preparation of study, problems used as a tool to achieve the required knowledge and problem-solving skills, and new information acquired through self-directed learning (Barrows 1986).

Prerequisite

PBL is not about problem solving per se; rather it uses appropriate problems to increase *knowledge and understanding* (i.e., acquiring knowledge). The focus of PBL is on learning. Real life problems are employed to facilitate learning of basic concepts and learning that integrates basic concepts with application. To ensure the effectiveness of PBL, a program such as the McMaster problem solving program should be designed to enable students to acquire problem solving skills before enrolling into the PBL curricula. It is also essential for students to master some generic skills of and cultivate good attitudes (Wood 2003) towards teamwork, chairing a group, listening, recording, cooperating, respect for peer's views, critical evaluation on the literature, self-directed learning, good use of resources, and presentation skills.

PBL Process

Group tutorials are adopted in the PBL learning process. Students are first introduced to ill-structured or real-life problems. They receive help from the tutor (facilitator) in identifying learning issues and learning objectives from the problem case. Then, they are expected to carry out independent study (or self-directed learning, e.g., reading on their own and doing library research). Subsequently, they share their learning with the group members, and together they come out with possible solutions to the learning issues. The following summarises the PBL learning cycle (Hmelo-Silver 2004):

- The students are represented with a *problem scenario.*
- They formulate and analyse the problem by *identifying the relevant facts* from the scenario.
- As students understand the problem better, they *generate hypotheses* about possible solutions.
- *Knowledge deficiencies* are the learning issues that students research during their self-directed learning.
- Students apply their *new knowledge* and evaluate their hypotheses in light of what they have learned.
- At the completion of each problem, students reflect on the abstract knowledge gained.

Student and Facilitator Roles

Students by adopting self-directed and collaborative learning resume an active role in seeking and acquiring new knowledge. The roles of a facilitator include modelling, scaffolding (e.g., using questioning techniques), group facilitation, and developing higher order thinking (Hmelo-Silver 2004). Specifically, in a PBL unit (Baker 2000), a scenario can be presented gradually during several sessions of problem presentations which always follow by self-directed learning and group meetings. A scenario can be divided into introduction scenario, intermediate or second scenario and concluding scenario. When learning begins, during *problem presentation* of the introduction scenario, the student group clarifies terms and concepts, identifies facts, develops hypotheses, and formulates learning issues. The tutor urges application of prior knowledge, provides corrective feedback, facilitates group process, interpret ignorance as a challenge, and questions plans for seeking information. After self-directed learning when *the student group reconvenes*, the student group collects and organises information, analyses information, maps concepts, tests, and refines hypotheses. The tutor is accessible for consultation, judges adequacy of information sources, pursues hypotheses acceptance or rejection.

Subsequently, the second scenario was presented. The students perform self-directed learning and then reconvene to the group for collaborative learning. They identify facts, reformulate hypotheses, use concepts, specify learning issues, collect and integrate information, analyse information, test hypotheses, and expand concept mapping. The tutor facilitates integration of expanded problem, evaluates plans for seeking information, and is accessible for consultation. S/he assesses adequacy of information sources, and proposes hypotheses acceptance or rejection.

When the concluding scenario was presented, the students synthesise case analysis and design action plan, while the tutor facilitates integration of expanded problem, critiques concept maps, and appraises reasoning.

A good facilitator is able to change her(his) facilitation style, according with group experience and the different stages of the PBL process (Haith-Cooper 2003a and 2003b). It has been suggested that scaffolding may relieve students' dissatisfaction experienced in the PBL process (Green, van Gyn, Moehr, Lau & Coward 2004) and hence gives significant motivational effects in students (Segers, van de Bossche & Teunissen 2003). Facilitators need to intervene when students are new to PBL, and later reduce the intervention level when students become mature (Haith-Cooper 2000; Segers, van de Bossche & Teunissen 2003).

The facilitator allows the learners to take control of the direction of discussions and agenda for solving the problem (Carder, Willingham & Bibb 2001). Students become more intrinsically motivated, active, and autonomous, when they feel that they are with a high degree of control (Segers et al. 2003).

Assessments

Implementing PBL entails the need for proper assessment. In almost every study investigating PBL and curricula, there is always a section presenting assessment modes. It is therefore appropriate to address this issue when deciding to implement PBL or incorporate it in curricula. Studies assessing the effects of PBL on the knowledge and skills of students have been conducted using various methods. Dochy, Segers, van de Bossche, and Gijbels (2003) found that assessments have been done in the forms of written examinations, multiple-choice questions (MCQ), modified essay questions (MEQ), essay questions, short answer questions, oral examinations, progress tests, performance-based testing, free recall, and cases.

In addition, student evaluation ranges from state board examination, teacher-made tests to self-assessments, journals, and peer reviews (Baker 2000). Group evaluation procedures range from group projects to group assessments and teacher evaluations. Tutor evaluations are performed by the tutor and the students. Interviews and focus groups have also been used for students and tutors to obtain feedback, discuss and ascertain their level of satisfaction (Conway & Sharkey 2002; Green, van Gyn, Moehr, Lau & Coward 2004; Price 2000; Sharp & Primrose 2003).

Assessment often drives learning and students' behaviour. For example, discipline specific assessment results in students tending to rote learn subjects, rather than develop deeper and integrated levels of understanding. Hence, assessment methods need to be compatible with the PBL approach, reflecting the PBL process and skills developed by the students (Murray & Savin-Baden 2000). The traditional methods of course assessment, such as examinations may not be very effective in assessing PBL approach (Major & Palmer 2001) as these traditional assessment strategies tend to examine what students have learned, rather than whether students can apply and analyse what they have learnt (Murray & Savin-Baden 2000). As a result, there is a need to consider how the effectiveness of PBL should be assessed and how outcomes should be regarded. Alternative approaches to assessments may provide additional insight into the effectiveness of PBL and other alternative pedagogies (Major & Palmer 2001).

Alternative assessment measures might include constructed response items, essays, writing samples, oral presentations, exhibitions, experiments, and/or portfolios. In a PBL classroom, these may be more relevant and authentic to a problem-solving setting compared to a traditional standardised MCQ test. While each particular PBL instructional environment is unique, and therefore merits its own unique assessment strategy, several alternative techniques appear well-placed in a PBL learning environment. Specifically, the use of outside evaluation by experts, content analysis of projects, focus groups, peer evaluations, journals or activity logs as well as personal reflections. Such techniques focus on the contextual nature of PBL, requiring students to produce an authentic product that is related to the problem and to make judgements about their performance (Major & Palmer 2001).

PBL Effectiveness

The efficacy of PBL is difficult to evaluate as it is generally introduced together with other changes in the curriculum and along with changes in student selection, staff development, and assessment procedures. The confounding factors make it difficult to determine the actual extent to which PBL contribute to any detected change in outcomes (Finucane, Johnson & Prideaux 1998). In a review paper, Hmelo-Silver (2004) described five important goals in PBL:

- Construct an extensive and flexible knowledge base.
- Develop effective problem-solving skills.
- Develop self-directed, lifelong learning skills.
- Become effective collaborators.
- Become intrinsically motivated to learn.

She considered the evidence for PBL in relation to each of the five purported goals of the method. She reported that much of the evidence came from research in medical schools and gifted education although a few studies involved other populations. However, less empirical evidence was available as to what students were learning and how.

Constructing an extensive and flexible knowledge base: According to Hmelo-Silver (2004), much evidence on constructing an extensive and flexible knowledge base came from evidence based on examination scores.

She revealed that several meta-analyses demonstrated that PBL students scored slightly lower than traditional medical students on multiple-choice (MCQ) measures of academic achievement such as the National Board of Examiners (NBME) Part I which investigated basic science knowledge. Other meta-analytical studies also demonstrated that PBL students performed slightly better than traditional medical students at tasks related to clinical problem solving such as NBME Part II and on ratings and tests of clinical performance. In addition to her review of meta-analytical studies, Hmelo-Silver (2004) gave an account of other studies with regard to the effectiveness of PBL in constructing extensive and flexible knowledge. A summary of some of the findings can be found in Table 4.1.

Developing effective problem-solving skills: An indicator of effective problem-solving skills is the ability to transfer strategies to new problems (Hmelo-Silver 2004). Another aspect is being able to define what the problem actually is, especially with ill-structured problems. Hmelo-Silver (2004) provided an account of studies that studied PBL in these arenas. The summary of this can be found in Table 4.2. Hmelo-Silver (2004) concluded that research on the influence of PBL on strategy transfer is limited; it does provide some evidence that students in PBL learn problem-solving and reasoning strategies that are transferable to new problems.

Developing self-directed, lifelong learning skills: Hmelo-Silver (2004) reviewed qualitative studies of SDL as well as quantitative indicators of self-directed learning (SDL). Some of the latter indicators include planning one's own learning, developing and applying strategies, and appropriately using learning resources. A summary of studies that were reviewed can be found in Table 4.3. Hmelo-Silver (2004) concluded that for students who are poor self-regulators, PBL is likely to pose difficulties if they try to develop without appropriate scaffolding. Scaffolding SDL is not likely to be especially important for younger learners but research points out that there are considerable individual differences even among adult learners. She further added that research in SDL in PBL has largely been confined to professional students, thus there is a need for research to investigate its wider application.

Becoming effective collaborators: Another goal of PBL is to help students become effective collaborators. However, according to Hmelo-Silver (2004), there is little available research that examines this area directly. Research has focused on factors that affect how well students learn collaboratively. In particular, group function has been identified as an

106

TABLE 4.1 Findings in the effectiveness of constructing extensive and flexible knowledge

Author(s)	Focus Area(s) / Measures	Participants	Findings
Constructing Extensive and Flexible Knowledge: Professionals in educational context			
Meta-Analyses (Albanese and Mitchell, 1993; Goodman et al. 1991; Mennin et al. 1993; Vernon and Blake 1993)	Learning outcomes/Academic achievement were assessed using MCS in NBME Part 1 (Science Knowledge)	Traditional medical students vs. PBL students	PBL students scored slightly lower than traditional medical students.
Meta-Analyses (Albanese and Mitchell 1993; Vernon and Blake 1993)	Learning outcomes in clinical problem-solving tasks were measured in NBME Part II as well as ratings and tests of clinical performance	Traditional medical students vs. PBL students	PBL students scored slightly better than traditional medical students
Patel et al. (1991, 1993)	Problem-solving skills were assessed through diagnostic explanations of a clinical problem	Traditional medical students vs. PBL students	PBL students were more error-prone but more elaborate in explanations than traditional students.

TABLE 4.1 Findings in the effectiveness of constructing extensive and flexible knowledge (cont'd)

Author(s)	Focus Area(s) / Measures	Participants	Findings
Constructing Extensive and Flexible Knowledge: Professionals in educational context			
Quasi-experimental longitudinal study Hmelo (1998)	Students generated causal explanations for each of 2 problems at each of 3 testing sessions that occurred during the 1st week of classes, and again after 3 and 7 months. Explanations were scored for accuracy, coherence, and use of Science concepts.	Students who self-selected into traditional and PBL tracks at a Midwestern medical school	Students did not differ on any measure at initial testing session. Students in PBL curriculum more likely to produce accurate hypotheses and coherent explanations than traditional curriculum students. PBL students were more likely to use science concepts in their explanations compared to traditional students.
Quasi-experimental study Schmidt et al. (1996)	Diagnostic accuracy was assessed on 30 case vignettes	Medical students in PBL and traditional curricula	PBL students found to be more accurate than students in traditional curricula.

TABLE 4.1 Findings in the effectiveness of constructing extensive and flexible knowledge (cont'd)

Author(s)	Focus Area(s) / Measures	Participants	Findings
	Constructing Extensive and Flexible Knowledge: Undergraduates		
Hmelo et al. (1995)	Pre-test, Post-test assessments on factual knowledge and problem-solving skills	Undergraduate engineering students using PBL in multidisciplinary teams	Students demonstrated increases on both measures.
Derry et al. (2000)	Pre-test, Post-test assessments on learning outcomes	Undergraduate students learning statistical reasoning	Students showed learning gains for some, but not all of the course content.
Derry et al. (2002)	Problem-based assessment pre and post test assessment – undergraduates viewed video of a student being interviewed before and after instruction along with excerpts from instruction. Participants were asked to explain why the student in the video failed to learn.	Pre-service teachers using video problems and web-based information resources.	PBL approach led to transfer and flexible use of course concepts. Students applied more relevant concepts and produced more sophisticated explanations at post-test than pre-test assessments.

TABLE 4.1 Findings in the effectiveness of constructing extensive and flexible knowledge (cont'd)

Author(s)	Focus Area(s) / Measures	Participants	Findings
Constructing Extensive and Flexible Knowledge: Undergraduates			
Controlled study Schwartz and Bransford (1998)	Pre and post test assessments on problem-solving tasks	Compared undergraduate psychology students in 3 groups: (a) students who solved only problems, (b) students who read a textbook chapter prior to attending a lecture and (c) students who solved problems prior to attending lecture	Students who solved problems prior to the lecture performed better on a problem-solving task than students who read the chapter or those who just solved problems
Constructing Extensive and Flexible Knowledge: Younger students			
Gallagher and Stepien (1996)	Student scores in MCQ used to assess learning outcomes	Gifted high school students from a problem-based American studies course were compared to students from traditionally instructed students	PBL students scored higher on the MCQ test than traditionally instructed students

TABLE 4.1 Findings in the effectiveness of constructing extensive and flexible knowledge (cont'd)

Author(s)	Focus Area(s) / Measures	Participants	Findings
Constructing Extensive and Flexible Knowledge: Younger students			
Dods (1997)	Information retention as a means of assessing learning outcomes	Gifted students from high school	Students tended to retain information presented in PBL units better than information presented from traditional units, despite the fact that the students thought they learnt more

SOURCE: Hmelo–Silver (2004)

TABLE 4.2 Findings in the effectiveness of PBL in developing effective problem-solving skills

Author(s)	Participants / Task	Findings
	Developing effective problem-solving skills: Ability to transfer strategies to new problems	
Patel et al. (1991, 1993)	Traditional and PBL students in medical school were asked to provide diagnostic explanations of a clinical problem.	Students in PBL were more likely to use hypothesis-driven reasoning than were students in a traditional curriculum.
Norman et al. (1994)	Students in medical school.	Students in a traditional medical school used more data-driven reasoning (characteristic of experts) but only on familiar problems.
Norman et al. (1998)	Medical students were employed in a laboratory experiment to test the notion that hypothesis driven reasoning supports learning. This was done through getting students to learn how to read electrocardiograms.	A hypothesis-driven strategy led to greater accuracy on a transfer task than using a data-driven strategy.
Hmelo (1998), Hmelo et al. (1997)	Students with and without PBL experience tested on ability to transfer strategy to unrelated problems and ability to generate coherent explanations	Students in PBL curricula transferred hypothesis-driven reasoning strategy to unrelated problems and generated more coherent explanations than students without PBL experience.

TABLE 4.2 Findings in the effectiveness of PBL in developing effective problem-solving skills (cont'd)

Author(s)	Participants / Task	Findings
	Developing effective problem-solving skills: Ability to define the problem	
Gallegher et al. (1992)	Gifted students who were traditionally instructed were compared to PBL students on problem-solving skills.	PBL students were more likely to include problem finding as a step when presented with a novel ill-structured problem

SOURCE: Hmelo-Silver (2004)

TABLE 4.3 Findings in the effectiveness of PBL in developing SDL Skills

Author(s)	Participants / Task	Findings
Dahlgren and Dahlgren (2002)	Students in PBL curricula in three different disciplines were interviewed	Students in two out of three disciplines felt a great sense of uncertainty about what to study.
Evenson (2000)	Medical students from PBL group were interviewed and analysed through oral learning logs and written notes. This analysis used grounded theory approach. It examined interactions of academic self-concept, learning strategies, learning opportunities provided by programme, and evaluation mechanisms of two students.	Both students developed strategies for coping with challenges to their self-efficacy and described the reflection on their learning and information-seeking strategies. Provides a glimpse into the lives of two students learning to adapt to the SDL demands of a PBL programme.
Evenson et al. (2001)	Medical students from PBL group were interviewed and analysed through oral learning logs and written notes. This analysis built a model of how students developed as self-directed learners using additional case studies.	The more reflective learners were about SDL, the more likely they could modify or invent strategies for SDL.

TABLE 4.3 Findings in the effectiveness of PBL in developing SDL Skills (cont'd)

Author(s)	Participants / Task	Findings
Ertmer et al. (1996)	Veterinary students' approach to learning	Students who were low self-regulated learners (SRL) had difficulty adapting to the kind of learning needed in problem-based instruction. They tended to focus on fact acquisition.
		High SRL students valued learning from problems and tended to focus on the problem analysis and reflection process.
		Low SRL students may have difficulty dealing with SDL demands of PBL curriculum.
Dolmans and Schmidt (2000)	First through fourth-year medical students were given a questionnaire with items relating to the different curricular elements. The authors wanted to see how other curricular elements might direct SDL.	Both problem discussion and course objectives had the greatest positive influence on SDL. Tests and lectures had the least positive influence.
		Over the four years of curriculum, students increased their emphasis on the functional knowledge they would need as physicians and decreased their reliance on external elements such as tests.
		Over time, students in a PBL curriculum become more self-reliant.

TABLE 4.3 Findings in the effectiveness of PBL in developing SDL Skills (cont'd)

Author(s)	Participants / Task	Findings
Hmelo and Lin (2000)	Medical students in traditional and PBL curricula who had completed a pathophysiological explanation task were compared.	PBL student transferred hypothesis-driven strategies from their problem solving into their SDL as they used their hypotheses to plan their learning.
		PBL students were more likely to integrate new information into a revised explanation than traditional medical students.
Blumberg and Michael (1992)	Traditional and PBL medical students were compared in terms of the learning resources they used.	PBL students were more likely to use self-chosen learning resources whereas students in the conventional curriculum used faculty-chosen resources.
		PBL students were more likely to report selecting the material to study themselves, whereas conventional curriculum students reported reading specific teacher-generated assignments.
Shikano and Hmelo (1996)	Engineering students in a PBL course in sustainable technology were studied	These students increased their use of expertise other than that provided by course instructors as the course progressed and tended to use a variety of student-selected resources through the course.

SOURCE: Hmelo-Silver (2004)

important factor as it affects learning outcomes and intrinsic motivation. Table 4.4 summarises the studies reviewed by Hmelo-Silver (2004) in this area.

Hmelo-Silver (2004) concluded that there was insufficient evidence supporting the hypothesis that PBL helps students to become better collaborators. However, there is evidence that students work together to provide collaborative explanations. There is also evidence showing that collaboration in tutorial groups is a key factor in student learning and motivation, although not all groups collaborate well. The author asserted that more research is necessary to examine whether PBL environments help all learners become better collaborators.

Becoming intrinsically motivated: Hmelo-Silver (2004) found little research evidence on the effectiveness of PBL on enhancing intrinsic motivation. In her review, she stated that most of the available research had instead, examined student satisfaction or confidence. A summary of these studies can be found in Table 4.5. Hmelo-Silver (2004) revealed that there has been insufficient work on motivation among K-12 PBL students. The results for medical students have been consistent. In general, medical students enjoy PBL and feel confident about their learning. The lack of empirical data about motivation in undergraduate and K-12 education makes it difficult to draw conclusions about motivation in these other contexts.

In summary, research evidence, according to Hmelo-Silver (2004), was found mainly in three of the five goals of PBL:

- *Construct an extensive and flexible knowledge base*: Increasingly flexible knowledge develops as individuals apply their knowledge in a variety of problem situations.
- *Develop effective problem-solving skills*: It includes the ability to apply appropriate meta-cognitive and reasoning strategies.
- *Develop self-directed, life long learning skills*: Meta-cognitive strategies are very important for developing self-directed, lifelong learning skills.

However, less research evidence was available for the remaining two areas:

- *Become effective collaborators*: Being a good collaborator means knowing how to function well as part of a team. Explaining one's

117

TABLE 4.4 Findings in PBL's effectiveness in helping students become effective collaborators

Author(s)	Details of study	Findings
Schmidt and Moust (2000)	Used path analysis to study group functioning	Group functioning is affected by the quality of the problem and facilitator functioning, but not by prior knowledge.
DeGrave et al. (1996)	Analysed videotape of a tutorial group and had students engage in stimulated recall while watching the video.	In the group meeting, students did not appear to attend to collaboration explicitly but their stimulated recall indicated that students were sensitive to collaborative process and their own part in the collaboration.
Hmelo-Silver (2002)	Two PBL tutorial sessions were analysed (case study).	Student discourse often focused on responding to and refining ideas that had been proposed. The case study provides an example of what is possible in well-functioning groups.

TABLE 4.4 Findings in PBL's effectiveness in helping students become effective collaborators (cont'd)

Author(s)	Details of study	Findings
Faidley et al. (2000)	In this pilot study, observational and self-report instruments that could be used to provide information on group processing were constructed to help students learn to be better collaborators.	There was a relationship between the two instruments.
	Learning Team Survey (LTS) is a self-report effect instrument designed to focus on behaviours and attitudes that are important to group learning.	There was a great variability in the groups studied, providing further evidence that not all groups are effective.
	Observational checklist focuses on substantive and group processing behaviours.	The facilitator had a large effect on how well the group worked.
	The observational checklist was used to determine whether group differences in LTS could be explained by attending to the behavioural variables.	

SOURCE: Hmelo-Silver (2004)

TABLE 4.5 Findings in PBL's effectiveness in helping students become intrinsically motivated

Author(s)	Details of study	Findings
Derry et al. (2000)	Students' reaction to a PBL course in statistical reasoning was studied.	Mixed results were yielded.
Ertmer et al. (1996)	The nature of students motivation was studied in relation to PBL.	Intrinsic motivation was associated to PBL. However, the nature of students' motivation in PBL may depend on their academic or professional discipline.
Albanese and Mitchell (1993), Hmelo (1994), Vernon and Blake (1993)	Medical students in PBL curricula and traditional curricula were compared in terms of their satisfaction with their learning, and confidence in their understanding.	Students in PBL curricula reported being more satisfied with their learning and confident in their understanding as compared to those in the traditional curricula.

ideas is important for productive collaboration and also serves to enhance learning.

* *Become intrinsically motivated to learn*: It occurs when learners work on a task motivated by their own interests, challenges, or sense of satisfaction. Hmelo-Silver (2004) found some strong evidence about the nature of knowledge construction and the development of problem-solving skills in certain settings. However, she proposed several caveats that need to be noted.

(1) The claims of PBL advocates are not supported by an extensive research base, and much of the research has been limited to higher education, predominantly in medical schools.

(2) There is little research conducted with K-12 populations.

(3) A significant amount of the research has employed case study, pre-post test, or quasi-experiment designs rather than controlled experiments. However, on a more positive note, these designs provide converging evidence about learning with PBL.

(4) Majority of research on PBL examines knowledge construction, problem solving, and SDL. There is lack of work done in the areas of motivation and collaboration. Further research is necessary to examine these aspects.

(5) There is a need for more information on the generalisability of the medical model of PBL into other settings, with considerations of local contexts, goals and developmental level of learners.

  * Using PBL in K-12 poses a problem in terms of constraints of classroom organisation.
  * The model of PBL in medical schools involves integrated, interdisciplinary curriculum organised around problems rather than subject domains. In K-12 situations, teachers often need to assess students in specific areas and problems do not map neatly onto these subject area divisions.
  * Careful planning is required to engage in PBL in short class periods allocated in K-12 settings.

(6) The PBL model should be tailored to the developmental level of the learners. Self-directed learning may prove particularly

difficult for younger learners who tend to have difficulty applying metacognitive strategies. Hence, scaffolding is important to help support student metacognition and reflection at this level. Some noteworthy research issues include:

i. Understanding the nature of adaptations as well as how the aspects of PBL may be scaffolded for different learners.

ii. A just-in-time basis needs to be considered. That is, as students grapple with a problem and are confronted with the need for particular kinds of knowledge, a lecture at a right time may prove beneficial (e.g. create a "time for telling" [Schwartz and Bransford 1998, cited in Hmelo-Silver 2004]). Research should consider at an empirical level how to incorporate this into a student-centred learning environment.

iii. More evidence-based instructional strategies that demonstrate which facets of PBL are important for particular outcomes so that educators can make informed choices in adapting PBL to their particular context is necessary.

(7) The lack of sufficient number of skilled facilitators poses a problem in using the technique. Challenges and possible solutions in this aspect are as follows:

- Classrooms usually have more students than one person can easily facilitate. Learning to facilitate may itself be a challenging task.
- Techniques, such as procedural facilitation, scripted cooperation, and structured journals may serve as useful tools to help facilitation.
- The PBL activity structure may be modified to support PBL for specific teaching goals and technology be incorporated to serve in adapting PBL for specific disciplines. For example, in the Secondary Teacher Education Programme (STEP) (www.estepweb.org, cited in Hmelo-Silver 2004), the activity structure was modified to help preservice teachers engage in instructional design as they learned about educational psychology.

Dochy, Segers, van den Bossche and Gijbels (2003) conducted a meta-analysis of 43 empirical studies, done at the tertiary level on real-life classrooms, using the core PBL model. These studies employed quasi-experimental designs. Dochy, Segers, van den Bossche and Gijbels' (2003) meta-analysis aimed at addressing the main effects of PBL on knowledge and skills (i.e., application of knowledge) and the potential moderators of the effect of PBL. Table 4.6 provides a summary of the meta-analysis in terms of the studies used, criteria for studies to be included, as well as the findings of the analysis in relation to each of the aims of the study.

Dochy, Segers, van den Bossche and Gijbels (2003) revealed that the main results of the meta-analysis are similar to the conclusions of the previous meta-analytic reviews in that *a robust positive effect of PBL on skills* was obtained. Furthermore, the team's meta-analysis made similar conclusions about the effect of PBL on knowledge and provides further validation of the findings from the previous meta-analytic reviews. Although converging results were yielded from this meta-analysis in relation to the earlier two reviews, the authors emphasised that the study had only included only field studies (quasi-experimental research). This statistical limitation implies that although the study had high ecological validity, some internal validity relative to more controlled laboratory studies was compromised. Thus, results from this study should be interpreted from such a perspective, from which investigators try to bridge the gap between research and educational practice.

PBL VERSUS PROJECT WORK

The main ideas underlying both project work and problem-based learning is their emphasis on *learning* instead of teaching. Learning is an active process of investigation and creation based on the learners' interest, curiosity and experience and should result in expanded insights, knowledge, and skills. The rudiments of problem-based learning are discussed above. The following delineates what project work is:

* Project work is a special way of organising learning characterised by an *active discussion and writing process in a group-based course.*
* Project work stresses both the process and the product in the form of a project report. The reason for this organisation of learning is based on the idea of teaching and learning as an active process of cognition,

TABLE 4.6 Meta-analysis by Dochy, Segers, van den Bossche & Gijbels (2003)

Number of Studies	Inclusion Criteria	Aims of Meta-Analysis	Methodology / Statistical Measures	Results/Findings
A total of 43 studies were used:	Work had to be empirical.	Main Effects of PBL on skills	A statistical meta-analysis was conducted, supplemented by more inclusive vote counts and the associated sign test.	33 studies presented data on knowledge effects.
14 were based on reading of articles' abstracts in first literature database search;	Characteristics of the learning environment had to fit the previously described core model of PBL.		Metric used to estimate and describe effects of PBL on knowledge and skills was the standardised mean and difference (d-index) effect size (for comparison of 2 means).	Vote count and combined effect size suggest a robust positive effect from PBL on skills of students. No single study reported negative effects.
17 based in "snowball method" by reviewing references in selected articles for additional work;	Dependent variables used in the study had to be an operationalisation of the knowledge and.or skills (i.e. Knowledge	Main Effects of PBL on Knowledge	The shifting method from Cooper (1989, cited in Dochy et al. 2003) was used in identifying independent hypothesis	25 studies reported data on effects concerning the application of knowledge. A tendency to negative results detected (combined effect size is significantly negative).
Second literature search was				Result strongly influenced by two

TABLE 4.6 Meta-analysis by Dochy, Segers, van den Bossche & Gijbels (2003) (cont'd)

Number of Studies	Inclusion Criteria	Aims of Meta-Analysis	Methodology / Statistical Measures	Results/Findings
conducted following the same procedure and authors contacted a few researchers in PBL field to request for relevant studies or to identify additional sources of studies—12 studies were yielded.	application) of the students. Subjects had to be students in tertiary education. The study had to be conducted in a real-life classroom or programmatic setting rather than under more controlled laboratory conditions.	Potential moderators of the effect of PBL	tests. Combined effect sizes across studies were obtained. The variability of the effect sizes via a homogeneity analysis was obtained to examine potential moderators. A Qt statistic (chi-square, N-1 degrees of freedom) was used to test if effect size is homogeneous. First category of moderators includes design aspects of the reviewed research (methodological factors).	studies and the vote count does not reach a significant level. The combined effect size for the effect on knowledge is non-robust. Category 1: In terms of methodological factors, there is a diminished negative effect of PBL on knowledge, if the quality of the research is categorised as higher. Category 2: Both for knowledge- and skills-related outcomes, the expertise level of the student is associated with the variation in effect sizes. Results for skills give a consistent positive picture.

TABLE 4.6 Meta-analysis by Dochy, Segers, van den Bossche & Gijbels (2003) (cont'd)

Number of Studies	Inclusion Criteria	Aims of Meta- Analysis	Methodology / Statistical Measures	Results/Findings
			The second category of moderators examined whether the effect of PBL differs according to the various levels of student expertise.	For knowledge-related outcomes, results suggest that the differences encountered in the first and second year disappear later on if the reproduction of knowledge is assessed in a broader context that asks all the students to apply their knowledge.
			The third category of moderators looked at the different types of assessment methods.	Category 3: Results seem to indicate that the more an instrument is capable of evaluating the skills of the student, the larger the ascertained effect of PBL. Although unclear, an analogue tendency was acknowledged for the knowledge-related outcomes. Students do better on a test if the test makes a stronger appeal on retrieval strategies.
			The fourth category addresses the influence of the insertion of a retention period.	Category 4: Moderator analysis indicated that students in PBL gained slightly less knowledge but remember more of the acquired knowledge.

SOURCE: Dochy, Segers, van den Bossche and Gijbels (2003)

126

searching, and acquiring knowledge instead of the traditional form of education.

- Project work usually requires more human resources, as analysis and solution of problem are more intensive, than the human resources required for solving a posed task. So *teamwork is an integrated part of the project work.*

- Characterising *project work involves "a type of problem-or objective"* because no project work can be practised without having a clearly described objective for what is going to be analysed or solved. This type of problem may cover a wide range of problem conceptions, from practical, theoretical and social problems to purely technical problems.

To highlight the uniqueness of project-based learning and to clarify its definition, five criteria are propounded (Thomas 2000, cited in Burns 2000):

- Centrality: Projects are central, not peripheral to the curriculum.
- Driving questions: Projects are focused on essential questions based on central concepts from one or more disciplines.
- Constructive investigations: Project activities must involve students in knowledge construction.
- Autonomy: Projects are student-driven to a significant degree.
- Realism: Projects are realistic or authentic, not school-like. Many include activities conducted beyond school walls.

Project activities are the important part of the project, where students work collaboratively to gather information for the project. The most extensive research on project-based learning comes from evaluation studies of whole-school reform efforts that feature Project-based learning as their primary form of instruction. These include Expeditionary Learning Outward Bound (ELOB) and Co-nect, which combines PBL with technology integration. According to Thomas (2000, cited in Burns 2000), nine of ten schools that implemented Expeditionary Learning in 1993 demonstrated significant improvement in students' test scores on standardised tests of academic achievement. Additionally, ELOB programmes were associated with positive changes in school climate, student motivation, attendance, and structural changes in schools. Similarly, Co-nect schools demonstrated significantly greater gains across subject areas compared to control schools.

127

The most comprehensive and important findings on project-based learning effectiveness were reported from a 1997 longitudinal study of mathematics learning in two British secondary schools serving similar populations but differed significantly in instructional practices. The key finding was that students taught with a more traditional, formal, didactic model developed an inert knowledge of mathematics that was of little use on complex problems, while students taught using open-ended projects seemed to develop a flexible knowledge of mathematics that could be applied more easily in a variety of new contexts (Thomas 2000, cited in Burns 2000).

With regard to implementation research, main findings were yielded from the University of Michigan. Research described the challenges faced by students as they participated and teachers as they enacted a published, project-based science program. Difficulties that students exhibited included: (a) generating meaningful scientific questions, (b) managing complexity and time, (c) transforming data, and (d) developing a logical argument to support claims. The findings point to the need to incorporate specific teaching strategies to help students overcome these deficiencies prior to and during the implementation of a project. Common challenges faced by teachers included the following:

- Time: Projects often took longer than anticipated.
- Classroom management: Student autonomy needs to be balanced with the teacher's need to maintain control.
- Control: Teachers often felt the need to control the flow of information while believing that students' understanding required that they build their own understanding.
- Support of student learning: Teachers had difficulty scaffolding students' activities, sometimes giving them too much independence and too little modeling and feedback.
- Technology use: Teachers had difficulty incorporating technology into the classroom, especially as a cognitive tool.
- Assessment: Teachers had difficulty designing assessments that required students to demonstrate their understanding.

We compared the two learning concepts (problem-based learning and project based learning) in four ways (Kolmos 1996), namely educational objectives, problem-solving, cooperation, and management. Similarities and differences of the two methods have also been discussed elsewhere

(Esch 1998) and differences are presented in Table 4.7.
    In terms of similarities,

- Both are instructional strategies that are intended to engage students in authentic, "real world" tasks to enhance learning.
- Students are given open-ended projects or problems with more than one approach or answer, intended to simulate professional situations.
- Both learning approaches are defined as student-centred, and include the teacher in the role of facilitator or coach.
- Students engaged in project- or problem-based learning generally work in cooperative groups for extended periods of time, and are encouraged to seek out multiple sources of information.
- Often these approaches include an emphasis on authentic, performance-based assessment.
- Both instructional strategies have their roots in the constructivist approach evolved from the work of psychologists and educators such as Lev Vygotsky, Jerome Bruner, Jean Piaget and John Dewey.

In fact, PBL and project work use a common problem and rely on the teacher to help guide the learning process (Hmelo-Silver 2004). PBL uses realistic, ill-structured problems, whereas project-based science uses the problem as a driving question as the focus for scientific inquiry. In terms of process, PBL uses the PBL learning cycle, and project-based science uses scientific inquiry cycles to design experiments, male predictions, observations, and then construct explanations of why their prediction was or was not correct. In terms of tools, PBL uses a simple tool, a structured whiteboard with lists of facts, ideas (hypothesis), learning issues and action plans to help structure the students' problem solving and learning. Project based science uses a variety of computer-based tools to scaffold students problem solving.

Project Work via PBL

In considering the implementation of problem- and project-based curricula, four design principles are important:

- Defining learning-appropriate goals that lead to deep understanding.

- Providing scaffolds such as "embedded teaching," "teaching tools," set of "contrasting cases," and beginning with problem-based learning activities before initiating projects.
- Ensuring multiple opportunities for formative self-assessment and revision.
- Developing social structures that promote participation and a sense of agency.

Taking these principles in consideration, one can then forward the notion of implementing a project-based curriculum via a PBL approach. Such a notion encapsulates the principles suggested above. Both methods are by and large similar in principles 1, 3 and 4. The second principle is, however, critical in considering project work through PBL. In particular, problem-based learning can serve as a scaffold for project work.

Relevant problem-based challenge can serve as a scaffold for more open-ended, subsequent projects for many reasons. A relatively circumscribed problem can support the initial development of vocabulary and concepts, and video-based problems. There are strong advantages to pairing problem-and project-based activities. By beginning with a simulated problem, students develop a level of shared knowledge and skill that prepares them to undertake actual project. By following the problem with a project, students will develop more flexible levels of skills and understanding. And if students know they will be completing real projects in their community, they are motivated to learn. Table 4.7 shows some differences between PBL project work and typical project work.

Literature on the implementation of project based work via PBL is scarce. However, Chin and Chia (2004) has attempted to illustrate the implementation of project work in Biology through problem-based learning at the secondary school level and their effort has brought a new perspective to the application of these learning strategies. The focus of the study was on how students carried out their investigative projects through PBL, how the teacher mediated these activities and how the students responded to this mode of learning. A class of 39 students worked in nine groups of four or five members each. Each group worked on a self-selected project topic related to a central theme (in this case "Food and Nutrition"). The procedure which is described in their paper was based on the PBL model. To reiterate, five stages were involved:

TABLE 4.7 Problem-based learning (PBL), project-based learning and PBL project work

	Problem-based learning	Project-based science/learning
(Nature of) Problem	Realistic ill-structured problem.	Driving question.
	Begins with a clearly-stated problem or problems and require a set of conclusions or a solution in direct response, where "the problematic situation is the organising centre for the curriculum."	Any number of problems will arise and students will require problem-solving skills to overcome them.
Role of problem	Focus on learning information and reasoning strategies.	Focus on scientific inquiry process leading to artefact production.
Process(es)	Begins with a problem for students to solve or learn more about.	Typically begins with an end product or "artefact" in mind.
	Identify facts, generate ideas and learning issues, self-directed learning, revisit, and reflect.	Prediction, observation, explanation cycles.
	End products are more summative and simpler. The inquiry and research is the primary focus of the learning process. E.g. groups report on their research findings.	End products are elaborate and shape the production process, and drives the planning, production, and evaluation process. Ex: computer animation piece.

TABLE 4.7 Problem-based learning (PBL), project-based learning and PBL project work (cont'd)

	Problem-based learning	Project-based science/learning
Models used	This approach uses the inquiry model: students are presented with a problem and they begin by organising any previous knowledge on the subject, posing any additional questions, and identifying areas they need more information.	This approach uses the production model. First, students define the purpose for creating the end product and identify their audience. They search their topic, design their product, and create a plan for project management.
Specific groups	PBL also used in K-12 classrooms, but has its origins in medical training and other professional preparation practices.	Tends to be associated with K-12 instruction.
Role of teacher	Facilitate learning process and model reasoning.	Introduce relevant content before and during inquiry. Guides inquiry process.
Collaboration	Negotiation of ideas. Individual students bring new knowledge to group for application to problem.	Negotiation of ideas with peers and local community members.
Tools	Structured whiteboard Student-identified learning resources.	Computer-based tools that support planning, data collection and analysis, modelling and information-gathering.

TABLE 4.7 Problem-based learning (PBL), project-based learning and PBL project work (cont'd)

Integrating	PBL and Project Work	Typical Project Work
PBL Project Work	Problems are identified by students themselves, and inspired by real life experiences.	Problems are identified by students or given by the teacher. Sometimes, problems are contrived
	Problems are ill-structured.	Problems are well-defined if given by teacher.
	Students role-play a character in the problem statement with whom they can identify.	No role-playing is usually involved.
	Students are required to generate questions and identify learning issues	Students are not required to pose questions and identify learning issues.
	Because students are required to offer a solution for an ill-defined problem, they are unable to use "copy-and-paste" strategies in the written report.	Some projects allow descriptive reporting on specific topics. This may lead students to resort to "copy-and-paste" strategies in the written report.

SOURCES: Chin & Chia (2004), Esch (1998), Hmelo-Silver (2004)

Stage 1: Identifying the problem to be investigated

- Students wrote down their ideas and questions individually onto problem logs.
- Students discussed ideas in groups, agree on a topic and jointly formulate their problem.
- In writing problem statements, students were encouraged to adopt real-life problem-solving roles.

Stage 2: Exploring the problem space

- Students organised ideas around three prescribed focus questions.
- Students were required to record their ideas and questions onto a worksheet regularly.
- Students were asked to identify the resources they used and the type of tasks they had to engage in to solve their problem.

Stage 3: Carrying out scientific inquiry

- Students gathered information to answer their own questions.
- Teacher set up an internet forum page for students to consult a panel comprising experts.
- Students used platform to ask questions related to research, and some used the science lab to carry out investigations. Others went on field investigations, conducted surveys and reviews, and searched for information from print and electronic resources.

Stage 4: Putting the information together

- Group members reported on what they had done, completed further worksheets and planned for further tasks.
- A notebook was used to track progress of inquiry.
- A learning log and project task allocation form was filled up at the end of every meeting or investigation with regard to what was learnt and discovered. They then planned the next steps in inquiry.

- These methods helped them review and consolidate information gathered.

Stage 5: Presenting the findings, teacher evaluation and self-reflection

- Each group gave a 15-minute oral presentation and answered questions posed by the rest of the class and the teacher.
- All groups used technology-based multimedia modes of delivery and submitted artefacts.
- A group project file documenting group's findings and details of inquiry process was submitted.
- Each student completed a self-evaluation form and a feedback questionnaire, wherein they assessed themselves on their knowledge application, communication and independent learning skills. This also helped students discover problems encountered while carrying out the project etc. The idea was to help students reflect on the learning process.

According to Chin and Chia (2004), the project aimed to help students acquire competence in identifying, accessing, and processing relevant information. Through this, students can use this information to solve authentic problems and construct new knowledge. Implementing project work via PBL, albeit with some difficulties, based on student-generated questions provides such an opportunity.

CONCLUSIONS

The pendulum of educational reform is swinging away from traditional approaches and towards PBL with much enthusiasm (Finucane, Johnson & Prideaux 1998). More importantly, there is evidence that PBL, in comparison to other instructional methods, has value for enhancing the *quality* of students' learning in subject areas, leading to the tentative claim that learning higher-level cognitive skills via PBL is associated with increased capability on the part of students for applying those learnings in novel, problem-solving contexts. Although conclusions on the effectiveness of PBL are tentative and there are questions left unanswered, the effect of a well-designed curriculum that incorporates PBL can facilitate learning. Such a notion should be considered carefully. The future of PBL in school curriculum, although requires more scrutiny, shows promise in various areas and in particular groups of students. With adequate preparation, training, resources, support and comprehensive evaluation, PBL may foster more innovative and enterprising learning environments in schools.

REFERENCES*

Baker, C. M. 2000. Problem-based learning for nursing: integrating lessons from other disciplines with nursing experiences. *Journal of Professional Nursing, 16(5)*, 258–266.

Barrows, H. S. 1985. *Now to Design a Problem-Based Curriculum for the Preclinical Years*. Springer Series on Medical Education. Springer Publishing Company: New York.

Barrows, H. S. 1986. A taxonomy of problem-based learning methods. *Medical Education, 20*, 481–486.

Burns, R. 2000. Project-based learning: a review of research. *The ITI Review, 2(3)*. Retrieved 13 November 2004 from http://www.ael.org/rel/iti/pbl0009.htm

Camp, G. 1996. Problem-based learning: A paradigm shift or a passing fad? MEO, 1(2).

Retrieved 6 November 2004 from www.med-ed-online.org/f0000003.htm

Carder, L., P. Willingham, & D. Bibb. 2001. Case-based, problem-based learning information literacy for the real world. *Research Strategy, 18*, 181–190.

Chin, C., & L. G. Chia. 2004. Implementing project work in biology through problem-based learning. *Journal of Biological Education, 38(2)*, 69–75.

Conway, J., & R. Sharkey. 2002. Integrating on campus problem-based learning and practice-based learning: issues and challenges in using computer mediated communication. *Nurse Education Today, 22*, 552–562.

Dochy, F., M. Segers, P. Van den Bossche, & D. Gijbels. 2003. Effects of problem-based learning: a meta-analysis. *Learning and Instruction, 13*, 533–568.

Esch, C. 1998. The Multimedia project: project-based learning with multimedia. Retrieved 6 November 2004 from http://pblmm.k12.ca.us/PBLGuide/PBL&PBL. htm

Finucane, P. M., S. M. Johnson, & D. J. Prideaux. 1998. Problem based learning: its rationale and efficacy. *MJA, 168, 445–448*. Retrieved 12 November 2004 from http://som.flinders.edu.au/HTML/COURSES/GEMP/PBL_Staff.htm

Green, C. J., G. H. van Gyn, J. R. Moehr, F. Y. Lau, & P. M. Coward. 2004. Introducing a technology-enabled problem-based learning approach into a health informatics curriculum. *International Journal of Medical Informatics, 73*, 173–179.

Haith-Cooper, M. 2000. Problem-based learning within health professional education. What is the role of the lecturer? A review of the literature. *Nurse Education Today, 20*, 267–272.

Haith-Cooper, M. 2003a. An exploration of tutors' experiences of facilitating problem-based learning. Part 1—an educational research methodology combining innovation and philosophical tradition. *Nurse Education Today, 23*, 58–64.

Haith-Cooper, M. 2003b. An exploration of tutors' experiences of facilitating problem-based learning. Part 2—implications for the facilitation of problem based learning. *Nurse Education Today, 23*, 65–75.

Hmelo-Silver, C. E. 2004. Problem-based learning: what and how do students learn? *Education Psychology Review, 16(3)*, 235–266.

Kolmos, A. 1996. Reflection on project work and problem-based learning. *European Journal of Engineering Education, 21(1)*, 141–148.

Major, C. H., & B. Palmer. 2001. Assessing the effectiveness of problem-based learning in higher education: lessons from the literature. *Academic Exchange Quarterly, 5*, 4–9.

Murray, I., & M. Savin-Baden. 2000. Staff development in problem-based learning. *Teaching in Higher Education, 5(1)*, 107–126.

Price, B. 2000. Problem-based learning the distance learning way: a bridge too far? *Nurse Education Today, 20*, 98–105.

Segers, M., P. Van den Bossche, & E. Teunissen. 2003. Evaluating the effects of redesigning a problem-based learning environment. *Studies in Educational Evaluation, 29*, 315–334.

Sharp, D. M. M., & C. S. Primrose. 2003. The "virtual family": an evaluation of an innovative approach using problem-based learning to integrate curriculum themes in a nursing undergraduate programme. *Nurse Education Today, 23*, 219–225.

Wood, D. F. 2003. Problem-based learning. *British Medical Journal, 326*, 328–330.

* Rajani and Valerie Ho assisted in literature search.

CHAPTER 5

Learning with the Information and Communication Technologies (ICT)

MAISIE TAN AND TAN AI GIRL

INTRODUCTION

To foster economic growth and global competitiveness, the Singapore government established the National Computer Board (NCB) in 1981 and developed an Information Technology (IT) policy in the same year to increase IT labour and industry. Later, in 1986, the first national IT plan was organised to further enhance national IT competence. In 1991, the NCB initiated the IT2000 vision to make Singapore an "Intelligent Island," electronically linking the island both locally and globally (National Computer Board 1992). Similarly, "Singapore ONE" was launched in 1997 to increase multimedia services in homes, business and schools (National Computer Board 1997). Today, the NCB, now renamed the Infocomm Development Authority (IDA) of Singapore, is set to make Singapore a digital hub of innovation and entrepreneurship. To achieve this aim, education is especially vital to train future workers and leaders to be competent in IT knowledge and usage. Thus, information and communication technologies are becoming increasingly commonplace in schools. Presently, there are four main categories of ICT: 1) informative (providing visual, audio, and text information, e.g., World Wide Web), 2) situating (creating an environment so students can experience the context and happenings, e.g., simulation games and virtual reality), 3) construction (manipulate and construct own knowledge, e.g. construct own webpage), and 4) communicative (e.g., email and forums) (Lim & Tay 2003).

Application of ICT in Education

Information and communication technologies (ICT) is a useful tool that can complement, support and supplement different pedagogies. The use of computers in Singapore primary schools was introduced in 1983. However, globally, drill-and-practice exercises have been the predominant use for computers in the classroom over the past two decades, owing to the traditional view of technology as facilitating instructional delivery (Chan SC 2002). Thus, computers were only used to build up basic skills that were assessed using standardised tests. For example, in 1993, the Curriculum Development Board of Singapore developed a drill-and-practice courseware named *Primary Mathematics Series*. However, in 1997, under the IT Masterplan in Education, the MOE proposed to use technology as a tool to enhance creative thinking, independent and lifelong learning in students at all levels of education. Also, with the current emphasis on student-centred learning, ICT has become a key tool in schools for teaching. For example, in a secondary two Gifted Education Programme literature class, poetry is taught using a visual art computer programme where students can make drawings to help them "visualise" the poem (Tan-Hoo 1999). Other computer programmes used for local teaching include *Midisaurus* for Music, *Crayola* for Art, *RoboLab* for Science, and *MathBlaster* for Mathematics (Lim & Chai 2004). The revised Mathematics Syllabus for Singapore primary schools (2001) also proposed that ICT use in primary schools should involve meaningful understanding of concepts and real life problem solving, teaching of thinking strategies, developing a sense of enquiry and inquisitiveness, group work and communication.

In an in-depth study of a geography web-based educational application *GeogDL*, Goh, Ang, Theng and Lim (2004) investigated the components of the programme that facilitate student-centred and collaborative learning. After being pilot-tested on a group of secondary school students, it was found that the vast store of information in the programme enabled students to access and to explore related supplementary information on their own. The programme also contained a wide range of past examination questions for students to attempt, and allows students to search for questions based on type or year. After attempting the questions, GeogDL presents both the answers and the explanations to the questions, links to related concepts and web sites and also the relationships between different concepts and questions. Students are also able to chat with other users to discuss concepts and ideas. In additional, navigational functions like zoom and pan make it easy and interactive for students to study geographical maps.

Another educational computer programme is "e-daf," the virtual self-access Centre for German as a Foreign Language at the National University of Singapore (Chan & Kim 2004). Besides linguistic training, e-daf also provides students with text processing such as spellcheck, cultural information, dictionary and thesaurus, so students can easily obtain all their information from a single source. In addition, e-daf is highly interactive. For example, students can construct their own conversations with virtual conversation partners by selecting different responses at each conversation turn. In this way, students are given the autonomy to be actively involved in their learning process. Conversations can also be contextualised by adding realistic sound effects of public destinations.

Virtual reality simulations can also be used to teach (Ong & Mannan 2004). In the Manufacturing Department at the National University of Singapore, a web-based interactive programme is used in teaching a manufacturing engineering class. The programme can create visualisations that traditional teaching materials are unable to achieve. Moreover, such virtual reality technology is especially useful in teaching automated machine tools, because students can then train without having to work on actual machines in the laboratory.

Besides teaching, ICT has also been used by teachers for grading assignments. For example, in the School of Computing in the National University of Singapore, an automated grading system called the *Online Judge* is used to grade students' computer programming exercises (Cheang, Kurnia, Lim & Oon 2003). This programme relieves teachers of their already heavy workload, and grades assignments with increased efficiency and accuracy. In addition, the system is capable of detecting plagiarism easily. However, it can be inflexible when grading (i.e., only one acceptable answer). Also, feedback to students can be limited (e.g., cannot explain source of students' errors).

Benefits and Issues in the use of ICT in Education

Meta-analytical research studies and studies in Singapore indicate that computer-assisted lessons can improve students' academic achievement and attitudes toward learning, and allow students to learn more in less time with more enthusiasm (Chan SC 2002). Much research has also shown that the use of ICT in schools can develop students' critical thinking skills, communication skills and self-confidence (Cheong 2001). For example, in mathematics classes, instead of having to make manual calculations and mechanically draw graphs, students can now focus on interpreting and analysing data, thus developing higher order thinking skills (Chan SC 2002). In addition, because students are given more autonomy in the learning process with the use of ICT (e.g., students can control their rate of learning and learning sequences), they are allowed to create their own knowledge instead of it being forced on them in ways that they do not comprehend or at rates at which they are unable to cope. In turn, students may develop more positive attitudes toward learning (Lim & Chai 2004).

This autonomy is possible because of the flexibility of computer-based learning. Individualised instruction can be designed to meet students' needs, interests and abilities (Chan LK 2002). Computer programmes can also provide immediate feedback on students' performance. The use of such interactive ICT thus allows students to engage in self-directed learning, and instead of teacher-centred learning, teachers are now facilitators in the classroom.

Computers can also facilitate class discussions (for example, via email and discussion forums) and thus collaborative learning. In turn, by engaging in collaborative learning, students build up their communication and teamwork skills. In addition to working with peers, colourful computer animations and other visual and audio effects create interest in learning and provide enjoyment for students (Tan-Hoo 1999). With multimedia, students are more able to have a tangible experience of the subject they are learning (Lim & Chai 2004).

Moreover, computer simulations of real-life events make learning relevant and also develop students' real-life problem-solving skills (Chan SC 2002). For example, students can access the internet to find real-life situations and information, so learning is no longer confined to the classroom, the teacher's knowledge, or even the resources available in the school. Students thus gain "useable knowledge" that can be applied to various real-life contexts.

An example of ICT being used to make learning relevant to real life is a computer simulation programme created by Brink (1994). To make learning mathematics more enjoyable, Brink (1994) created a flight simulation programme that required students to read cockpit instruments, calculate altitude, convert measurements, draw maps, and estimate arrival time among other problems that involved mathematical concepts. It was found that through this programme, misconceptions could be corrected almost immediately, and students were able to apply their mathematics knowledge to real life situations by combining concepts and principles that they already knew in new and different ways.

In fact, Jonassen (1996) terms such computer learning programmes as "mindtools." Mindtools increase students' cognitive functioning by requiring them to formulate new knowledge that they would not have achieved otherwise. Students are brought into a learning environment where they are expected to reflect on new knowledge intentionally and meaningfully, elaborate on already acquired knowledge, and observe relations between both old and new knowledge. Moreover, by being constantly exposed to novel situations, students will be more motivated to engage in lifelong learning.

However, much time and money must be spent both on infrastructure and teacher training to use ICT in teaching. The implementation of ICT in schools also requires time-consuming, careful and systematic planning, and teachers must plan their lessons according to available equipment (Cheong 2001). Drill-and-practice computer-based lessons can also become boring and unchallenging for students (Chan SC 2002). Lastly, learning to use the technology and technical difficulties may reduce the amount of time available for actual learning during lessons (Chan SC 2002).

Studies of the Application of ICT in Singapore Schools

Studies have been conducted on the use of ICT in Singapore schools. In particular, the effectiveness of using ICT in the classroom has been investigated. For example, Yeo (2003) compared secondary four students who used *LiveMath*, an interactive algebra computer programme, with those who did not receive any form of computer-based instruction in mathematics. It was found that, although both groups of students had undergone a guided discovery method of learning (where the teacher guides the students to discover and develop Mathematical formulae), the students who used *LiveMath* showed significantly greater conceptual and procedural knowledge than the students who did not use the programme. Students also developed moderately positive affect towards the use of IT. This shows that even when student-centred teaching methods are used, the use of ICT can yield even greater improvements in students' achievement.

142

In another study of the effectiveness of ICT in teaching mathematics, Lee (2002) studied a group of 40 primary four students in a SAP school who used the programme LOGO for studying geometry and angles. It was found that students mastered "traditional" procedural knowledge as competently as students who did not use LOGO under the same time, class size and curriculum content constraints. Moreover, it was found that students who used LOGO showed greater increases in subject understanding and thinking skills compared to those who did not use LOGO.

ICT-based lessons have also been utilised for subjects other than mathematics. A study by Divaharan (1999) investigated the effect of IT-based writing activities in a constructive classroom setting on students' written English. The study involved 103 secondary school students, 37 from the Express stream, 38 from the Normal (Academic) stream and 28 from the Normal (Technical) stream. It was found that the use of IT does improve students' grammar, and that the Normal (Academic) students displayed the greatest improvement. IT also helped the students become independent learners.

Studies have similarly been done on students' attitudes toward both ICT-based lessons and subject material. Teng (2000) found that after using ICT in a primary five Mathematics class, students' attitudes toward attending lessons improved. Moreover, Etheris (2002) found that, after using an electronic forum for collaborative learning and problem solving in a class of 45 primary six students in a neighbourhood school, students' attitudes toward Mathematics became more positive.

Studies have also been done on the design of computer-based instructional material. Adal (2002) conducted a software review, and also observed and interviewed ten-year-old children using three different mathematical software. Adal (2002) found that children were more engaged in the programme when 1) children perceived more control and challenge in the programme, 2) there was fantasy involved in the programme, 3) children's curiosity was aroused, and 4) children were confident of how to use the programme. Adal (2002) also found that surface features did not affect student engagement, no matter how sophisticated the graphics and sounds are.

Chan LK (2002) investigated the extent to which ICT should be used in teaching, also particularly in the subject of Mathematics. In a study concerning seven primary schools, it was found that a wide range of ICT facilities were available for teachers, teachers had basic skills to use ICT, teachers use computers regularly during lessons (93 per cent of the time), and that teachers' attitudes toward ICT use was generally positive. However, Chan SC (2002) also found that teachers still mainly used ICT only for presenting drill-and-practice exercises, and suggests that this limited use of ICT was due to teachers' lack of understanding of alternative uses of ICT. Nonetheless, students found the IT-based lessons interesting because lessons were animated and presented using cartoon characters. There were also excessive sound effects to keep students interested in the exercises. None of the added special effects were meant to enhance students' understanding of Mathematical concepts. To expand teachers' use of ICT in the classroom, Chan SC (2002) proposed that teachers should assume a constructivist approach to instruction. Teachers should focus on the learning process when using ICT instead of the technology itself, be aware of the benefits of ICT and should also broaden their knowledge of the wide range of ICT and uses. For example, teachers should be aiming to develop students' higher order thinking skills instead of teaching them how to use the technology competently. It is also unnecessary for teachers to be able to use technology expertly before they begin using it in the classroom.

In another study of two primary schools by Lim and Chai (2004), it was found that students require autonomy over their learning processes to nurture their higher order thinking skills (such as creativity), and that "orienting activities" support that autonomy. These activities include introductory lessons to ICT tools so students can use the technology independently and confidently, advance organisers and instructional objectives so students understand what is required of them, worksheets to test their knowledge, checklists to ensure they are learning what they are expected to know, communication among students, and tools to aid post-lesson reflection so students can consolidate what they have learnt on their own.

It has been found that students generally have positive attitudes towards the use of ICT in classrooms. In a polytechnic e-learning initiative for an engineering module, students preferred e-learning to traditional lecture style because the e-learning programme was free from mistakes, allowed students to have greater control and interactivity with their own learning and also with the programme, and information via e-learning was up to date, clear, and easy to access (Ong 2003).

Factors facilitating the use of ICT by teachers have also been researched. Wang and Chan (1995) collected responses from 117 secondary school teachers, and found that teachers appreciate computer-based lessons providing immediate feedback to students, as well as avenues for alternative teaching methods. It was also found that teachers appreciate support both from MOE and the school, and ample time and resources to execute ICT-based lessons.

Other studies investigated the barriers to ICT usage by teachers. Ang (1999) proposed that psychological and behavioural factors such as "anxiety, self-efficacy, willingness to make time commitment and take personal risk, computer competency, beliefs, knowledge and perceived needs and relevance in the use of IT in teaching and learning" may hinder teachers from using ICT in the classroom. Ang (1999) also found that increased teaching experience without computers is significantly related to decreased perceived confidence and competence in computer usage, and negative beliefs in the relevance of computers in teaching. However, increase in computer usage for teaching is significantly related to decreased anxiety and increased competence and confidence in ICT usage. Such teachers are also more willing to learn about newer technologies, and are usually younger and have only been teaching for a few years. Similarly, Rahmat (1998) concluded that teachers' experiences with computers determined their attitudes toward using computers for teaching.

In a related study, Tan-Gibson and Miiko (1997) found that teachers were not against using technology, but nonetheless still had fears, anxieties and insecurities regarding the use of new equipment in the classroom instead of teaching in the traditional drill-and-practice manner. In fact, Yeo (1999) reported that computer anxiety and feelings of lack of ICT knowledge were the two main reasons for teachers not using ICT. Wang and Chan (1995) reached the same conclusion, and also add that teachers dislike the lack of human interaction in ICT-based lessons, as well as the large financial investment in procuring ICT equipment.

Research has also been done on teacher training in the use of ICT. A study by Cheong (2001) sought to organise a staff development structure so teachers can use ICT effectively in two institutes of the Institute of Technical Education (ITE). Firstly, there must be a focused vision clearly expressed by the Principal, so staff will share in the vision of becoming ICT competent and its meaning. Secondly, teacher readiness must be addressed. Thirdly, teachers must undergo hands-on practice and post-training development to be kept up to date with ICT developments. Fourthly, teachers can also learn from their colleagues through interaction, encouragement, collaboration, support groups, peer tutoring, sharing and reflection. Lastly, schools must provide sufficient infrastructure support and encouragement to teachers to use ICT.

In addition, the effectiveness of teacher training and how such training is perceived by teachers has also been researched. While Yeo (1999) found that training sessions conducted by MOE showed improvements in attitudes and perceptions of teachers towards ICT, Ang (1999) interviewed 83 teachers who felt that training sessions were not adequate in helping them learn different strategies to use ICT for teaching.

Suggestions for the Future

Research shows that teachers' readiness for change is most crucial for the effectiveness of the use of ICT (Cheong 2001). Lang (1992; in Cheong 2001) found that teachers will only use the technology if it makes sense to them. Hence, most importantly, there must be increased teacher training in ICT usage, and research into teacher development programmes (e.g., Cheong, 2001) for ICT to be effectively used in the classroom. Teachers must also have positive exposure to computers and ICT to reduce their fears and anxieties, and for them to develop positive attitudes towards ICT being used during lessons. Moreover, besides using the technology, teachers should also be trained in classroom management, because proper management is necessary for the effective implementation of ICT in the classroom (Pek 2003).

In addition, students must also be trained to use ICT effectively for learning. For example, Lim and Chai (2004) suggest that students must change their views of the learning process, from simple and fixed to complex and continuous. Also, students must be equipped with skills for self-directed learning, such as the ability to judge their progress accurately. Lastly, students must be motivated to learn. Thus, it is not only a matter of supplying ICT resources to classrooms. Mindsets and attitudes of both students and teachers must also change with changing teaching methods.

Schools must also be supportive of the use of IT and provide appropriate infrastructure for teachers. Equipment should be easily accessible, and teachers must be provided with ample time to prepare lessons and execute them in the classroom, given the novelty and more time-consuming nature of ICT-based lessons (Chan SC 2002). Moreover, more research should be done to investigate the effectiveness of ICT in schools in other subject areas besides Mathematics, since most local studies have been conducted on that subject. More research can also be conducted into developing appropriate teaching software. For instance, Chan and Kim (2004) outline five guidelines for programme development: 1) maximise interactivity and learner involvement, 2) cater to individual preferences and abilities, 3) facilitate acquisition and use of strategies, 4) encourage inductive learning, and 5) aid cognitive processing and increase metacognitive awareness (e.g., students become more aware of their individual learning styles).

Teachers must also exercise discernment in choosing the specific computer programmes that they use during their lessons. Many programmes display sophisticated technology, yet lack pedagogical usefulness and depth (Chan LK, 2002). Even though teachers acknowledge that educational software must be judged beyond surface appearances (e.g. graphics, audio, video, images and animations), many teachers are still nonetheless greatly influenced by such factors when selecting computer programmes (Chan LK, 2002). In addition, teachers must determine the authenticity of information found on the internet. This is also an example of how teachers can facilitate ICT-based lessons.

Teachers should also be aware of how they are using the technology, and they must ensure that ICT is not used simply for drill-and-practice. For example, the revised Mathematics syllabus for Singapore primary schools (2001) warns that "care has to be taken to ensure that [IT-based] activities which provide consolidation and practice fundamental skills is not over-emphasised." Instead, ICT activities should engage in real-life problem solving and develop higher-order learning and thinking skills. The National Council of Educational Technology, UK, also suggests that ICT can enhance learning effectiveness and enjoyment only when children have the autonomy to control their learning, explore and experiment, take risks, make mistakes and learn from them, collaborate with friends, share ideas and develop confidence in subject competency. In this way, students will be prepared to adapt to novel situations and will be encouraged to engage in lifelong learning, making them capable of succeeding in this knowledge-based era.

REFERENCES

Adal, J. 2002. *Design factors affecting learner engagement in educational software*. Unpublished Master's Dissertation. Singapore: National Institute of Education (NIE).

Ang, K. H. 1999. *An investigation into the psychological barriers related to teachers' use of computer technology in the school.* Unpublished Master's Dissertation. Singapore: National Institute of Education.

Brink, J. 1994. Applying Mathematics with flight simulators. *Computer Teacher,* 21, 29.

Chan, S. C. 2002. *Evaluation of the motivational aspects of educational software: Is this CD-ROM and website suitable for my audience?* Unpublished Master's Dissertation. Singapore: NIE.

Chan, L. K. 2002. *Beyond drill-and-practice: The use of ICT in enhancing mathematics concept learning.* Unpublished Master's Dissertation. Singapore: NIE.

Chan, W. M., & D. H. Lim. 2004. Towards greater individualization and process-oriented learning through electronic self-access: Project "e-daf". *Computer Assisted Language Learning,* 17(1), 8–108.

Cheang, B., A. Kurnia, A. Lim, & W. C. Oon. 2003. On automated grading of programming assignments in an academic institution. *Computers and Education,* 41, 121–131.

Cheong, H. Y. 2001. *Staff development in using information technology for teaching: The management perspective.* Unpublished Master's Dissertation. Singapore: NIE.

Divaharan, S. 1999. *Impact of Information Technology and constructive learning tools on the learning of written English.* Unpublished Master's Dissertation. Singapore: NIE.

Etheris, A. I. 2002. *Computer-supported collaboration problem solving and anchored instruction in a Mathematics classroom: An exploratory study.* Unpublished Master's Dissertation. Singapore: NIE.

Goh, D. H., R. P. Ang, Y. L. Theng, & E. P. Lim. 2004. GeogDL: A web-based approach to geography examination revision. *Computers and Education* (in press).

Jonnasen, D. H. 1996. *Computers in the classroom: Mindtools for critical thinking.* New Jersey: Prentice-Hall Inc.

Lee, Y. K. 2002. *An evaluation of a secondary school mathematics e-learning project.* Unpublished Master's Dissertation. Singapore: NIE.

Lim, C. P., & C. S. Chai. 2004. An activity-theoretical approach to research of ICT integration in Singapore schools: Orienting activities and learner autonomy. *Computers and Education,* 43, 215–236.

Lim, C. P., & L. Y. Tay. 2003. Information and communication technologies (ICT) in an elementary school: Students' engagement in higher order thinking. *Journal of Educational Multimedia and Hypermedia,* 12(4), 425–451.

National Computer Board. 1992. *IT2000—A vision of an intelligent island.* [Online]. Available: http://www.ncb.gov.sg/ncb/vision.asp.

National Computer Board. 1997. *Singapore ONE: One network for everyone.* [Online]. Available: http://www.ncb.gov.sg/ncb/press/1997/pm.asp, 1997.

Ong, E. T. 2003. *Engineering students' attitudes toward e-learning in a polytechnic.* Unpublished Master's Dissertation. Singapore: NIE.

Ong, S. K., & M. A. Mannan. 2004. Virtual reality simulations and animations in a web-based interactive manufacturing engineering module. *Computers and Education,* 43(4), 361–382.

Pek, M. S. 2003. *Classroom management issues in ICT-based learning environment.* Unpublished Master's Dissertation. Singapore: NIE.

Rahmat, H. 1998. *The impact of computers on teachers: A general computer attitude study of some teachers in Singapore.* Unpublished Master's Dissertation. Singapore: NIE.

Tan-Gibson, R., & T. Miiko. 1997. *A case study of the initial efforts to develop an innovative IT environment in Singapore schools.* Unpublished Master's Dissertation. Singapore: NIE.

Tan-Hoo, J. 1999. IT, modern art and the unseen poem. In *Localising pedagogy: Teaching literature in Singapore.* Edited by S. H. Chua & W. P. Chin. Singapore: NIE.

Teng, L. K. 2000. *The relationship between the nature of the classroom learning environment and relevant attitudes in primary five computer-assisted classrooms.* Unpublished Master's Dissertation. Singapore: NIE.

Wang, P., & P. S. Chan. 1995. Advantages, disadvantages, facilitators, and inhibitors of computer-aided instruction in Singapore's secondary schools. *Computers and Education,* 25(3), 151–162.

Yeo, B. W. 2003. *The effect of exploratory computer-based instruction on secondary four students' learning of exponential and cognitive curves.* Unpublished Master's Dissertation. Singapore: NIE.

Yeo, K. L. 1999. *Managing teacher development to integrate IT into the curriculum.* Unpublished Master's Dissertation. Singapore: NIE.

6

Does Class Size Really Matter?

JULIAN LIM, JOHN HERDBERG,
AND TAN AI GIRL

INTRODUCTION

The argument for class size reduction in Singapore according to our search on Lexis-Nexis using two key terms "class size" and "Singapore" first appeared in the media in 1998, when the *Straits Times* called for the Ministry of Education (MOE) to re-examine its class size policy. In response to the readers' queries, the Director of Personnel from the MOE highlighted that reducing class size was impractical given the recruitment rate of teachers at the time, and that many other factors are determinants of the quality of education a child receives. The vast majority of relevant articles were published in the *Straits Times* within the past four years, indicating a recent surge of public interest in the topic. In particular, a rash of letters in January and February of 2001 prompted a spokesman from the Education Ministry to reinforce the Government's stand at the time, namely that research has not turned up any significant causative relationship between class size and pupil achievement, and positive results to date (e.g., the Student Teacher Achievement Ratio project or project STAR) have shown that the benefit of reductions is minimal unless the reduction is fairly drastic (i.e., to single-digit class sizes). MOE policy is to target weaker students with quality teachers rather than spread these teachers out too thinly. The Learning Support Program is an example of this targeted intervention.

The issue surfaced again in the 2001 Budget Debate and General Election, during which an opposition leader criticised the Singapore education system, and made specific mention of large class sizes. Once again, the rebuttal from the then Education Minister was that a sudden increase in the recruitment of new teachers would lead to a substantial dip in the quality of instruction and a poorer learning experience overall.

In September 2002, the *Straits Times* reported on "mega classes" in a secondary school (lower primary classes with over 60 students in them), and painted these (on the whole) as positive learning experiences. There was one reply to the article speaking against the school's move. The public debate on class size continued with sporadic letters to the press throughout 2003 and 2004, all of which highlighted various benefits of reducing class size (in particular trimming teacher workloads).

In March 2003, the MOE announced its plan to hire 700 new teachers in preparation for reducing primary one and two class sizes and eliminate afternoon session classes for upper primary students. They cited falling enrolment rates and a larger pool of teachers as reasons for this change. On 11 June 2004, the plan was put into action, and starting from 2005, class sizes for primary one and two students will be reduced from 40 to 30. Thus, it can be seen that large class sizes in Singaporean schools have clearly been an area of concern for parents, teachers, and administrators for some time now, with the move to decrease class size at the most elementary levels being the first concrete response to this concern made by the MOE in recent years.

Class size is a quantitative variable that seems, intuitively, as if it should have a significant impact on achievement and behaviour in the classroom. As such, a substantial amount of educational research over the past three decades has focused on how manipulating class size affects varying aspects of teacher and student development. The results of this research have been wide-ranging and controversial. While there are those who see small classes as a panacea for learning-disadvantaged children, there are others who think that the effects of class-size reduction are negligible and not worth the oftentimes-staggering costs incurred.

It is not difficult to understand why the results are so varied. Educational research is not a hard science with variables that can be easily controlled and manipulated. Altering class size leads inevitably to a suite of other changes (Bennett 1998). Teachers adjust their instructional styles; students act differently in different environments. Above all, it must always be remembered that behavioural and sociological studies will never produce results that can be used to make predictions—they can at most offer us recommendations based on statistical certainty.

Learning as a Social Process

The school system does not operate in a vacuum, and the children within it are not blank slates. To provide the best possible environment for children to learn in, therefore, it is necessary for educators to understand the invisible motivators (beyond classroom processes) that drive a child. Culture norms and personal values play a large part in determining what works in the classroom and what is destined for failure. Biggs (1998), for instance, highlights the differences in student mindsets between Western and "Confucian" cultures—in particular that in the latter culture students are brought up to be more obedient and educators more authoritarian. As Singapore is a country that still operates largely within this tradition, great care must be taken in applying the results of research from the West to our local situation.

Children entering primary schools also carry with them the influences of their family—their parents' expectations, hopes, and the moral and ethical codes that have been inculcated in them from young. In the Singaporean society, the expectations of parents, teachers, and elders include among other things that children be brought up to be productive members of society and a contributing citizens of our country. Aside from this, children beginning their academic careers with personal family and social experiences and cannot easily "unlearn" the lessons from home through the rewards and punishments of the educational system alone. Therefore the school needs to function as a social system that acknowledges and understands the individual backgrounds of its pupils before it can proceed to educate them. Teaching in a small class may boost teacher morale and improve their interpersonal interactions with individual students and the class, further promoting academic and social engagement. There are contextual factors to be considered: the family-community environment that the child comes from and whether appropriate space for learning activities exists in school and at home. These factors are important, for instance, bad parenting can be a serious impediment to a child's attitude towards learning, and poor infrastructure can hamper a teacher's ability to give off her best. Such obstacles can prevent optimal outcomes from being realised even after class sizes are reduced. (Finn, Pannozzo & Achilles 2003)

CLASS SIZE RESEARCH: SOME LESSONS

One concern among class-size researchers is the long-standing confusion between the terms "class size" and "pupil-teacher ratio" (PTR). The two terms are *not* interchangeable; for example, schools may keep class size smaller by increasing teacher workload (which does not change PTR), or by hiring more teachers (which does). For the purposes of this report, we will concern ourselves with class size *only*, since it is this variable that has the stronger positive effect on learning outcomes (Achilles & Nye 1998). In this chapter, reflectively, we elaborate only on the major class size findings in the international research literature with a focus on the three propositions; these are class size and achievement, class size and pedagogical strategies and class size and students at risks.

Class Size and Achievement

One of the chief motivations for manipulating class size is to improve student academic outcomes. As such, student test scores have been the dependent measure on most major class size studies to date. Here, we present the highlights of what research has to say on the subject of the impact of class size on achievement.

The Student Teacher Achievement Ratio project or the Project STAR was a four-year, experimental study conducted statewide in Tennessee. This was one of the most comprehensive, large-scale studies of its kind, and is held up by many researchers as the gold standard of class-size experimentation. In it, more than 7,000 students were randomly assigned to one of three conditions: *small class* (13 to 17 students per teacher), *regular class* (22 to 25 students per teacher) and *regular-with-aide class* (22 to 25 students with a full-time teacher aide). (The average class size in the USA as of 2002 was 22 students (Heritage Foundation 2002). The study began when the students entered kindergarten and followed them subsequently through grades one, two and three.

The results of Project STAR (Word, Johnston, Bain, Fulton, Zaharias, Lintz, Achilles, Folger & Breda 1990; Mosteller, Sachs & Jason 1996; Reichardt 2001) convincingly suggest that being in a small class significantly enhances a student's academic achievement and development. At the end of grade one, students in small classes outperformed students in regular and regular/aide classes, and students in regular classes with a full-time teacher aide outperformed students in regular classes in reading and mathematics achievement. This result was both significant and meaningful. Many educationists cite the STAR outcomes as strong evidence supporting the long-held notion that class size should be reduced preferentially in the early grades (kindergarten and grade one) (Biddle & Berliner 2002). The earlier in their academic career students are placed in small classes, the greater the potential for a positive impact on their achievement (Finn, Gerbre, Achilles & Boyd-Zaharias 2001).

Follow-up studies indicate that after the conclusion of Project STAR, enduring benefits for children were found right through to Grade 9 (Nye, Hedges & Konstantopoulos 2001a). Thus, students in small classes in the early grades not only learned more, but also continued to have an advantage over the rest of their peers, showing that small class benefits do not disappear over time.

In a subsequent paper, Nye, Hedges and Konstantopoulos (2001b) took a different statistical approach to analysing the STAR data, holding achievement in previous grades at *each grade level* constant. Using this method, the researchers found that the positive effect of being in a small class was *still* statistically significant for *every* grade level (Nye, Hedges & Konstantopoulos 2001b), suggesting that the effects of being in a small class are cumulative. This point is reiterated by Finn, Gerbre, Achilles and Boyd-Zaharias (2001), who note that positive effects increase with each additional year in a small class.

The current class size reduction initiative in Singapore may be more effective if extended by several years, into the upper primary levels. As moving into a larger class from a smaller one in primary three may have a *detrimental* effect on student outcomes (our own projection and speculation), this matter should take on even more urgency.

Peter Blatchford, a forerunner in United Kingdom class size experiments, pioneered a recently concluded longitudinal study in his country of nearly 10,000 children in two cohorts. This study, which ran until 2003, dealt with many facets of the class size issue, including pupil and teacher behaviour, social development, peer relations, and within-class grouping.

The early motivation behind Blatchford's studies was to discover the *links* between class size and their apparent effects of academic attainment in order to tease apart the mechanisms underlying these gains. In an early paper, he identified the following possible links, namely, that in small classes there is more individual attention and more individualized teaching, high quality of teaching, richer coverage of curriculum, increased pupil attention, better teacher control and less time spent disciplining students, more time for teachers to prepare for classes, increased student and teacher morale, and better pupil-pupil relations (Blatchford & Martin 1998).

In subsequent papers, Blatchford expanded on these topics. His elaborations are summarised below.

Classroom dynamics: There were significant differences between the quality of teacher-pupil and pupil-pupil interactions in small and large classes (Blatchford 2003). In small classes:

- Teacher-child contacts were found to be more frequent/ personalised.
- Children were more likely to be on-task, although they interacted less extensively with their peers.
- Children were more likely to interact with their teachers on a one-to-one basis.
- Children experienced more teaching overall. There was more task-related talk, and more social talk to teachers.
- There was about twice as much teacher "task preparation."
- There was less child-child contact, both on and off-task.

Pupil attentiveness: Children tend to be more attentive in smaller classes. This is mostly the case because those in large classes are more likely to engage in peer interaction, which distracts them from on-task work (Blatchford, Edmonds & Martin 2003). Smaller classes also offer more opportunities for student participation, which in turn encourages pupils to focus their attention on the lesson (Blatchford & Martin 1998)

Social development: Academic achievement is not the sole measure of the success of education. Young children must be taught social skills and norms in order that they may function at higher levels of school and in society at large. The first two years of primary school are an important transition period, and must be the time in which the foundations of this social education are established. Blatchford, Edmonds and Martin (2003) suggest that smaller classes help with this adjustment, since teachers find it easier to manage disruptive children and draw out quiet ones in smaller settings. In general, the quality of relationships between children in smaller classes tends to be higher (Smith, Molnar & Zahorik 1989), and this is especially true of elementary school pupils.

Somewhat surprisingly, the UK longitudinal studies fail to confirm this hypothesis. In an analysis of pupil behaviour ratings (PBRs) by class teachers, there was no evidence that peer relations were better in smaller classes. In actual fact, there was a slight tendency for peer relations to be *worst* in the smallest classes (Blatchford, Edmonds & Martin 2003), with students in these classes most likely to be aggressive, asocial, or excluded.

The authors propose two possible reasons for this anomaly:

- In smaller classes, teachers may have a clearer picture of their children and are thus more aware of their antisocial tendencies.
- Children in smaller classes may grow overly reliant on their teacher and thus be less capable in learning from (and interacting with) each other—stunting their social development and promoting antisocial/excluded behaviour.

It is therefore possible that there exists a *trade-off* between social development and academic achievement as class size changes.

Teacher morale: Finally, an important point that runs in an undercurrent through all of the class size literature is that small classes bring about important intangible benefits in terms of teacher morale (Blatchford, Baines, Kutnick & Martin 2001, 1998; Blatchford & Martin 1998; Slavin 1989). Those who teach in smaller classes have a lighter workload and less negative interaction in the classroom, thus lowering their stress and raising their enthusiasm for the job. In general, boosting teacher morale will lead to better performance at work, and a higher quality of teaching, and this is a factor worth considering when contemplating class-size reduction as policy.

Direct evidence that class size is perceived as an important educational issue comes from a survey by Bennett carried out in 1996. This survey aimed to uncover the perceptions of teachers (411), head teachers (160), parents (1,264) and administrators (100) of how class size affects educational processes and outcomes. When these groups were asked about optimum size of primary school classes, the response ranged from 18–28 (with the mean centred around 22–23). All groups believed that class size was an important factor that has a strong effect on the quality of teaching and learning. Among teachers, 84 per cent thought that it was the most important issue, and 82 per cent said that they would change their classroom practices if class sizes were smaller (e.g., by providing more individual attention, reorganising the classroom, doing more group work etc.) There was a concern among both administrators and teachers that the government would raise the maximum class size because of the bottom line.

How Small is Small?

When tackling the issue of class size, we must first be sure of how we define our terms. "Small" is relative, and different countries may have dissimilar ideas of what a "small" class really is. Project STAR, for example, defined a small class as one with 13–17 students in it—this size would be normal for countries like Luxembourg (mean class size 15.8) or Iceland (17.3) (OECD, 2003). On the other hand, in Singapore, decreasing class size to below 30 in primary and secondary schools would already be a significant reduction from current numbers.

Although most experimental studies have shown that reductions only have a significant effect when class size dips to 15, it is also important to note that relative changes may be as important as absolute ones. Jin and Cortazzi (1998) bring up the point that when comparing Asian and Western cultures, teachers' perceptions of class sizes varied depending on the size of their largest class. The greater this maximum size was, the larger the number that teachers cited as an ideal class size, and the larger a class had to be before they deemed it problematic. Pupils also have different perceptions of what a "normal" class size is depending on the expectations and norms they have been brought up to accept.

A minor but valid point that many class size researchers make is that the holy grail of an "optimum" class size probably does not exist—or if there does, it is likely to be one (Slavin 1989). Preece's (1987) theoretical model of class size versus learning deficits corroborates this fact, as do researchers like Blatchford and Mortimore (1994) who espouse the effectiveness of peer tutoring (which effectively sets up a class of one) as a learning strategy for pupils. We discuss the merits and drawbacks of one-on-one tutoring in a subsequent chapter of this report.

Counter-evidence

Not all researchers see promise in the evidence that being in a small class bolsters students' academic achievement. Prais (1996) argues that the effects of the Project STAR studies are negligible when *relative* as opposed to *absolute* changes in students' performance are considered. Moreover, he claims that the gains that manifest themselves by changing other aspects of education (e.g., improving teaching methods/materials) are far greater, and these should be pursued as a first-line option.

Other findings also indicate that small classes might not be as beneficial as the literature might suggest. In particular, the few studies that have been conducted in Asian school systems appear to be in staunch opposition to the opinions and results obtained by the West.

As an example, Pong and Pallas (2001) set out to examine the relationship between class size and mathematics achievement in nine countries (Australia, Canada, France, Germany, Hong Kong, Iceland, Singapore, the USA and South Korea) using a cross-sectional design. They found that beneficial effects of small classes were seen *only* in the United States, and in contrast, countries such as Australia, France, Germany and Hong Kong showed higher achievement levels in *larger* classes. Even after controlling for non-random assignment of students, those in larger mathematics classes in Hong Kong and Singapore still outperformed their counterparts in smaller classes. Furthermore, there was no linear relationship between class size and mathematics achievement in any of the countries studied. As a caveat, however, it should be noted that this analysis was conducted using data from the TIMSS (Third International Maths and Science Study), meaning that it was both *post hoc* and correlational.

Other papers written on class size in Asia include Jin and Cortazzi's (1998) review on how talk and culture mediate learning in large classes in China. The authors develop this idea with reference to current attempts to reduce class size in countries such as Britain. They argue that large classes are successful in China because of interactive techniques in classroom dialogue and the underlying Confucian culture of learning. Chinese pupils have a more cognitive-centred, learner-listening approach as compared to the more skill-centred, learner-talking communicative approach of Western students. This increases learner responsibility rather than fostering dependence on the teacher.

In the same paper, Jin and Cortazzi discuss the differing perceptions of teachers and students in Western and Confucian society (1998). Good Chinese teachers are thought to have deep knowledge and answers are held up as moral examples; good British teachers are seen more as arousing students' interest, explaining clearly, and organising activities. Correspondingly, good Chinese students study independently, develop independent thinking, prepare for classes, and respect the teacher while good British students merely pay attention and obey. These cultural differences may well account for the variations observed when international comparisons of class size and academic achievement are carried out, since the values of the good Chinese student make him well suited to cope with education in a large class (Pong & Pallas 2001; Wößmann & West 2002).

Thus, while most of the available literature states that smaller classes help students perform better academically, it is vital in policy-making that the approach taken by Singapore is not unconsciously shaped by norms and expectations which are culturally different from our own, as this may lead to detrimental effects instead of benefits.

We must also emphasise once more that most investigators of class size define a large class size as containing around 26 students and a small class size as one with about 15 students. There is a dearth of literature on the dynamics of classes of other sizes, and as such, further investigation into the matter is required. The recent local reduction of primary one and two classes from 40 to 30 may serve as a chance to test certain new hypotheses, and we recommend that the MOE grasps this opportunity to broaden our understanding on this important issue.

Group Size

We conducted a search of the literature using key terms such as group size and learning, teaching, and dynamics. Our search uncovered numerous articles that are useful justifications for keeping class sizes large but dividing them into groups for certain types of activities.

First of all, it should be noted that there is a general relationship between class- and group size. As class size increases, the number of within-class groups also increases until a threshold is reached—following which *group size* increases (with the number of groups staying the same) (Blatchford & Martin 1998). This is because there is a critical number of groups (usually four or five) that teachers can handle before the classroom situation becomes unmanageable.

Experimentally, there is convincing evidence that within-class group size may be as important as class size *per se* in affecting learning outcomes. Lou, Abrami and d'Apollonia (1996) conducted a meta-analysis on 145 studies in order to discover which students benefit the most from instruction in small groups. The authors noted that there was great variability in the magnitude of group size effects, and aimed to unearth the underlying trends by controlling for factors that varied across the studies. Within-class grouping was seen to be more effective in improving achievement in certain subjects, in particular math and science. More importantly, the results of the analysis strongly support the proposition that students in *large classes* benefit *more* than those in small ones from being arranged in groups. The precise reasons for this impact are discussed in the later section on class size and pedagogy.

In one of the smaller experiments within his longitudinal study, Blatchford, Baines, Kutnick and Martin (2001) discovered that within-class group size plays a large role in influencing classroom dynamics. In a sub-sample of students (n = 3157), the average group size across the three grade levels observed (reception year, year one and year two) was just over five; groups in classes with *older* children were significantly smaller, despite the fact that *class size* was smaller for reception year and year two. Furthermore, children in classes of >25 students were more likely to be in a group of 7–10; those in classes of <25 students were more likely to be in a group of 11+.

Blatchford, Baines, Kutnick and Martin (2001) found that being in a larger group at the primary levels was detrimental to learning and academic attainment. He observed (and confirmed quantitatively) that pupils in large groups were much less likely to work together. This result corroborates that of Moody, Bausell and Jenkins (1974), who also concluded that group size has a considerable effect on learning, citing similar reasons as Blatchford's.

As part of the same study (Blatchford, Baines, Kutnick & Martin 2001), a survey of teachers uncovered their opinions that bigger groups affect the quality and amount of teaching they could do, the quality of children's work, children's contribution to the class, and their overall level of concentration. The dilemma for teachers, however, is that many small groups are much harder to manage than fewer large ones, thus there is a trade-off between the quality of learning and overall classroom discipline.

If a class is to be split up into small groups, the next logical question is what size these groups should be. Unfortunately, in the same way that it is nearly impossible to determine what optimum class size is, optimum within-class group size is also extremely hard to ascertain. Blatchford, Baines, Kutnick and Martin (2001) suggest (from observation) that 4–6 students is, in fact this optimum number, and certainly, groups larger than that do produce the negative repercussions mentioned above. Woods (1994) also asserts that groups or 5–6 are ideal when members are engaged in problem-based learning.

A quantitative experiment conducted by Sindelar, Rosenberg, Wilson and Bursuck (1984) more clearly illustrates the trend of how achievement varies with group size, as well as how it interacts with the mode of instruction. In this study, teachers had to cover five objectives in a 15-minute mathematics lesson under four conditions: lesson-only, lesson plus teacher-led follow-up, lesson plus independent follow-up and supervised seatwork follow-up. Groups of one, three and six children were allocated to each of these conditions. In terms of achievement, mean scores for the children taught individually were the highest across the board (a result successfully replicated by Lou, Abrami & d'Apollonia, 2001), and there was no significant difference in the scores of children placed in groups of three and six.

Although the obvious conclusion from this study is that children learn better when given individual instruction than in larger groups, another important message is that *there is no negative impact on learning outcomes when group sizes are doubled from three to six*. This has important implications for the Singaporean classroom. In effect, a class of 15 split into five groups of three should function *as well as* a class of 30 split into five groups of six (although, of course, issues of discipline, diversity of student achievement and so forth would be more significant in the larger class). However, given that classes cannot be efficiently managed if more than five groups exist in the class, a teacher with a class of more than 30 students in it *cannot profitably make use of small-group learning*. This is a clear justification for reducing class sizes from 40 to 30, even though there is no literature documenting in a direct way how this change might be beneficial.

Thus, we are now more confident in asserting that appropriate grouping practices can counterbalance the negative effects that Singaporean students may experience from studying in (relatively) large classes of 30 or so students. Moreover, this finding has important implications for alternative pedagogical methods, which can be just as important, if not more so, than the manipulation of class size on its own. We now proceed to discuss the possible impacts group seating may have on classroom teaching methods, and how pedagogy must change along with this physical rearrangement.

CLASS SIZE AND PEDAGOGICAL STRATEGIES

Class size and organisational changes are insufficient in and of themselves to affect learning outcomes. In tandem with these reforms, teachers must be able to tailor their instruction to their new situation in order to fully exploit the benefit of small classes or classes in small groups. In the following section, we aim to provide a synopsis of some of these revised pedagogical strategies which may be useful in local classrooms.

Group Size and Pedagogy

The new 30-student primary one and two classes provide teachers with increased opportunities to divide their classes into small groups. Small group instruction is valuable in numerous ways. Not only does it allow the teacher to individuate instruction, it also allows for cooperative and collaborative learning among students. This in turn encourages students to be more actively engaged in their lessons. Being in a small group may also promote achievement because it maximises opportunities for students and teachers to interact (Sindelar, Rosenberg, Wilson & Bursuck 1984) (which is in stark contrast to the current over-reliance on whole class teaching).

If teachers are to fully utilise this new and powerful tool, they must know how best to teach and organise their classes. It is *not* an effective strategy, for example, to rely on a fixed arrangement of grouped furniture in the classroom to physically separate students into clusters (Hastings & Wood 2002). Although this *does* facilitate teaching, allow ability grouping, and promote collaborative learning within a classroom, the method is also far too inflexible for the changing needs students have over the course of a day. The effectiveness of group work is highly dependent upon the nature of the task or activity at hand. Collaborative learning is an unsuitable method for many lessons in our current curriculum, thus, there must be "strategic flexibility" (Hastings & Wood 2002) in the way that teachers deploy their in-class groups. They should call for children to arrange themselves into groups when a task demands it, and not have clusters of furniture as permanent fixtures within the room.

Types of Groups

Even after teachers decide on assigning children to small groups for an activity, there are still decisions to be made on the kind of groups that ought to be created. In a review article on the subject, Mosteller, Sachs and Jason (1996) summarise the types of *skill groups* that can be created in schools. They are, in brief heterogeneous groups (high achievers with low achievers) within grades, homogeneous groups (same-ability students together) within grades (XYZ skill groups), homogeneous groups across grades (cross-grade groups), homogeneous groups within classes (within-class groups), and heterogeneous groups within classes (project teams).

There is conflicting evidence and opinion in the literature as to which of these groups is most effective (or if this kind of grouping is an effective practice at all). Moreover, there are few studies in general that explore this topic, and many of these studies are doctoral dissertations written on poorly funded, small-scale studies. The results that are available are summarised below.

Heterogeneous vs. homogeneous groups within grades/classes: For the purposes of this review, we do not make a distinction between groups within grades and classes (particularly since the results are almost identical anyway). Leonard (2001) conducted a study to examine how to whether homogeneous or heterogeneous groups are better in maximising students' learning potential. He found that low-achieving and middle-achieving students performed better in heterogeneous groups than in homogeneous groups. For high-achievers, there was no difference in performance between the two conditions. This study confirmed the findings of a very similar experiment that was carried out in Israeli junior high schools (Linchevski & Kutscher 1998).

Mosteller, Sachs and Jason's (1996) meta-analysis of the subject, however, yielded slightly different results. Over the ten studies considered, the authors concluded that there was a slight positive effect for high achievers in homogenous groups as opposed to heterogeneous groups, suggesting that these high-skilled students get "held back" when grouped with their weaker counterparts. They agree that low- and medium achievers suffer when assigned to homogeneous skill groups. Adding to the controversy, Lou et al. (1996) found that *medium*-achievers benefit more in homogeneous groups (although it must be added that this may be a problem of definitions rather than an actual artefact of their experiment). Although the results are disparate, we would like to emphasise that the latter studies (Lou, Abrami, Spence, Pouslen, Chambers & d'Apollonia 1996; Mosteller, Sachs & Jason 1996) have greater credence, since they are meta-analyses of numerous group composition experiments. It is extremely likely, both from the results and our intuition, that high-skilled students would prefer, and perform better in homogeneous groups, and that there *is* a drawback to assigning to them to mixed-ability groups.

Homogeneous groups across grades: Another alternative for educators is to form groups outside the bounds of the class. This arrangement bears some resemblance to pull-out programs (e.g., for reading), but on a wider scale. Experiments on cross-grade, homogeneous groups (otherwise known as Joplin groups) are extremely scarce, but these have found that such groups may have substantial benefits for all children (Hillson, Jones, Moore & Van Devender 1964; Morgan & Stucker 1960).

On the far end of the scale, a minority of researchers is of the opinion that forming traditional skill groups in the class has almost no effect on learning at all (Slavin 1993). These researchers believe that other alternative pedagogies (e.g., peer tutoring) are far more useful in improving achievement outcomes.

Academic improvements aside, Mosteller, Sachs and Jason (1996) stress that there are important non-cognitive gains to be accrued in creating between-class skill groups. These include improving students' metacognitive ability, their attitudes towards group learning, as well as their levels of participation. Skill-grouped students tend to score higher in self-reports, both on how much they enjoy school as well as how much they perceive themselves as learning (Marascuilo & McSweeney 1972). Teachers, too, report that skill-grouped classes are easier to teach and more facilitative for learning (Barton 1964; Lovell 1960; Peterson 1966).

Two issues arise from these findings. First is the issue of *equity*. As we have stressed, homogeneous groups tend to benefit higher achievers (who do not have to spend time guiding their weaker peers, and who might feel bored because of the slower pace of learning), whereas heterogeneous groups benefit slower learners (Mosteller, Sachs & Jason 1996). Moreover, dividing a class into homogeneous groups also tends to sort students according to SES and ethnicity. If small-group teaching is adopted in the classroom, teachers must make an ethical choice as to how they want to allocate students to these groups (or possibly reassign groups depending on activities or lesson aims). Second, teachers need to be sensitive to the needs of individual students and flexible in how they group them if conflicts in the classroom should arise. Grouping students does not always work, and doggedly following this practice may be counterproductive in a classroom where it is not appropriate.

Small Group Instruction

When using small-group instruction, teachers must decide which particular methods of instruction are most beneficial for their particular subject area. The effects of small group learning are significantly enhanced when the right methods are used for this instruction (Lou, Abrami & d'Apollonia 2001). Some of these strategies include:

- *Think-pair-share* (Lyman 1981): Question/discussion issue posed during a lecture, individuals think about it, adjacent pairs made to discuss, and some pairs share their answer. The benefits of this method include greater student involvement and allowing the teacher to assess how well the lesson is getting across on the spot.
- The *Minute Paper* (Wilson 1986): Involves having students answer two questions in the last one to three minutes of class (e.g., What was the most important thing you learned in this class?").
- *Cooperative Learning:* Small groups of three to five students work together on activities carefully designed to promote positive interdependence as well as individual accountability (Abrami, Chambers, Poulsen, de Simone, d'Apollonia & Howden 1995). Students are rewarded for the group's performance and not individual performance. This strategy has been shown to be more effective than other small-group instruction methods where students are not positively interdependent (Lou, Abrami, Spence, Pouslen, Chambers & d'Apollonia 2000).
- *Teacher-led follow-up:* In a study conducted by Sindelar, Rosenberg, Wilson and Bursuck (1984) where students were placed in three conditions: (A) lesson-only, (B) lesson and teacher-led follow-up and (C) lesson and supervised seatwork follow-up. There were three group sizes in each condition: one, three and six children. Findings indicate that children under condition (C) were, on average, more attentive. At group size one, findings suggest that a teacher-led follow-up is more beneficial to students' performance than no follow-up or supervised seatwork. Having supervised seatwork also results in significantly higher scores than having no follow-up at all.

165

Learning Tasks and Class Size

From the studies quoted above, it would appear that small group experiences are great facilitators of learning in the classroom. However, these experiences cannot take up the entirety of a student's time in the classroom, as the arrangement is not suitable for many academic activities. For instance, a survey of teachers in the UK revealed that certain exercises (e.g., physical education classes) were in fact facilitated by having larger numbers (Charlton & Bullivant 2000). Given that class size in Singapore is likely to remain at around 30, teachers must also be provided with the pedagogical skills to cope with classes of this size. Listed below are brief summaries of three useful methods for teaching in large classes. For a more detailed look at these alternative pedagogies, we refer you to the later section of this report that is so titled.

Problem-based learning (PBL): PBL is a method of group learning that uses true-to-life problems as a stimulus for students to learn problem-solving skills and acquire knowledge. PBL experts recommend groups of five to six learners, and preferably less than nine (Woods 1994). Students benefit because of increased autonomous learning, and the development of critical thinking, problem-solving and communication skills (Morales-Mann & Kaitell 2001).

Scaffolding: This teaching strategy involves the following:

*   Recruitment of an adult of a child's involvement in meaningful and culturally desirable activity beyond the child's current understanding or control.
*   Titration of assistance provided by the adult during interaction, i.e., a process of "online" diagnosis of the child's understanding and/or skill level, together with careful calibration of the support provided to help him or her accomplish the goal or sub goal.
*   Provision of a range of types of support, depending on the nature of the task; this might include nonverbal assistance, or extensive dialogue.
*   Gradual withdrawal of the support the adult provides, so that there is a transfer of responsibility from adult to child.

Use of technology: Many present-day educationists espouse computer-based learning as a means of catering to the needs of large classes, especially when students in these classes have different achievement levels and progress rates. Providing children with computers in the classroom allows for individual and group-based learning to proceed simultaneously (Roth 1999). It allows children to proceed at their own pace, to have access to tailored instruction at any time (even at home), and provides opportunities for integrated learning that can consist of seeking solutions for real-life problems (Roth 1999).

In a meta-analysis, Lou, Abrami and d'Apollonia (2001) found that when students used computer technology in the classroom, small group learning had significantly more positive effects than individual learning on individual student achievement, as well as a moderate positive effect on group task performance. Historically, the most common instructional strategy has been to have one computer to each student (Skinner 1961); however, these results suggest that when working with Computer Technology (CT) in small groups, students in general gain more individual knowledge, and produce substantially better group products than individual products.

In particular, when using CT, students learned more working in pairs than in three to five member groups (Lou, Abrami & d'Apollonia 2001). This finding appears contradictory to previous within-class grouping research where the optimal group size was larger (Lou et al. 1996). However, this inconsistency may be due to the physical constraints associated with computer use.

Kassner (2000) highlights other possibilities for structuring a class during computer-aided instruction. He brings up the "single-computer concept), where only one computer is used by the entire class, either by allowing the teacher to operate the software, or through rotating students through "learning stations," the computer activity being just one of these.

In summary, it is vital that teachers are well equipped and knowledgeable in using these and other strategies, both for teaching small groups as well as handling large classes as a whole.

CLASS SIZE AND STUDENTS AT RISK

In the class size literature, there is modest though by no means definitive evidence that academically weaker students benefit more from being in small classes than normal learners. We hasten to point out that this evidence does not have any bearing on *learning-disabled* children, who in developed countries are typically given special instruction in extremely small classes (usually five students or fewer). "Academically weak" students have nothing intrinsically or psychologically wrong with them, rather, they lack the skills or motivation to fulfil their academic potential.

Supporting the notion that these weaker students should be in smaller classes is the Wisconsin Student Achievement Guarantee in Education (SAGE) study (Smith, McMillan, Kennedy & Ratcliffe 2003). SAGE set out to improve the academic achievement of low-income students (who are typically most at risk of failure) through a number of structural educational reforms. These reforms included setting up schoolhouses that were open for longer hours than the normal school day, developing more rigorous curricula, and setting up programs to develop the skills of school professionals. A comparison between SAGE students and students from a control group showed significant differences in their achievement both during and after the experiment. SAGE first graders performed 25–30 per cent better on reading, language arts and mathematics subjects of the Comprehensive Test of Basic Skills (CTBS) at the end of their first year, and maintained that difference throughout the course of the program. The effects were found to be especially powerful in narrowing the achievement gap between African Americans and their white classmates (and between the disadvantaged and normal children in general) (Smith et al. 2003).

The results of this experiment are highly credible; the study was well controlled and had a large sample size (21 school districts). However, this does not mean that they are immediately applicable to our local context. The authors of this study identified students at risk by considering exogenous factors (socio-economic status, ethnicity), and not their achievement *per se*; thus, it is unclear whether there is a direct link between small class size and improved performance from the academically weak.

Surprisingly, Project STAR, the large-scale Tennessee study, completely failed to confirm the hypothesis that being in a small class is a boon to slower learners. Repeated measures analyses on the STAR data suggested no statistically reliable pattern of differential effects of small classes on both median and very-low achievement students, when pooled across grades (Nye, Hedges & Konstantopoulos 2002). From this result, the principal researchers concluded that small classes are not enough to close achievement gaps between the very low and higher achieving students in reading or math achievement.

One possible reason for this finding is that classes *smaller* than 13 may be needed before weaker students show signs of improvement (recall that the STAR study involved small classes of 13–17 students). Otherwise, it could be that teachers of small classes must be trained in alternative teaching methods before the class size reduction shows its effects (see previous section). Thus, while the STAR results are discouraging in this respect, this analysis is by no means the final word on the subject.

Finally, the UK longitudinal studies revealed some evidence that "disadvantaged" students benefit more from being in small classes. However, the trend was not very strong and disappeared completely in classes of over 28 students (Blatchford, Goldstein, Martin & Browne 2002).

All in all, the data do not support the reduction of class size based on academic performance alone; it appears, in fact, that allocating some *small-group* time to weaker children is, in fact, more effective than placing them in marginally smaller classes (where they stay put throughout the school day). The LSP currently available to primary one and two students who do not possess a high-enough level of English literacy, is already effective in fulfilling this niche. Two independent projects from graduate students in Singapore have confirmed the success of this intervention (Ang 2002; Yang 2004).

Thus, we would *not* recommend class-size reductions below 30 based on the needs of the academically weak. A more economically sound solution may be to extend the LSP to the upper primary levels (and possibly beyond) so that students who require more individual and personalised attention can be given the help they need.

CONCLUSIONS

The relationship that exists between class size and academic achievement remains a contentious issue, especially since academic achievement should not be our only concern. It is crucial that students' social, behavioural, and personal developments are taken into account. That said, there is no way a small class in itself will bring about better academic achievement; other factors such as teaching style and forms of assessment contribute as well.

However, based on the findings so far, we reiterate that being in a small class is most crucial for early primary school students, and that there are lasting benefits for keeping these children in small classes up till primary three or four. As there is no existing research to support the implementation of small class size locally, there remains a need for a study to be put in place here. Moreover, in future studies, it is imperative that we look not only at student outcomes, but teacher outcomes as well.

The findings about students-at-risk illustrate that there is no advantage for them to be put in smaller classes. Rather, implementation of withdrawal teaching programmes such as the LSP has been shown to be promising. Longitudinal efficacy studies can be carried out to examine the benefits of such programmes.

In lieu of reducing class size, the MOE may consider altering the way in which large classes are managed and taught. One possibility is to encourage teachers to divide classes into groups of 4–6 students—a technique which has proven to increase attentiveness and enthusiasm in students towards their work. Research is not clear on whether arranging for homogeneous or heterogeneous groups is in the interest of educators, and the decision is ultimately an ethical one —do teachers want to help weak students or encourage the strong? Besides group work, other pedagogical strategies such as PBL, scaffolding, and computer-aided instruction should also be considered.

Finally, as studies have shown, and as many well-known specialists in education have pointed out, class size effects are largely related to the culture and norms of the country. The bulk of class size research has come from the western world; consequently, careful thought must be applied before drastic class size changes are implemented in Singapore.

REFERENCES*

Abrami, P. C., B. Chambers, C. Poulsen, C. De Simone, S. d'Apollonia, & J. Howden. 1995. *Classroom connections: Understanding and using cooperative learning.* Toronto, Ontario: Harcourt Brace.

Achilles, C. M., & B. A. Nye. 1998. Attempting to understand the class size and pupil-teacher ratio (PTR) confusion: a pilot study. Paper presented at AASA Conference Within A Convention in San Diego, CA.

Ang, M. K. 2002. *Effectiveness of primary 2 learning support programme (English) in a neighbourhood primary school in Singapore.* Unpublished Masters Dissertation, National Institute of Education, Nanyang Technological University, Singapore.

Barton, D. P. 1964. *An evaluation of ability grouping in ninth grade English.* Unpublished doctoral dissertation, Brigham Young University, Hawaii.

Bennett, N. 1996. Class size in primary schools: perceptions of headteachers, chairs of governors, teachers and parents. *British Educational Research Journal*, 22(1), 33–55.

Bennett, N. 1998. Annotation: class size and the quality of educational outcomes. *J. Child Psychology & Psychiatry*. 39(6), 797–804.

Biddle, B. J., & D. C. Berliner. 2002. Small class size and its effects. *Educational Leadership*, 59(5), 12–23.

Biggs, J. 1998. Learning from the Confucian heritage: so size doesn't matter? *International Journal of Educational Research.* *29*, 723–738.

Blatchford, P. 2003. A systematic observational study of teachers' and pupils' behaviour in large and small classes. *Learning and Instruction, 13*, 569–595.

Blatchford, P., & C. Martin. 1998. The effects of class size on classroom processes: 'It's a bit like a treadmill—working hard and getting nowhere fast!' *British J. of Educational Studies, 46(2)*, 118–137.

Blatchford, P., & P. Mortimore. 1994. The issue of class size from young children in schools: what can we learn from research? *Oxford Review of Education, 20(4)*, 411–428.

Blatchford, P., E. Baines, P. Kutnick, & C. Martin. 2001. Classroom contexts: connections between class size and within class grouping. *British Journal of Educational Psychology, 71*, 283–302.

Blatchford, P., H. Goldstein, C. Martin, & W. Browne. 2002. A study of class size effects in English school reception year classes. *British Educational Research Journal, 28(2)*, 169–176.

Blatchford, P., S. Edmonds, & C. Martin. 2003. Class size, pupil attentiveness and peer relations. *British J. of Educational Psych, 73*, 15–36.

Charlton, T., & R. Bullivant. 2000. Teachers' perceptions of the impact of class size on specific curriculum activities. *Education 3–13, 28(2)*, 46–51.

Finn, B. A., S. B. Gerbre, C. M. Achilles, & J. Boyd-Zaharias. 2001. The enduring effect of small classes. *Teachers College Record, 103(2)*, 145–183.

Finn, J. D., G. M. Pannozzo, & C. M. Achilles. 2003. The "why's" of class size: student behaviour in small classes. *Review of Educational Research. 73(3)*, 321–368.

Hastings, N., & K. C. Wood. 2002. Group seating in primary schools: an indefensible strategy? Paper presented at the Annual Conference of the British Educational Research Association, University of Exeter, 12–14 September 2002 in England.

Hillson, M., J. C. Jones, J. W. Moore, & F. Van Devender. 1964. A controlled experiment evaluating the effects of a non-graded organization on pupil achievement. *Journal of Educational Research, 57*, 548–550.

Jin, L., & M. Cortazzi. 1998. Dimensions of dialogue: large classes in China. *International Journal of Educational Research, 29*, 739–761.

Kassner, K. 2000. One computer "can" deliver whole-class instruction. *Music Educators Journal, 86(6)*, 34–40.

Leonard, J. 2001. How group composition influenced the achievement of sixth-grade mathematics students. *Mathematical Thinking and Learning, 3(2&3)*, 175–200.

Linchevski, L., & B. Kutscher. 1998. Tell me with whom you're learning, and I'll tell you how much you've learned: Mixed-ability versus same-ability grouping in mathematics. *Journal for Research in Mathematics Education, 29*, 533–554.

Lou, Y., P. C. Abrami, J. C. Spence, C. Pouslen, B. Chambers, & S. d'Apollonia. 1996. Within-class grouping: a meta-analysis. *Review of Educational Research, 66(4)*, 423–458.

Lou, Y., P. C. Abrami, & S. d'Apollonia. 2001. Small group and individual learning with technology: A meta-analysis. *Review of Educational Research, 71(3)*, 449–521.

171

Lovell, J. T. 1960. The Bay high school experiment. *Educational Leadership, 17,* 383–387.

Lyman, F. 1981. "The responsive class discussion." In *Mainstreaming Digest.* Edited by S. E. Anderson. College Park: College of Education, University of Maryland.

Marascuilo, L. A., & M. McSweeney. 1972. Tracking and minority student attitudes and performance. *Urban Education, 6,* 303–319.

Moody, W. B., R. B. Bausell, & J. R. Jenkins. 1974. The effect of class size on the learning of mathematics: a parametric study with fourth-grade students. *Journal for Research in Mathematics Education, 4,* 170–176.

Morgan, E. F. Jr., & G. R. Stucker. 1960. The Joplin Plan of reading vs. a traditional method. *Journal of Educational Psychology, 51,* 69–73.

Mosteller, F. L., R. J. Sachs, & A. Jason. 1996. Sustained inquiry in education: Lessons from skill grouping and class size. *Harvard Educational Review, 66(4),* 797–842.

Nye, B., L. V. Hedges, & S. Konstantopoulos. 2001a. The long-term effects of small classes in early grades: Lasting benefits in mathematics achievement at Grade 9. *The Journal of Experimental Education, 69(3),* 245–257.

Nye, B., L. V. Hedges, & S. Konstantopoulos. 2001b. Are effects of small classes cumulative? Evidence from a Tennessee experiment. *The Journal of Educational Research, 94(6),* 336–345.

Nye, B., L. V. Hedges, & S. Konstantopoulos. 2002. Do low-achieving students benefit more from small classes? Evidence from the Tennessee Class Size Experiment. *Educational Evaluation and Policy Analysis, 24(3),* 201–217.

Peterson, R. L. 1966. *An experimental study of effects of ability grouping in grades seven and eight.* Unpublished doctoral dissertation, University of Minnesota.

Pong, S. L., & A. Pallas. 2001. Class size and eight-grade math achievement in the United States and abroad. *Educational Evaluation and Policy Analysis, 23(3),* 251–273.

Prais, S. J. 1996. Class size and learning: The Tennessee experiment—what follows? *Oxford Review of Education, 22(4),* 399–414.

Preece, P. F. W. 1987. Class size and learning: a theoretical model. *J. Educational Research, 80(6),* 377–379.

Reichardt, R. 2001. *Reducing class size: choices and consequences.* California: Rand Corp.

Roth, W. F. 1999. Computers can individualize learning and raise group-interaction skills. *Education Digest, 65(3),* 27–31.

Sindelar, P. T., M. S. Rosenberg, R. J. Wilson, & E. D. Bursuck. 1984. The effects of group size and instructional method on the acquisition of mathematical concepts by fourth grade students. *Journal of Educational Research, 77(3),* 178–183.

Skinner, B. F. 1961. Why we need teaching machines. *Cumulative Record.* New York: Appleton Century-Crofts.

Slavin, R. E. 1989. Class size and student achievement: small effects of small classes. *Educational Psychologist, 24(10),* 99–110.

Slavin, R. E. 1993. Ability grouping in the middle grades: Achievement effects and alternatives. *Elementary School Journal, 93*, 535–552.

Smith, A. B., B. W. McMillan, S. Kennedy, & B. Ratcliffe. 1989. The effect of improving preschool teacher/child rations: an 'experiment in nature'. *Early Child Development and Care 41*, 123–38.

Smith, P., A. Molnar, & J. Zahorik. 2003. Class size reduction: a fresh look at the data. *Educational Leadership, September*, 72–74.

The Heritage Foundation. 2002. Education Statistics. Retrieved 3 August 2004 from http://www.heritage.org/Research/Education/WM134.cfm#2

Wilson, R. C. 1986. Improving faculty teaching: effective use of student evaluations and consultants. *Journal of Higher Education, 57(2)*, 192–211.

Woods, D. F. 1994. *Problem-based Learning: How to Gain the Most from PBL.* Hamilton, Ontario: W.L. Griffin Printing.

Word, E., J. Johnston, H. Bain, B. Fulton, J. Zaharias, N. Lintz, C. M. Achilles, J. Folger, & C. Breda. 1990. *Student/Teacher Achievement Ratio (STAR): Tennessee's K-3 class size study.* Final summary report. Nashville, TN: Tennessee State Department of Education.

Wößmann, L., & M. R. West. 2002. Class-size effects in school systems around the world: evidence from between-grade variation in TIMSS. Unpublished manuscript.

Yang, P. C. T. 2004. *Effectiveness of the Learning Support Programme in a Primary School.* Masters thesis submitted to the NIE, Singapore.

---

* Radhi Raja and Tammy Kwong assisted in the literature search.

CHAPTER 7

Benefits of Pre-Referral Interventions

LEVAN LIM, POON-MCBRAYER KIM FONG,
AND AHELON ANNATHURAI

INTRODUCTION

Pre-referral Intervention is a process used to help students who are identified to be "at risk" before determining whether they should be formally referred to special education (McDougal, Clonan & Martens, 2000). Pre-referral interventions are normally discussed and implemented by a team in the schools known as Teacher Support Team, Child Study Team, Mainstream Assistance Team, School Wide Assistance Team, Student Study Team, and Intervention Assistance Team, to name but just a few. These pre-referral intervention teams stemmed out from the Teacher Assistance Team (TAT) Model, a pre-referral intervention model introduced by Chalfant, Pysh, and Moultrie in 1979 (see Phillips, McCullough, Nelson & Walker 1992). Pre-referral intervention teams use a consultation-based approach to providing behavioral and/or instructional support to students before considering their eligibility for special education placement (McDougal, Clonan & Martens 2000). The main purpose of these teams is to give teachers support in preventing inappropriate referrals of "at risk" students to special education (Sindelar, Griffin, Smith & Watanabe 1992).

Since the mid-1980s, the pre-referral intervention process has been implemented in schools to more effectively meet the diverse needs of students who experience academic and behavioural problem in the general education setting (Nelson, Martella & Marchand-Martella 2002). The expectation is that the pre-referral intervention process will minimise the number of inappropriate requests for special education assessments made by school personnel while increasing student success in general education. Several published studies indicate that rates of referral to special education decrease when pre-referral intervention is implemented (Kovaleski, Gickling, Morrow & Swank 1999; McDougal, Clonan & Martens 2000). There is evidence that at schools with pre-referral teams, students made significant improvement particularly at comprehension and completion of a given task (Kovaleski, Gickling, Morrow & Swank 1999). A basic conceptual framework of the pre-referral intervention process is given below for better understanding of the whole process.

Before a formal referral for eligibility determination for special education, the student who is experiencing difficulties in the mainstream education program is referred to the pre-referral intervention team in the school. This team helps teachers to establish successful programs for "at risk" students within the regular classroom. Normally, the principal of the school is responsible for ensuring that the pre-referral process occurs and that it is documented in the student's regular education record. Any student who is identified for formal referral to special education must have gone through the pre-referral intervention team first. It is expected that early intervention by the school's pre-referral intervention team can prevent formal referrals to special education.

Basic conceptual framework defining the pre-referral model (Buck, Polloway, Smith-Thomas & Cook 2003):

- A process that is preventive (i.e., interventions are developed and implemented before a formal, special education evaluation).
- A problem-solving approach that is team-based (i.e., team members review data on a referred student, hypothesise causes to explain the student's difficulties, and develop strategies to remediate those difficulties).
- An approach that is action-research oriented (i.e., a team develops specific interventions that the referring teacher is expected to implement in her(his) classroom [either with or without outside assistance] and then evaluate in terms of its effectiveness).
- An intervention process that is centred upon the enhanced success of students and teachers within the general education setting and in the general education curriculum.

TEACHER ASSISTANCE TEAMS

The Teacher Assistance Team (TAT) which is a pre-referral intervention team was designed to respond systematically and effectively to the complex challenges faced in schools. The purpose of the team is to provide support to classroom teachers before any child is referred for an evaluation under special education. It is important to note that the TAT is not part of the special education process but a general education responsibility. The TAT can serve as a mechanism to recommend interventions to staff for children experiencing difficulties and when making appropriate referrals to school services, including special education.

Rationale behind the TAT

The kinds of challenges teachers and other staff face today are very complex, challenging and require a team effort. The most valuable assistance is rendered when educators assist one another in solving difficult classroom problems, as in a pre-referral intervention model like the TAT. Studies indicate that there are children entering school who can be expected to need individual help; and fewer than half of these students have a disability to such a degree that they require special education (Safran & Safran 1996). Hence, the majority of students who are referred to the TAT can be prevented into being referred to special education. With this objective in mind, the TAT was implemented in schools.

Teachers and other school staff are faced with a variety of challenges during each school day and should seek assistance when strategies they have used are not working (Lane, Mahdavi & Borthwick-Duffy 2003). Usually assistance is given through informal contacts with peers, principals, counsellors, special education staff, and others. Many problems are not resolved because of a lack of time or expertise in dealing with the issue. A more effective and systematic process for assisting teachers is the TAT process. Though studies have pointed the rate at which these TATs and other pre-referral intervention teams have taken effects in schools (Harris 1995; Myers & Kline 1996), it has to be noted that different schools have different ways of forming a TAT process based on the situation in the school. However there are certain basic common guidelines to look at when forming a TAT process in schools. The following segment of this report describes the TAT process that has been implemented in a number of schools in America.

Teacher Assistance Team process

The team and referring teacher (also known as consultee) collaborate in identifying and defining the problem, brainstorming solutions, and discussing possible interventions for children experiencing instructional and behavioural difficulties (Copenhaver 2003). Students, parents, and other specialists can also be involved in the process. The nature of the student's problem determines which team members are needed to explore and recommend possible solutions. The interventions recommended by the team may include school, home, and community resources. Follow-up meetings are held with the consultee to decide whether or not recommendations are working. The consultee should first attempt interventions on his or her own before referring a child to the TAT. Many problems are solved without assistance or support. The following diagram depicts the relationship between the degree of the problem and the possible service options.

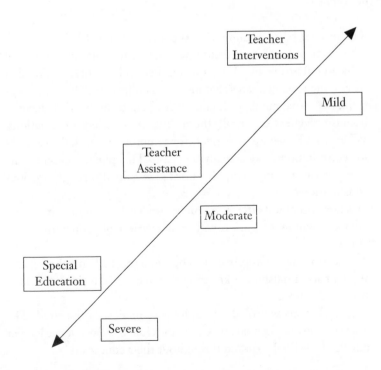

Benefits of the Teacher Assistance Team

Several researchers have stated some of the benefits of the TATs (Copenhaver 2003; Myers & Kline 2001/2002; Noll & Kamps 1993). These benefits are categorised and stated below.

For the child and family

- The child remains in the general classroom and benefits from instruction and peer interaction. Children with mild learning and/or behavioural difficulties can learn best within the general education classroom.
- Many problems that occur at school also occur at home. With parents participating on the team, the TAT helps to define the problems and provides valuable information. The school and parents can work in partnership to help the child.
- The TAT also provides guidance with non-academic challenges such as transition to a new grade or child/teacher conflicts.

For the teacher

- The teacher receives immediate support from the TAT.
- The teacher gains new techniques for addressing academic and behavioural problems. When one teacher finds an intervention that works, the teacher shares that idea with colleagues. Over the long-term, the actual number of requests for help from the TAT declines because teachers can apply these skills to a variety of situations. When a TAT operates effectively for a number of years, the requests for consultations may actually decrease. This phenomenon occurs as educators are able to apply knowledge gained through previous consultations.
- Teachers become better communicators and problem-solvers and are more willing to work together in a variety of cooperative team efforts.
- The school climate improves: teachers and the TAT members gain a sense of accomplishment knowing they have positively affected the lives of children.
- The TAT process provides for a long-term view of the child. The interventions are focused on helping the child be a productive learner during the school year and throughout their education.

For the school

- The implementation of a support system for teachers, parents, and other school staff can help meet the variety of educational challenges. By using a team of professionals trained in consultation and intervention techniques, the range of educational options for children increases.
- Using the TAT, resources can be directed in a more cost-effective fashion. Testing for the purpose of special education diagnosis is time consuming and expensive. Evaluation services are expensive.
- The TAT is an effective method to provide information needed to verify that a child needs special education. The best way to know if a child's difficulty cannot be corrected without special education (a requirement prior to determining eligibility for special education) is to try a number of appropriate interventions before making a referral for evaluation. The support team process provides documentation of the school's efforts to work with children in the general classroom.
- The TAT focuses on the identified needs of the child. The process defines and clarifies the child's problem and provides documentation of what works and what is ineffective. This improves the special education evaluation by providing a focus on a specific area of concern, leading to more accurate evaluations.

For the Community

- The TAT is proactive and preventative in nature; interventions and solutions occur before problems become serious and extend to the community.

Below are the common terms used in the TAT process as well as the roles and responsibilities of the members (core and optional) of the TAT.

Common terms in TAT process

TAT: A team of general education staff trained to assist school personnel and parents in solving difficult instructional and behavioural challenges. TAT is also referred to as step one, school wide assistance team, building based support teams, and pre-referral team.

Consultation meeting: The TAT meets with the consultee to clarify the challenge, determine the goal and suggest possible interventions.

Consultee: The staff member making the referral to the Teacher Assistance Team. The consultee becomes a member of the team and ultimately decides which interventions will be tried.

Interventions and: Modifications to instructional curriculum,
accommodations classroom/school environment, and/or behaviour expectations that result in the child benefiting from their education.

Problem solving: A process that leads to effective interventions and solutions.

Referral: A formal recommendation for an individualised evaluation that determines if a disability exists and there is a need for special services. This normally takes place after numerous unsuccessful interventions have been attempted.

Special education: Specially designed instruction to meet the unique needs of an eligible child with a disability.

Team leader: The TAT leader does the scheduling and arranges a meeting place and time. The leader also facilitates the meeting process.

Core Members of the Teacher Assistance Team
Classroom teacher: Teachers should be chosen who are willing to commit, have knowledge of evidence-based instructional and behavioural techniques, and have good communication skills.

School counsellor: Counsellors have knowledge of academic and behavioural interventions and have information about scheduling, curriculum, and graduation requirements. Their advice on selecting classes and matching children with particular teachers is very helpful.

School principal: If the school principal participates on the TAT, care should be taken not to evaluate teacher performance based upon their referrals to TAT. Teachers must feel safe to bring problems to the team without fear of evaluation. Principals make good members because they understand the resources available at the school.

Optional Team Members

Parent or guardian: Parents must be notified of their child's referral to the TAT and should be encouraged to participate in the TAT process. Parents should be involved whenever possible, since they know the child best and can offer valuable advice.

Student: The student's participation is recommended only when the parents and team agree such involvement might result in a benefit for the student. The student's involvement will increase the personal ownership of the problem and may yield some insights into possible solutions.

School nurse: The school nurse should be involved whenever there is a health care concern. The nurse can provide expertise in developing child health care and emergency plans. School nurses have knowledge of medical conditions that might contribute to a child's problems in school.

School psychologist: School psychologists have knowledge of human development, behavioural and educational interventions. The psychologist can assist in developing behaviour management plans and provide consultations to classroom teachers.

Social worker: School social workers often are able to gather detailed knowledge of the family and child. This individual can support interventions that match family needs and resources.

Speech therapist: Many of the problems typically presented to the TAT can be understood as issues in expressive and written communication. The

181

speech therapist will be an excellent resource when addressing language problems.

Special education: teacher

It is not recommended that the special education teacher be part of the core team, but should be used as a resource to suggest instructional and behavioural interventions.

Paraeducator:

The paraeducator instructional assistant may have valuable insights and be in a position to work with the child in ways a teacher cannot.

Studies on the Effectiveness of TATs and Pre-referral Intervention Teams

As mentioned, pre-referral intervention teams are known by many names, and these names have stemmed from the TAT model introduced by Chalfant (1979 as cited in Phillips, McCullough & Nelson 1992). Their members typically include general teachers, parents, administrators, and experts such as special education teachers, school psychologists, and counsellors. These teams meet on a regular basis to (a) discuss referred students' strengths and weaknesses and (b) generate academic and behavioral intervention ideas that the classroom teacher may implement in the general education classroom (Chalfant & Pysh 1989, cited in Nelson, Smith, Taylor, Dodd & Reavis 2002).

TATs are designed to support the regular education teacher who needs strategies and support for students who exhibit academic, emotional or behavioural difficulties. It's an interdisciplinary approach which involves a team consisting of teachers, psychologist, social workers, parents and counsellors to help and improve student's academic and behavioural outcomes. TATs can be viewed as a compilation of all the support available in the schools itself to help the students needs instead of placing the child in pre established models. In some instances the teacher assistance teams are viewed as "push-in" model rather than "push-out" model as it gives the child greater access to the general education curriculum (Sindelar, Griffin, Smith & Watanabe 1992). Promising findings suggest that the TAT and other pre-referral intervention teams are effective in reducing both the number of unnecessary special education referrals and placements and consequently

FIGURE 7.1 Stages of the TAT process

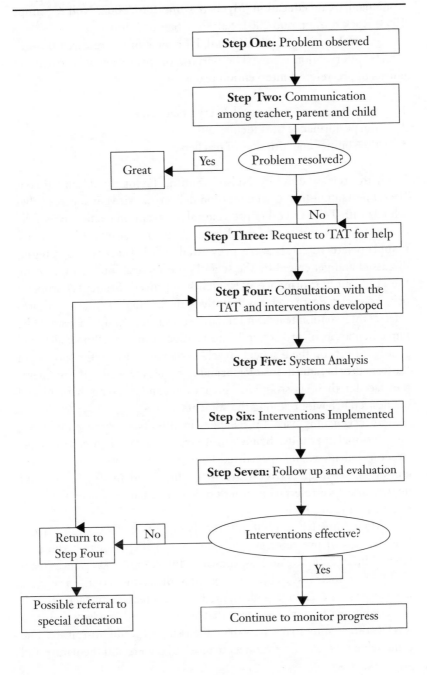

unnecessary stigmatisation due to labelling and separation of the child from mainstream education (Myers & Kline 2001/2002; Noll & Kamps 1993; Rock & Zigmond 2001; Safran & Safran 1996).

Nelson and Smith (1991) did a review of the research on pre-referral intervention teams. The purpose of this review was to see the effects of pre-referral intervention teams on:

1. special education service delivery practices;
2. the performance of students; and
3. the abilities and attitudes of teachers.

From the review done by Nelson, Smith, Taylor, Dodd and Reavis (1991) pertaining to special education delivery services, it was seen that schools with TATs and other pre-referral intervention teams successfully decreased the number of formal referrals to special education. Hence inappropriate referrals were prevented. With successful strategies discussed and generated by the school's pre-referral intervention team, the academic performance of students improved. Students' problem behaviour also decreased significantly with the implementation of pre-referral intervention teams and the measures taken up by the team. The implementation of pre-referral intervention teams in schools also had positive effects on the teachers. Teachers shared that with the support of the team they became more tolerant and were able to redefine the problems they faced in their classroom to a great extent and by doing this achieved the desired behaviour among the students.

Interventions used by teachers in the above review included, instructional methods, behavioural strategies, academic strategies, structural changes and specialised help. Studies showed that teachers conferred with special education teachers and professionals and implemented pre-referral interventions before actually going on to formal referrals if the need arises.

Myers and Kline (2001/2002) also conducted research on the effectiveness of pre-referral interventions. In their research the pre-referral intervention team was known as Intervention Assistance Team (IAT). From their research, it was seen that the team served as a support for teachers for exchanging ideas, methods, techniques, and activities. It was established from the research that assistance with student problems was less threatening to teachers than discussing with administrators. The team helped the teacher to conceptualise and understand the nature and underlying problem of the students. With support from this pre-referral team in the school, there was a significant reduction in frustration in the teachers over the handling of student problems as well as teacher burnout. The IAT allowed the students to achieve without an unnecessary special education label (Myers & Kline 2001/2002). Besides the benefits to the teachers and the students, it was found from the research that the pre-referral team approach was also cost-effective. The IAT approach not only improved the outcomes for current students, but also served to benefit future students by increasing teachers' competencies in dealing with students with problems. Hence the work of the team replaced the time and money spent on in-service that did not meet the expressed needs of all teachers.

Despite the overwhelming support and benefits of the TAT model and other pre-referral intervention team models, it has to be noted that there have been some concerns presented in the literature. Chalfant and Pysh (1989, cited in Nelson, Smith, Taylor, Dodd & Reavis 2002) identified frequent barriers to pre-referral intervention implementation such as insufficient time, no useful intervention strategy, interference with special education referral process, lack of readiness to properly initiate teams, and insufficient impact on student performance. Ross (1995) also identified several obstacles to successful pre-referral interventions. These obstacles included loss of funding from reduced student enrolment in special education classes, the increased job responsibilities without increased compensation for the educators and teacher attitudes to the pre-referral process. Hence one has to bear these impediments to pre-referral intervention in mind when designing successful pre-referral intervention teams in schools.

STAGE MODEL OF INTERVENTION

Similar to the TAT model in America, many schools in Singapore follow a pre-referral intervention model known as the Stage Model of Intervention (SMI) which was officially launched as a pilot phase in the year 2000. The SMI has been introduced to altogether 107 schools in Singapore. There are three main stages in the model. In the first stage the teacher proceeds to help the students who have academic and behavioural difficulties and may consult with a member of the CMT for suggestions and strategies to equip herself when helping the student. If the student still faces problems, then the second stage is introduced

185

where the Learning Support Coordinator, Teacher Counsellor, the Discipline Master or any other member of CMT may take on an active role by directly engaging with the student. If after these two stages, the student still has difficulties, then an external formal referral is made to the Multi Skilled Team (MST) from the MOE Psychology and Guidance Services Branch (PGSB).

FIGURE 7.2 Stages at the SMI

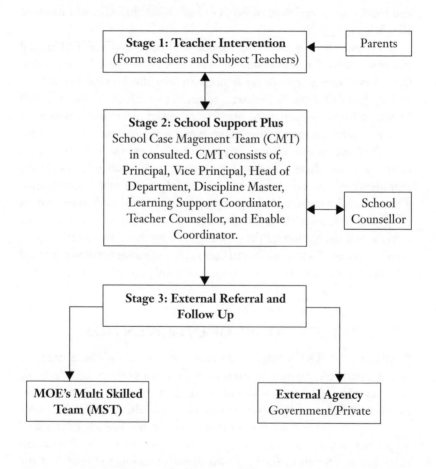

Literature on pre-referral intervention teams shows that there are very similar characteristics between both these models of pre-referral intervention, thus enabling this report to draw parallels from both models. One similarity which can be noted is that, one of the main functions of the SMI and the TAT is to provide a framework for the systematic identification and support of pupils with learning, behavioural and emotional difficulties thus preventing inappropriate referrals to special education. There is also a team of people in the SMI (Case Management Team, CMT) serving to empower the referring teacher similar to the TAT model. Some of the key differences between both models are also discussed below. A more detailed table of comparisons can be found in Table 7.1.

Some key differences between US based TAT Models and the Singapore Stage Model of Intervention.

-   In the Stage model the LSC, TC and DM directly intervenes in the classroom, whereas in the TAT models, the consultee (the referring teacher) is the person who provides the intervention in the classroom. The TAT will provide other personnel of the team to assist the classroom teacher only if the teacher requests for assistance.
-   A formal referral and assessment may be conducted at in the second stage of the Stage model and students may be provided LSP. Under TAT models, there are no formal referrals until the last stage.
-   In the TAT models, the consultee chooses the appropriate intervention to implement since s/he is the one who takes full responsibility for her(his) class. Based on the documents received from the Stage model, it is unclear as to whether the consultee always decides.
-   One of the stages in the TAT models is called System Analysis where there is an understanding that some problems are the result of variables other than the student. The team will analyse the student's *environment* to determine if other factors are causing the problem. Hence possible levels of intervention in schools can constitute the following.

Level of intervention	Specific examples
State	Funding, policies and procedures.
Community	Law enforcement, understanding cultural differences in the community.
School district	Funding, policies, curriculum materials, parental involvement.
School	Adequacy of school building, school climate, services.
Classroom	Physical arrangement of classroom, seating of students, instructional materials and other resources, number of students.
Teacher	Instructional strategies, expectations of students, interactions with students, tolerance, reinforcement and feedback schedule, classroom management strategies.
Student	Academic achievement, emotional development, social development, organisational and study skills, situational stressors, family, cultural factors.

So during the problem identification stage, the team identifies the levels of intervention that contribute in solving the problem. Using System Analysis, the team members receive a more global view of students' difficulties. This analysis is very critical if long-term change has to occur for the student. This approach also improves the teacher's skills and benefits the climate of the entire classroom. A similar approach is mentioned in the role and responsibilities of the CMT (i.e. identify key problems at a systematic level). However a description of this approach was not elaborated in the Stage model.

CONCLUSION

The chapter defines the process of Pre-referral Intervention which has proven to be of success in the research studies conducted. Many students who were identified to be "at risk" managed to fit into mainstream settings due to strategies and interventions (both academic and behavioural) implemented by TATs. Singapore schools also follow a form of Pre-referral Intervention known as the Stage Model of Intervention. This model's main objective is to help students who face learning and behavioural challenges. The chapter introduces two

TABLE 7.1 Comparisons of Two US.based models to Singapore Stage Model of Intervention

Teacher Assistance Team Model 1 (US based)	Teacher Assistance Team Model 2 (US based) also known as Teacher Support Team	Stage Model of Intervention (Singapore)
7 stages **Stage 1: Problem identified** - Problem/challenge is observed. - If the problem is at school, the teacher will inform the parents. - If it is noticed at home and involves the school in some way, the parents should call the teacher. - If the situation is not resolved, it is appropriate to ask for help from the TAT. **Stage 2: Parent Involvement** - Parental involvement should begin when the teacher encounters persistent problems, and should continue for as long as the TAT meets.	**3 stages** **Stage 1: Teacher tries to solve** classroom problems - Isolated Ongoing Problem Solving. - Switches student seating. - Modifies assignments. - Works in small group or 1:1. - Provides extra practice. - Provides extra attention/praise. - Works with parent/guardians. - Few resources. - Less severe problems. **Stage 2: Teacher asks for help from TST and TST addresses the problem.** - An initial interview is conducted with the referring teacher and child's parents.	**3 stages** **Stage 1** - Initial concern can be from parent or teacher. Other concerns pertaining to the children are identified here. - Teacher interventions take place here. - Teacher monitors pupil progress and may consult the appropriate key school personnel such as LSC & TC. - Some assistance LSC can offer is advice to teacher on learning difficulties and teacher's concern about pupil. - Some assistance TC can offer is offer advice to teacher on emotional difficulties, make a home visit with the teacher or observe a pupil in the class. **Stage 2** - More direct intervention by key school

TABLE 7.1 Comparisons of Two U.S.based models to Singapore Stage Model of Intervention (cont'd)

Teacher Assistance Team Model 1 (US based)	Teacher Assistance Team Model 2 (US based) also known as Teacher Support Team	Stage Model of Intervention (Singapore)
Stage 3: Referral to TAT - If the problem cannot be resolved by the teacher, student, or parent, a referral is made to the TAT. - Preferred method to request assistance from the team for the teacher is to approach the team leader or school principal. The contact person should be easily accessible and should have an opportunity for frequent contact with team members. - Usually a brief verbal description of the problem(s) is given to the contact person. - Once the request for assistance is made, meeting times are coordinated with the various individuals involved in the team	- Background data are reviewed (work samples, cumulative records, etc.). **Questions to address** - Before intervention. What? How? Who? When? Where? - During Intervention. Is it working? - After Intervention. Did it work? An Instructional Intervention (II) is begun when a student is identified as: - likely to have difficulty meeting expected benchmarks, or	personnel such as LSC, TC, and DM etc. - LSC inputs may include implementation of IEP, classroom observation, direct assessment of the child to investigate problem further etc. - TC inputs may include direct counseling of pupil and direct work with parents - Case is made known to CMT which meets regularly and discusses cases. CMT makes appropriate decisions (e.g. Return to teacher for further intervention, engage school's external counsellor or refer to MST or other external agency. **Stage 3** - Formal referral to the MST or other external agencies. - Clear documentation of Stage 1 and Stage 2 interventions is required

TABLE 7.1 Comparisons of Two US-based models to Singapore Stage Model of Intervention (cont'd)

Teacher Assistance Team Model 1 (US based)	Teacher Assistance Team Model 2 (US based) also known as Teacher Support Team	Stage Model of Intervention (Singapore)
meeting. These include the core members, consultee (referring teacher), parents, and optional members. **Stage 4: Consultation Meeting** - Problem is clarified in measurable terms, a goal is determined, and interventions are generated. - After studying each alternative, the **consultee** chooses the appropriate intervention(s) to implement. - The team discusses if materials are needed (e.g., computer, pencil grip, rewards, etc.), when the intervention will begin, how long it will be tried, and what support the consultee will need in carrying out the interventions.	- Having difficulty in meeting expected benchmarks. Steps to Problem Solving are initiated by TST. 1. Define the Problem. 2. Develop a Plan. 3. Implement the Plan. 4. Evaluate Effects. **Define the Problem** - A data-based classroom observation has been conducted. - Curriculum-based assessment has been conducted in the target area. - Based on data collected, has the identified problem been precisely defined? - Has a measurable goal been	- Parental consent - Direct assessment by MST. - Liaison between CMT and MST/ external agencies or professionals. - Continued support by classroom teachers. **Monitoring & Follow up stage** - Implementation of learning/ behavioural strategies recommended by MST, by teachers and parents. - Implementation of exceptional school arrangements/ accommodation. - Monitoring of targets and review of strategies by teachers as appropriate. - For pupils assessed as ESN, LSC follows up with application procedures to APSN. - For pupils requiring additional specialist intervention, LSC assists in the referral process. LSC monitors progress and

TABLE 7.1 Comparisons of Two US.based models to Singapore Stage Model of Intervention (cont'd)

Teacher Assistance Team Model 1 (US based)	Teacher Assistance Team Model 2 (US based) also known as Teacher Support Team	Stage Model of Intervention (Singapore)
Sometimes the consultee will not be the only team member with a role in carrying out an intervention. For example, the school counsellor may provide counselling, or the playground supervisor may be involved in reinforcing the student for appropriate playground behaviour if the consultee asks for such assistance. - Anyone given responsibility for carrying out an intervention needs to agree to provide the intervention. - The TAT chooses a team member who will monitor the progress of the intervention(s). This team member works with the consultee and provides support. This individual will keep the team informed of the	developed based on realistic expectations for success? - Based on all existing data, which instructional variables (curricular, instructional, student, environment) can be hypothesised as potential areas for intervention? - Has an intervention been designed based on the data collected and on the hypothesised instructional variables? - Has a data monitoring system been devised to track the student's rate of acquisition and rate of retention? - Who will assist the classroom teacher to establish the intervention and monitor the student's progress?	outcomes. - Case is closed when targets are met (in consultation with MST) - Continued support by classroom teachers.

192

TABLE 7.1 Comparisons of Two U.S.based models to Singapore Stage Model of Intervention (cont'd)

Teacher Assistance Team Model 1 (US based)	Teacher Assistance Team Model 2 (US based) also known as Teacher Support Team	Stage Model of Intervention (Singapore)
results of the interventions. - A summary document outlining the identified problem dates, and specifics of the intervention(s) must be completed by the team leader. This information is subject to the confidentiality requirements that apply to all student records. Documentation is important if the student moves to a different school or if the student is referred to other programs or agencies. **Stage 5: Systems Analysis** Some problems are the result of variables other than the student. Inappropriate instruction, poorly designed curriculum, or personality conflicts could cause certain students	**Develop a plan** - The team works with the classroom teacher to establish the intervention. - The classroom teacher and team members incorporate the strategy into the classroom routine. - Other support services are involved in the intervention. - Data are collected on a regular and frequent basis during the intervention. Changing the learner will require a temporary change to: - instructional conditions, - curriculum conditions, and - environmental conditions.	

TABLE 7.1 Comparisons of Two US.based models to Singapore Stage Model of Intervention (cont'd)

Teacher Assistance Team Model 1 (US based)	Teacher Assistance Team Model 2 (US based) also known as Teacher Support Team	Stage Model of Intervention (Singapore)
to misbehave. - TAT analyses the student's environment to determine if other factors are causing the problem. This part of the process is critical if long-term change is to occur for the student. A careful analysis of the system should be made by the team. - Using systems analysis, support team members acquire a more global view of students' difficulties; if interventions are aimed at highest level, problems can be solved more efficiently and similar issues may be prevented in the future. This approach also improves the teacher's skills and benefits the climate of the entire classroom.	The Teacher Support Team will determine appropriate interventions based on information such as: - existing educational record, - curriculum based assessment, - parent information, - screening instruments, and - direct observations and functional assessments. Does the team, by virtue of their collective experience and expertise, have the capacity to address the priority behaviour? If **Yes:** - Continue through intervention design steps, and if circumstances warrant, consider the additional behaviours.	

TABLE 7.1 Comparisons of Two U.S.based models to Singapore Stage Model of Intervention (cont'd)

Teacher Assistance Team Model 1 (US based)	Teacher Assistance Team Model 2 (US based) also known as Teacher Support Team	Stage Model of Intervention (Singapore)
Stage 6: Evidence based Interventions - Recommended interventions are implemented. - The assigned team member provides support and resources as needed during this phase. - Team members assist the consultee in implementing and fine tuning the intervention(s). - During implementation, the consultee records the student's response to the plan and then prepares the information for the follow-up meeting. The team might assign an individual team member to work closely with the consultee and follow the progress of the intervention.	If No: - Determine auxiliary personnel whose experience or expertise might assist in resolving the problem. - Identify available resources/information the team might access. - Schedule a follow-up meeting and secure teacher permission to invite selected auxiliary personnel. - Consider the additional behaviours identified by the teacher. When considering the additional behaviours identified by the teacher, look for the following: - behaviour for which remediation would result in a domino effect; - behaviour most easily/quickly ameliorated; and	

a

TABLE 7.1 Comparisons of Two U.S.based models to Singapore Stage Model of Intervention (cont'd)

Teacher Assistance Team Model 1 (US based)	Teacher Assistance Team Model 2 (US based) also known as Teacher Support Team	Stage Model of Intervention (Singapore)
Stage 7: *Follow up and Evaluation* - The follow-up meeting is designed to review and evaluate the effectiveness of the intervention(s). The team determines who will monitor the child's progress to ensure that the success is maintained. - Interventions will be continued into the following school year. - It is important to arrange for a meeting with the next year's teacher, preferably in the spring of the current year. The receiving teacher should know what worked and what was ineffective with the child. If the goal was not met, attempts to further clarify the problem are made, and a new goal may be set.	- behaviour the team is most confident about solving. - How precisely has the concern been described? - What are the salient features of the student's described performance? - What features of the instructional environment (curriculum, instruction) may be possible areas for intervention? - What features of the instructional environment need further analysis? - What types of assessments should be conducted with the student? - Who will conduct the assessments? **Implementation and Monitoring** - Is the intervention being implemented as planned?	

TABLE 7.1 Comparisons of Two US.based models to Singapore Stage Model of Intervention (cont'd)

Teacher Assistance Team Model 1 (US based)	Teacher Assistance Team Model 2 (US based) also known as Teacher Support Team	Stage Model of Intervention (Singapore)
- A decision is then made to try other interventions, and the process continues. - If the solutions attempted are unsuccessful and the child's needs are not accommodated within a reasonable amount of time, the team makes a **referral to special education.**	- What do the data indicate? - Is the student making the expected rate of progress? - Do we need to revisit the intervention and fine tune it? - Was the problem resolved? - Reduced discrepancy between student and peers - Should we continue the intervention? - Do we need a more intense intervention? - Is a referral for special education appropriate? Four Kinds of Assessments will be conducted before moving on to Stage 3.	

TABLE 7.1 Comparisons of Two U.S.based models to Singapore Stage Model of Intervention (cont'd)

Teacher Assistance Team Model 1 (US based)	Teacher Assistance Team Model 2 (US based) also known as Teacher Support Team	Stage Model of Intervention (Singapore)
	- Outcome Assessments - provide a bottom-line evaluation of program effectiveness. These include standardised tests. - Screening Assessments - determine which children might need additional intervention. - Diagnostic Assessments - provide in-depth information about skills and needs. - Progress Monitoring Assessments - determine if students are making adequate progress or need additional intervention. **Stage 3** - Intensive resources for resistant problems - Special Education Services	

TABLE 7.1 Comparisons of Two US.based models to Singapore Stage Model of Intervention (cont'd)

Teacher Assistance Team Model 1 (US based)	Teacher Assistance Team Model 2 (US based) also known as Teacher Support Team	Stage Model of Intervention (Singapore)
	- Low ratio instruction - Individualised Goals - Evaluated annually - Weekly monitoring - Emphasis on remediation	

examples of TAT Models from the United States compared to the Stage Model of Singapore. When compared, it was seen that there were many similarities. There were also some key differences which were noted between the models presented. In conclusion, it can be seen from the report that Pre-referral Intervention is a crucial step towards the direction in providing good support both to the students as well as the teachers who are directly responsible for them in the classrooms. Furthermore the risk of students being branded and stereotyped when being referred to special education is significantly reduced with the implementation of Pre-referral Interventions.

REFERENCES

Buck, G. H., E. A. Polloway, A. Smith-Thomas, & K. W. Cook. 2003. Prereferral intervention processes: A survey of state practices. *Exceptional Children, 69*(3), 349–360.

Copenhaver, J. 2003. Teacher Assistance Team (TAT). *Primer for School Staff and Administrators.* 1780 North Research Parkway.

Harris, K. C. 1995. School-based bilingual special education teacher assistance teams. *Remedial and Special Education, 16*(6), 337–344.

Kovaleski, J. F., E. E. Gickling, H. Morrow, & P. R. Swank. 1999. High versus low implementation of instructional support teams: A case for maintaining program fidelity. *Remedial and Special Education, 20*(3), 170–183.

Lane, K. L., J. N. Mahdavi, & S. Borthwick-Duffy. 2003. Teacher perceptions of the prereferral intervention process: A call for assistance with school-based intervention. *Preventing School Failure. 47*(4), 148–155.

McDougal, J. L., S. M. Clonan, & B. K. Martens. 2000. Using organizational change procedures to promote the acceptability of prereferral intervention services: The school-based intervention team project. *School Psychology Quarterly, 15*(2), 149–171.

Myers, V. M., & C. E. Kline. 2001/2002. Secondary school intervention assistance teams: Can they be effective? *High School Journal, 85*(2), 33–43.

Nelson, J. R., R. M. Martella, & N. Marchand-Martella. 2002. Maximizing student learning: The effect of a comprehensive school-based program for preventing problem behaviors. *Journal of Emotional and Behavioral Disorder, 10*(3), 136–148.

Nelson, J. R., D. J. Smith, L. Taylor, J. M. Dodd, & K. Reavis. 1991. Prereferral intervention: A review of research. *Education and Treatment of Children, 14*(3), 243–253.

Noll, M. B., & D. Kamps. 1993. Prereferral intervention for students with emotional or behavioral risks: Use of a behavioral consultation model. *Journal of Emotional and Behavioural Disorders, 1*(4), 203–215.

Phillips, V., L. McCullough, C. M. Nelson, & H. M. Walker. 1992. Teamwork among teachers: Promoting a statewide agenda for students at risk for school failure. *Special Services in the Schools, 6*, 3–4.

Rock, M. L., & N. Zigmond. 2001. Intervention assistance: Is it substance or symbolism? *Preventing School Failure, 45*(4), 153–162.

Ross, R. P. 1995. Best practices in implementing intervention assistance teams. In *Best practices in school psychology (4th ed.)*. Edited by A. Thomas & J. Grimes., National Assistance of School Psychologists, Silver Spring, MD, 227–237.

Safran, S. P., & J. S. Safran. 1996. Intervention assistance programs and prereferral teams. *Remedial & Special Education, 17*(6), 363–370.

Sindelar, P. T., C. C. Griffin, S. W. Smith, & A. K. Watanabe. 1992. Prereferral intervention: Encouraging notes on preliminary findings. *The Elementary School Journal, 92*(3).

Epilogue

TAN AI GIRL

In epilogue we present some reflection upon the theme of this book: What matters in learning? In the introductory chapter, we advocate that learning is for developing personhood, to become a person, and to optimise potentials. Learning is personal and social. We highlight the importance to create *spaces* for dialogue, adopting an *evidence-based* educational policy and having a good grasp of *research methodology*. Singapore's educational ministry in the past several years have attempted to create spaces for dialogues among school leaders, teachers, teacher educators, and ministry offices. Workshops and focus group discussions were conducted for the recent initiatives such as the innovation and enterprise (I & E) and teach less and learn more (TLLM) visions. During such meetings, the participants brainstormed their conceptions of I & E or TLLM, and often the dialogues as such would bring forth among others teachers' main concerns of the essence of education, the needs to assist less advantaged children, curricula, pedagogies, and assessments. These dialogues often begin and end with inconclusive remarks but passionate aspirations to a certain extent serve as a platform for teachers, school leaders, and policy makers to share their views openly.

Our book identifies themes pertinent to the Singapore's educational initiatives, i.e., self-directed learning, psycho-educational group, school counsellors, problem-based learning and project work, information and communication technologies (ICT), class size, and pre-referral interventions. We are especially interested to find out evidence-based literature to support the lay aspirations to promote various forms of learning as discussed above. For each of these themes we search relevant papers from the international databases, and approached Singaporean teacher educators and researchers who published and had the expertise.

For most chapters, our search began with key terms pertinent to the field and relevant to the Singapore's educational contexts. In chapter 1 "self-initiated learning" we identified self-regulation, self-efficacy, and self-directed learning. Cooperative learning, group guidance and counselling, and streaming have been a culture of learning in Singapore. In chapter 2, we refer to literature in social psychology for some insights into sociological and psychological perspectives of grouping and group work. Specifically, we were interested in understanding effectiveness of grouping and in eliciting some theoretical frameworks of group guidance. We agree with the notion that "disability" is cultural, and hence, in chapter 3, we refer to the Vygotskian discourse on disability, reviewed Singapore's learning support program and its efficacy, as well as benefits of school counsellors in assisting children with learning difficulties.

Project work has been part of the Singapore's school curricula. Some Singaporean researchers (Chin & Chia 2004) witnessed beneficial integration of problem-based approach to project work. In chapter 4, we specifically refer to Hmelo-Silver's (2004) review and Dochy, Segers, van den Bossche and Gijbels' (2003) meta-analysis for some insights into effectiveness of problem-based learning. In addition, we review commonalities of problem-based learning and project-based learning as well as some findings on the integration of these learning approaches. We examine in chapter 5 effectiveness of ICT in teaching and learning referring to some studies conducted by our graduate teachers. This chapter complements our review on some theoretical frameworks of ICT and creativity education (Tan & Law 2004). In chapter 6 we review some studies on class size reduction and its inconclusive findings. We also elicit possible ways to group students of large class size for effective learning. This chapter serves as an integrated chapter as its discussion includes among others views on group size and problem-based learning. Learning problems need to be identified early. So are children's disciplinary problems. Finally in chapter 7, we elicit possible benefits of pre-referral intervention models and compare differences between the US and Singaporean models.

The discussion of developing personhood as the ultimate aim of learning is indeed beyond the scope of this book. In epilogue, we revisit the notion of full personhood within the context of the discourse of including special needs children into mainstream schooling. We also like to highlight the importance of family and other factors such as socio-economic status (SES) and social support in learning.

Collaborative Teaching

To include children with learning difficulties to mainstream classrooms, Singapore in the next few years will deploy hundreds of special education officers and school counselors to mainstream schools. Likely collaborative teaching models are adopted to facilitate cooperation between mainstream teachers and the specialists. Collaborative teaching involves working with learning disabled individuals. There are various forms of collaborative teaching: one teaching, one assisting; station teaching; parallel teaching; alternative teaching; and team teaching (Murawski & Swanson 2001). Research on collaborative teaching examined aspects such as the teacher-student interaction process (see Kenneth & Forness 2000), what makes an effective teacher dyad (e.g., Murata 2002), the role of classmates in a disabled child's well-being (Kenneth & Forness 2000), and the influence of additional administrative support provided by the school and principal on the outcome of such an initiative (Murata 2002). Also essential is to examine how collaborative teaching can serve the needs of children with a wide spectrum of learning disorders (e.g., autism, dyslexia, or attention deficit hyperactive disorder) each with differing outcomes (see Kenneth & Forness 2000). In the Singapore's contexts, learning difficulties can be due to children's familiarity with the languages of instruction. For a child whose main home language is the English language, s/he may face difficulty or be less advantaged in her(his) early years of learning when the main language of instruction is the English language. One may also cautious about mainstreaming children with special needs. Mainstreaming may not be suitable for severely disabled children who need one to one attention and interactions. Individuals with poor social skills can be a disruptive to a learning atmosphere (Kenneth & Forness 2000). Rather than merely aiming for acceptance, an intervention could be developed to encourage pro-social behaviours among children. The teacher for instance could make the class aware of characteristics of learning difficulties or mild disabilities, and accordingly introduce cultivation of empathy toward children with such disabilities or learning difficulties.

It is necessary to provide a comprehensive skills training package to the teachers before actual implementation of any special program. Developing a sense of self mastery and competency in working with disabled children would be a boon to a teacher's confidence and performance.

Additional concerns for co-teaching or having the teacher dyad include the following:

- Division of professional responsibility and performance assessment of teacher dyads.
- Should the dyad be evaluated as a whole or how much of individual performance should be factored in?
- How are teacher dyads formed? Teacher dyads work best when teachers are free to choose the partners they wish to work with

(Murata 2002). The Murata study however involved only four teacher pairs. Implications for a national-wide implementation in Singapore?

It is widely documented that people are resistant to change and seek to maintain the status quo. It would be unwise to enact a reform and expect automatic compliance. In brief, several strategies to improve receptivity to the change would be to:

- engage teachers in the dialogue and decision making process,
- provide adequate training and support facilities,
- have a charismatic leader announce the change,
- get each individual teacher to make a personal commitment to the initiative, and
- maintain performance logs, reward good performance.

School leaders such as principals and vice principals should be informed and knowledgeable in inclusion education and have a personal commitment to its success.

Family

The family is a moderating factor in any program whereby their child is involved. With respect to co-teaching, families with learning disabled children need to be convinced that mainstreaming is an appropriate system for their child. Parents whose children have a learning disabled classmate should be reassured that the mainstreaming arrangement will not be negative on their child's education. The family could also enhance a child's compassion for the disabled. Should a child's learning disability be first discovered in school, it would be necessary to work closely with the family and explaining the intricacies of the disorder.

Finally, adopting the spirit of collaborative teaching we wish to highlight the importance of parental involvement beneficial to the children's developmental processes and academic achievement. It was evident that kindergarten children whose parents volunteered time to participate in the classroom showed gains in reading achievement relative to a control group (DeCusati & Johnson 2004). Likewise children whose parents were interested in their school activities (e.g., Ho & Willms 1996) had higher levels of academic achievement.

Parents can be involved in many different aspects of their child's upbringing and education. Epstein (1987, 1992, & 1994; cited in Fan 2001) proposes six ways in which parental involvement can be conceptualised. They are:

- [Schools] assisting parents in child rearing skills.
- School-to-home communications. (e.g., parent-teacher meetings).
- Involving parents in school volunteer opportunities.
- Involving parents in home-based learning.
- Involving parents in school decision making.
- Involving parents in school-community collaborations.

The degree to which parents are involved in their children is moderated by, in a large part, the socioeconomic status (SES) of the family (e.g., Grolnick, Benjet, Kurowski & Apostoleris 1997). SES encompasses variables such as the type of housing families stay in, the mean monthly family income and whether the family is receiving financial assistance from the government. A low SES family can overcome some of their difficulties if a strong social support network exists (e.g., extended family, Grolnick et al. 1997).

Parent volunteers can be directly involved in assisting teachers in classroom activities (DeCusati & Johnson 2004) or helping out with school related activities such as field trips or excursions. Classes and schools with parent volunteers have a beneficial effect on a child's academic achievement (e.g., DeCusati & Johnson 2004). The willingness and ability of parents to volunteer is varied. Parents who were employed were less likely to volunteer (Castro et al. 2004) due to the lack of time and work commitments. Personal characteristics of parents such as their level of self-efficacy can affect their confidence in volunteering their help (Grolnick et al. 1997). Teachers who were more experienced in interacting with parents in the classroom (a form of team teaching) encouraged parent volunteers to return for subsequent sessions (Castro et al. 2004). Schools which made concerted efforts to encourage volunteerism, such as having teachers personally inviting parents over the telephone, were more likely to attract parent volunteers (Feuerstein 2000).

Parents differ in ways they can volunteer. When working with younger children (kindergarten to lower primary) parents can facilitate small groups by either reading to the children or encouraging discussion (e.g., DeCusati & Johnson). When working with older children parents could present an alternate perspective to a teacher's discussion by drawing upon their own life and work experiences. Despite general agreement that parent volunteerism is beneficial, there lacks a prescriptive set of guidelines in which a parent is to contribute in a class (e.g., Mattingly, Prislin, McKenzie, Rodriguez & Kayzar 2002). We know that parents can be effective in a classroom. More empirical research is necessary to find out which specific activities hold the potential for including parents. Some considerations for Singapore schools are discussed.

In pursuing a policy of encouraging parents to volunteer it is important to consider several key issues.

- In what capacity do we wish to employ parents (e.g., participating in the classroom or facilitating school activities like field-trips)?
- If we choose to have parents as participants in the classroom, what roles do they play, as a co-educator, an administrative teacher or a teacher-aide?
- What is the frequency of parent participation? Does the same parent participate in a class on a regular basis or do parents come as and when they are able?
- How committed are parents who volunteer for the sake of earning credits in getting their children into the school?

Providing comprehensive training to potential parent volunteers is important as it raises their levels of self-efficacy to their continued commitment (Grolnick et al. 1997). Conducting workshops and preparing lesson plans is important to ensure consistency in parents' teaching material and techniques. Other suggestions to promote parent volunteerism include having an open-door policy in which parents can volunteer according to their own schedules, and having teachers show genuine interest and appreciation for parents (DeCusati & Johnson 2004).

Socioeconomic status describes the resources an individual or a family has at its disposal for everyday needs. Low SES families may not be able to afford the costs of putting their children through school (Buchmann & Hannum 2001). If both parents are working they can be less involved in their child's schooling (e.g., Feuerstein 2000), for example volunteering in schools (e.g., Ho & Willms 1996). Likewise if a family has several children to support, not all the children may get an adequate schooling if resources are limited (Buchmann & Hannum 2001).

Social support can buffer the negative effects of a low SES. A strong social support network is positively associated with the provision of a nurturing family environment (Grolnick et al. 1997). Relatives and friends could provide financial and/or other forms of assistance to families in need.

Differing levels of SES accounts for considerable variance in parental involvement (Feuerstein 2000), particularly in the area of parent volunteering (Feuerstein 2000; Ho & Willms 1996). Parenting values play a role in parental involvement. Despite a low SES, Ho and Willms (1996) found little support that these parents were less involved in their children's schooling relative to higher SES families. Ho and Willms (1996) concluded that though SES can affect how much time a parent has to volunteer at school, it is less likely to affect the degree of home supervision they provide their children. Cross-cultural factors affecting parent involvement, such as parenting values were subsequently discussed. It is not made explicit, yet it can be suggested that immigrant families (to the USA) may place a higher emphasis on education as a means of upward social mobility. If a parent and a child place a high value on education, it could offset the negative effects of a low SES.

Family size and can affect the academic attainments of children. In large families with many children, there may be insufficient resources to allow the children to actualise their academic potential. Occasionally the eldest child bears the burden of bringing up the younger siblings, hence s/he drops out of school early (Buchmann & Hannum 2001). Child labour is another prominent issue. A child at school incurs the opportunity cost of not putting the child to work. In lower SES families, depending on the emphasis placed on education, a parent could either invest in a child's schooling or put her(him) to work for immediate financial returns. Large families with many children need not necessarily be disadvantaged if the extended family contributes. Schools can involve parents in varying degrees. It is suggested that "major structural differences among schools in relation to the social class they serve... wealthy areas favour more [parent] participatory forms of governance and pedagogy" (Bowles & Gintis 1976; cited in Feuerstein 2000).

In summary, it is likely that low SES families face significant obstacles in putting their children through school if aid is not given by either the extended family or government. Parents have different attitudes to education, and unless parents encourage their children to maximise their academic potential, they may drop out of school to supplement the family income. For parents who value education, it is likely that they will be involved in their child's education both in school or at home to the best of their ability. Low SES parents display the same levels of home supervision as do high SES parents (Ho & Willms 1996). In today's knowledge driven society, a child's education is an asset in social mobility. For a low SES family not to invest in their children, it could mean the perpetuation of the cycle of poverty.

In concluding this book, we stress strongly that learning has to be conceptualised within the milieu of social and individualised. In enriched socio-cultural and familial environments, individualised learning takes place. Meaningful learning for self-development and personhood demands humanistic interactions of many stakeholders: among teachers and learners, among learners, and among learners and their caregivers and others in the community. We hope this book has stimulated continuous thoughts, questioning, and quest for the search for what really matters in learning and its relatedness to personhood, growth, inclusion, and full development.

REFERENCES

Buchmann, C. & E. Hannum. 2001. Education and stratification in developing countries: A review of theories and research. *Annual Review of Sociology, 27,* 77–102.

Castro, D. C., D. M. Bryant, E. S. Peisner-Feinberg, & M. L. Skinner. 2004. Parent involvement in Head Start programs: the role of parent, teacher and class room characteristics. *Early Childhood Research Quarterly (in press).*

Chin, C., & L. G. Chia. 2004. Implementing project work in biology through problem-based learning. *Journal of Biological Education, 38(2),* 69–75.

DeCusati, C. L. P., & J. E. Johnson. 2004. Parents as classroom volunteers and kindergarten students' emergent reading skills. *The Journal of Educational Research, 97(5),* 235–246.

Dochy, F., M. Segers, P. Van den Bossche, & D. Gijbels. 2003. Effects of problem-based learning: a meta-analysis. *Learning and Instruction, 13,* 533–568.

Fan, X. 2001. Parental involvement and student's academic achievement: A growth modelling analysis. *The Journal of Experimental Education, 70(1),* 27–61.

Feuerstein, A. (2000). School characteristics and parent involvement: Influences on participation in children's schools. *Journal of Educational Research, 94(1),* 29–39.

Grolnick, W. S., C. Benjet, C. O. Kurowski, & N. H. Apostoleris. 1997. Predictors of parent involvement in children's schooling. *Journal of Educational Psychology, 89(3),* 538–548.

Hmelo-Silver, C. E. 2004. Problem-based learning: what and how do students learn? *Education Psychology Review, 16(3),* 235–266.

Ho, S. C. E., & J. D. Willms. 1996. Effects of parental involvement on eight-grade achievement. *Sociology of Education, 69(2),* 126–141.

Kenneth, K. A., & S. R. Forness. 2000. History, rhetoric, and reality: Analysis of the inclusion debate. *Remedial and Special Education, 21(5)*, 279–296.

Mattingly, D. J., R. Prislin, T. L. McKenzie, J. M. Rodriguez, & B. Kayzar. 2002. Evaluating evaluations: The case of parent involvement programs. *Review of Educational Research, 72(4)*, 549–576.

Murata, R. 2002. What does Team Teaching mean? A case study of Interdisciplinary Teaming. *The Journal of Educational Research, 96(2)*, 67–77.

Murawski, W. W., & H. L. Swanson. 2001. A meta-analysis of co-teaching research. *Remedial and Special Education, 22(5)*, 258–267.

Tan, A. G., & L. C. Law. 2004. *Creativity for teachers.* Singapore: Marshall Cavendish Academic.

About the authors

Tan Ai Girl, Jason Tan, and Levan Lim are associate professors at the National Institute of Education (Singapore).

John Herdberg and Poon-Mcbrayer Kim Fong were faculty members of the National Institute of Education (Singapore).

Ahelon Annathurai, Bryan Thang, Chua Kia Chong, Julian Lim, Laura-Lynn Lee, Maisie Tan, and Wong Soo Fei worked on the chapters in the capacity of research associates.

Index